Archives and Museum of the Polish R. C. Union

THADDEUS KOSCIUSZKO
by Joseph Peszka

KOSCIUSZKO

LEADER AND EXILE

by

MIECISLAUS HAIMAN

Polish Institute of Arts and Sciences in America
New York
1946

" . . . it is pusillanimity and indecision which destroy Nations, but never their valor and ardor."

KOSCIUSZKO TO
THOMAS JEFFERSON,
ab. 1807

PREFACE

This is the second and the last part of a biography of Kosciuszko, the first part of which has been published under the title *Kosciuszko in the American Revolution* by the Polish Institute of Arts and Sciences in America, in 1943. The present volume is intended to mark and to honor the bicentennial of Kosciuszko's birth in 1746.

The author feels greatly indebted to Prof. Oscar Halecki, Director, Polish Institute of Arts and Sciences in America, for his most valuable advice; to the Rev. Prof. Joseph Swastek, St. Mary's College, Orchard Lake, Mich., and to the Rev. Samuel Bonikowski, Associate Editor, the Seraphic Chronicle, Detroit, Mich., for reading and revising the manuscript; to the Rev. Sisters M. Neomisia Rutkowska, of Philadelphia, Pa., and M. Liguori Pakowska, of Washington, D. C., Sisters of the Holy Family of Nazareth, who devoted much of their time to help the author in his researches; to Miss Marion Thompson Wright of Montclair, N. J., for information on the proposed Kosciuszko School in New Jersey; to Miss Eva W. Maupin, Clerk, Circuit Court, Albemarle County, Charlottesville, Va.; Miss Emelia E. Wefel, Librarian of the Main Library, Cleveland Public Library; Miss Carolyn E. Jakeman of the Houghton Library, Harvard University, Cambridge, Mass.; Mr. R. N. Williams 2nd, Acting Director, the Historical Society of Pennsylvania; Messrs. A. K. Gray, Librarian, and Barney Chesnick, Acting Librarian, Library Co. of Philadelphia, Ridgway Library; Mr. St. George L. Sioussat, Chief, Division of Manuscripts, and Frederick R. Goff, Chief, Rare Books Division, Library of Congress; Miss Mae Gilman and Miss Marian B. Rowe, Librarians, Maine Historical Society; Mr. Allyn B. Forbes of the Massachusetts Historical Society; Miss Brenda Richards, Assistant Archivist, Missouri Historical Society; Mr. P. M. Hamer, Director of Reference Service, The National Archives, and his staff; Miss Ethel L. Scofield, Curator, and Mr. W. Herbert Word, Acting Curator, New Haven Colony Historical Society; Miss Dorothy C. Barck, Librarian, New York Historical Society; Mr. Paul North Rice, Chief of the Reference Department, The New York Public Library; Miss Ellen M. Rollins, Collector for the Hall of History, North Carolina State Department of Archives and History; Mr. Zoltan Haraszti, Keeper of Rare Books, The Public Library of the City of Boston; Miss Elizabeth H. Jervey, Secretary and Treasurer, South Carolina Historical Society; Mr. J. G. de Roulhac Hamilton of the Library of the University of North Carolina; Miss Edna L. Jacobsen, Head, Manuscript and Historical Section, The New York State Library; Miss Louise Savage, Acting Director, and Mr. Harris H. Williams, in Charge of Manuscripts, Alderman Library; Miss Anne S. Pratt, Reference Librarian, Yale University Library; Miss Lois North, Curator, Henry Whitfield State Historical Museum, Guilford, Conn.; Mr. Herbert C. Schulz, Curator of Manuscripts, Henry E. Huntington Library and Art Gallery, San Marino, Cal.; and to all others who helped him to collect the necessary materials.

CONTENTS

ILLUSTRATIONS

I.

BACK HOME

Upon his return to Poland in 1784, Kosciuszko, like many of his comrades-at-arms in the American Revolution, settled at Siechnowicze, which his kin, the Estkos, managed to save from the creditors of his brother, Joseph. The long and meritorious service of the General in the ranks of the American army was now only a memory. It brought him much military experience and some fame, but no financial rewards. It widened greatly the horizon of his thoughts. Above all, it impressed him with new notions of human freedom and deepened his political wisdom.

For the next five years, however, he was forced to lead the quiet and monotonous life of a small Polish landlord. With special fondness he tilled his garden, and read much. Sometimes he visited his relatives or neighbors, and in turn, entertained them in his modest house. His friend, Charles Kniaziewicz, who subsequently gained glory as a leader of the Polish Legions under Napoleon, remembered that he liked company and youthful games, that "his behavior was full of simplicity. He was very courteous, he often bowed, he was meek and looked like a poor insignificant noble."[1]

Though seemingly so idyllic, at least on the surface, those years were not without their thorns. Kosciuszko had continuous financial difficulties; the income from his small estate was insufficient even for his modest wants and the expected interest on his American arrears did not arrive. Were it only for this, he still might have borne his burden with an easy heart; his affectionate sister, Anna Estko, was always ready to help him out. What was worse, however, he suffered spiritually. After so many years of travel, action and adventures, he now was subjected to comparative inactivity. Only so recently had he felt himself an actor on a great historical scene, while now, enclosed within the narrow borders of a Polish village, he vainly searched for an occasion to devote his energy, talents and virtues to some high purpose. He never was "pliant enough for politics"[2] and there was no place for him in the small Polish army. His life at this period undoubtedly appeared to him rather aimless and useless.

---

[1] Korzon, *Kosciuszko,* 183 and note 374.
[2] Joseph Ossolinski to Thugut, May 1, 1794, Korzon, *Kosciuszko,* 332 and note 594.

1

The emptiness of his home also weighed heavily on him. He had never yet felt the warmth of his own family hearth, though, no doubt, he longed for it. Somehow he had no luck in love. When a few years after his return from America he was at the point of marrying a Miss Thecla Zurowska, the marriage again was prevented by the ill will of his fiancee's father.

But, above all, he grieved over the sad plight of Poland. Like Mickiewicz's Wallenrod, "happiness ne'er could he find in his home, with his country unhappy."[3] True, her internal condition was greatly improved since he left her in 1775; the Permanent Council, though disliked by the nation as a creature of Russia, at the very least introduced some order in the government; the famous Commission of Education completely reorganized the Polish school system and made it one of the most progressive in Europe; there was a marked intellectual and industrial revival; some social improvements were introduced and others, still more radical, were discussed and demanded by able political writers. However, this internal progress seemed too slow to satisfy Kosciuszko; like all enlightened compatriots, he clearly saw the constant danger of destruction of the country's independence by its powerful and militaristic neighbors.

Undoubtedly very disagreeable to him, too, was the complete silence of his American friends. Whether it was neglect on their part, or the fault of slow and imperfect mail systems of those times, no letters from America reached him. There were moments when he felt completely disgusted. "Be sure that nothing keeps me here in Poland, but you," he wrote afflictingly to Anna Estko.[4] To his dear old commander, Gen. Greene, he complained on January 20, 1786:

"It surprise me very much that to this time, I have not one line from you, I am alarmed and my friendship for you puts Thousands disagreables thoughts into my head. Who knows, you may be sick or dead,... perhaps you have forgot me as I am no more in your Country... Do write me, my dear General, of the Situation of your Country, because I heard many bad things; hoever when our King has asked me, I gave him the best description I could. Write me of yourself, of your family, and of my friends. As to myself am in good health, something richer, but very inhappy of the situation of my Country which I believe *nulla redemptio* as well as I am, somuch am attached to your Country, that I would leave every thing behind, and would fly this very moment even in the Baloon to embrace you, Could I obtain an honorable rank in your Country's Army. . . . My respects to your

3 Adam Mitskievitch, *Conrad Wallenrod*, transl. by Michael H. Dziewicki, London, 1883, 64.
4 Korzon, *loc. cit.*, 183 and note 374.

2

Lady to Mrs. Moris[5] in Charstown tel her I propose to mary her when hers Husband dies and if he is in Life, which would be the most surprising thing to live so long in that Country, my best Compliments to him."[6]

The letter shows how hopeless the situation of Poland seemed to him at that time. But amid all these discouraging conditions and in his small circle of influence he tried to keep abreast of the spirit of the times in Poland and to introduce some social amelioration of his own. He could never reconcile his mind with the serfdom of peasants then existing in Poland and other European countries. "A subject— the word should be cursed in all enlightened nations," he wrote to one of his friends.[7] "The happiness of others is in my greatest respect and I am ready to sacrifice mine," he wrote to Miss Zurowska on another occasion.[8] He was eager to set his peasants completely free, without regard to his own financial loss, but he saw that it was too early yet for such a radical reform; he had to compromise by reducing their forced labor.

On September 20, 1787, Kosciuszko tried to remind the American Congress of the interest due on his certificate for the arrears of his pay, complaining that "he has not these three years received" anything, contrary to promises[9]. His letter was referred to the Board of Treasury and it had only a partial effect; the interest for one year, that of 1784, to the amount of little over seven hundred dollars, reached him sometime in Poland[10]. Perplexing as the matter was to Kosciuszko, as he never had too much, this did not, nevertheless, weaken his love for America. "It is my second country," he assured one of his American friends.[11]

Toward the end of 1788, Major Elnathan Haskell of Massachusetts, one of Kosciuszko's companions of the Ticonderoga Campaign, appeared in France to try his luck at speculating in United States funds, as did many Americans then living in Europe.[12] Remembering Kos-

---

5 The former Miss Nancy Elliott, wife of Maj. Lewis Morris.

6 Huntington Library, Greene Papers, HM 8056.

7 To Michael Zaleski, in 1789, Korzon, *loc. cit.*, 196; the original in Polish.

8 In 1791, Korzon, *loc cit.*, 213, the original in Polish.

9 Report of the Secretary of Congress, Library of Congress, Papers of the Continental Congress, ser. 180, p. 73.

10 Felix Oraczewski to Gouverneur Morris, Aug. 15, 1792, *American State Papers*, class 1, vol. I, p. 335; ct. also Rives, *Abridgement of Debates*, II, 192.

11 Kosciuszko to Elnathan Haskell, August 10, 1789, Archives and Museum of the Polish R. C. Union, hereafter referred to as Polish R. C. U. Museum, Kosciuszko Papers, no. 6A. Most of these letters reprinted in *Memorial Exhibition, Thaddeus Kosciuszko . Being the Collection Formed by Dr. and Mrs. Alexander Kahanowicz*, New York (1927), and in "Listy Kosciuszki," *Przegląd Historyczny*, VI, 86-106, ed. by A. M. Skałkowski.

12 Morris, *Diary*, I, 31 and passim. Morris calls him erroneously Hasgill. Haskell became associated in France with Daniel Parker of Massachusetts *(ibid.,* I, 518), a contractor for supplies to the Continental and French armies during the Revolution. In 1790, Haskell left France and settled in Charleston, S. C. (Family correspondence in the hands of Mrs. Frances G. White of Charleston). A few biographical details concerning him are given by McCrady and Ashe, *Cyclopedia of Eminent Men of the Carolinas*, I, 93. Most probably to him pertain references to a Brigade Major Haskell as present at White Plains, N. Y., in August 1778 *(State Records of No. Carol.*, X, 529 and 539).

ciuszko, he wrote him of Greene's death. The General had died on June 19, 1786, most probably before Kosciuszko's aforementioned letter reached America. The Pole felt happy that at least one of his old friends did not forget him, but the sad information touched him deeply. He answered Haskell on May 5, 1789:

"My Dear — Dear Haskell, Happy I am that once in five years can have at last the news of the country to which I am so much attached. — Hearteli I thank you for the obliging letter, your person was alway dear to me, and am not disapointed in your character. Few — very few such exemples in the world, of the lasting friendship at such a distance... He is gone my good friend Greene, rains begins to fall heavy from my eyes whenever I think of. You ought to make a statue or a Mausolium for his memory. I knew his Merit perhaps better than any one, and shall think always very ungratefull Country if she will not crown him with a title of a Great General and Citizen.[13] What is about your Congress do writ me. It is not famous, that to this date according to the Certificates given to the officers dont chuse to pay, nether the interest nor the somme due to them. I do not speak for myself, but I heard great many complains, and ill languages of my beloved Country, her reputation is dear to me, and I suffer myself more than great many in Congress perhaps. For God sake writ to your friends in Congress, I suppose you heard great deal in Paris yourself not to be convinced of the propriety in discharging the debt.[14] — My respecte to Mrs. Greene, Moris of Charlestown, and my love to Williams, Armstrong and if is living to Gates."[15]

Though his purse was meager, indeed, Kosciuszko wished to honor the memory of his dead friend and commander. He ordered an engraving of Greene to be made in Paris, copies of which he subsequently sent to his friends in America.[16] David Humphreys, who in

---

[13] Kosciuszko forever preserved a tender heart for Greene. A quarter of a century later Carlo Botta, the Italian historian of the American Revolution, asked him for his opinion of Greene; Kosciuszko answered: "I am hurrying to give you information on him out of regard for his most exalted character; he had all the qualities necessary for a statesman, a general, a republican and a man of science; he was truly compassionate, generous, a good citizen, a good friend, he had deep insight, just judgment, resolution, energy and necessary initiative, his spirit was ingenious in solving difficulties, his eye was keen, moreover he was modest in his manners, affable and polite." (Kosciuszko to Molineri, March 17, 1809, N. Y. Public Libr., Misc. MSS; the original in French).

[14] Kosciuszko probably referred to French officers who about that time became so impatient with the long and fruitless waiting for the payment of their arrearages that they called a meeting at Paris, "the object of which was . . . to address Congress in terms which would have been very disagreeable, and at the same time to present a petition to the King, claiming his interposition." With the help of Col. Gouvion, Jefferson appeased them only with difficulty. (Jefferson to the Board of Treasury, May 16, 1788, Lipscomb, *Writings of Jefferson,* VII, 10; hereafter referred to as Lipscomb).

[15] Polish R. C. U. Museum, Kosciuszko Papers, no. 30. The above is the only known letter which Kosciuszko signed as "Count." This caused some of his biographers to accuse him of using the title illegally and to put to doubt the sincerity of his democratic convictions (Skałkowski, *Kościuszko w Świetle,* 30). Wittlin, *The Torch of Freedom,* used this little incident as one of the main subjects in his brief biography of Kosciuszko. "Count of Poland" was the nickname given to Kosciuszko by the Southern Army (Tarleton, *History,* 147) and the use of the title should be regarded as rather an innocent reminiscence.

1790 returned to Europe as American Minister at Lisbon, helped the General in this regard. He wrote to Kosciuszko:

"I hope you received the Engravings of your good friend Gen. Greene, which were put into the train of transmission at Paris, which you directed. His untimely Death was the universal subject of regret in his own Country. It is a fortunate circumstance, that the Print which you caused to be taken of him, is the best likeness now existing of that excellent man. Indeed it is pronounced to be a perfect resemblance by all his friends in America."

At the same time Humphreys consoled him:

"Your acquaintances and friends in America all remember you with great affection. And the more so from the honorable agency you had in assisting to establish the Independence of that Country, — a Country, which now, in reality begins to enjoy the fruits of its Revolution."[17]

There are traces that William Carmichael, the American charge d'affaires at Madrid, also corresponded with Kosciuszko at the time.

At least a chance appeared of Kosciuszko receiving a commission in the national army. In 1788 the Great Diet assembled at Warsaw, and in response to universal demands for reforms, began its memorable work of reconstructing the mouldy national institutions. Increase of the army and the revenues of the treasury; a series of laws for the benefit of the bourgeoisie, the peasants, the Jews and the dissidents; improvement of the administrative system; these were the most important achievements of the Diet. In the words of an eminent historian, it "displayed an energy, a patriotic enthusiasm, a liberal enlightened spirit, and a high appreciation of its task, such as no Polish parliament had shown for two centuries."[18] Kosciuszko was highly satisfied with the reforms. Writing to Haskell again, he assured him that "we are upon the means to be respectable abroad, to give more energi for the execution of the established Laws and to destroi forever any hope for raising a Monarchique Pouvoir." Referring to the general European political crisis of 1789, which seemed so auspicious to Polish hopes, he added: "every Patriotique breast pray Almyty for the Continuation for three years of war amongst" powers.[19]

The increased army needed good officers and the eyes of the patriots turned to Kosciuszko. The King was favorably inclined to his appointment and publicly commended his behavior in America.[20]

---

16 It seems that the original of the picture was drawn by Kosciuszko himself.
17 Oct. 1, 1791, The Polish Academy of Sciences, MS 1171, no. 88.
18 Lord, *The Second Partition*, 488.
19 August, 1789, Polish R. C. U. Museum, Kosciuszko Papers, no. 6A.
20 Louise Lubomirska to Kosciuszko, May 21, 1789, Korzon, *loc. cit.*, 611.

During the debates in the Diet in the beginning of December 1788, prominent members spoke in his favor. Kosciuszko "has great personal virtues," said one of them; "if he knew how to shed his blood for a foreign country, he undoubtedly will not spare it for his own."[21] On October 1, 1789, he was appointed Major General in the Polish Army.

To this period belongs Kosciuszko's written project of a Polish national militia based on American patterns.[22] Opposed to the idea of a "regular army recruited by violence," he knew well that from the military point of view the value of a militia was rather small. But the American militia was comprised of all classes of men called to arms in defense of their country; its ranks leveled social differences: the rich and the poor, the educated and the ignorant, served as equals. That was a great social lesson for Poland. Kosciuszko's plan provided for the mobilization not only of nobles, but also of the burghers and peasants. He wanted to unite "all forces" of the nation "in the spirit of Patriotism, of civicism and fraternity."[23]

During one of his visits to Warsaw in connection with his nomination, Kosciuszko met John Paul Jones, then returning from his Russian service. He valued Jones' courage, but felt highly offended at the thought that an American, so strikingly distinguished in a war for freedom, should stoop so low as to accept a command under a despot and in a war of pure conquest. "The brave Paul Jones is at Petersburg," he wrote to Maj. Haskell from Warsaw on August 10, 1789. "I am sorry he is in the service of Russia, a Republican and American — it is sufficient to draw Conclusion."[24]

Still Kosciuszko was one of the first to extend a helping hand to the victor of the Serapis, when John Paul Jones, bitterly disappointed and painfully humiliated after his Russian experiences, passed through Warsaw on his way to Paris. The King entertained the American hero, Warsaw society treated him "with greatest hospitality and politeness,"[25] but it was Kosciuszko who endeavored to reestablish him. At one of their meetings, Kosciuszko openly pointed out to Jones that his Russian service was a false step. Poland had no navy and therefore could not use his talents, but Sweden was then at war with Russia and she would certainly be glad to accept his services; such employment, reasoned Kosciuszko, would be far more honorable to a famous veteran of the American Revolution.

21 *Ib.*, 201.
22 The original in the Polish Academy of Sciences, MS 647.
23 The Act of Insurrection, March 24, 1794, Haiman, *Fall of Poland*, 126.
24 Polish R. C. Museum, Kosciuszko Papers, No. 6A.
25 Jones to Chevalier Bourgoing, undated, De Koven, *Jones*, II, 370.

At first Jones hesitated. Actuated by a false notion of allegiance to Russia and the Empress which he was unable to shake off until his death, he had grave scruples. Slowly, however, these disappeared under the weight of Kosciuszko's arguments. Finally, Jones gave the General permission to act. Kosciuszko then contacted Count Lawrence Engestrom, the Swedish Minister at Warsaw. But before Engestrom could communicate with his government, Jones left Warsaw, leaving the following note at Kosciuszko's dwelling:

"I intend to set out this day[26] for Vienna, where I shall only stop a few days. I shall then go to Strasburgh, and from thence to Holland, where I expect to arrive before the 1st of December. My address in Holland is under cover to Messieurs Nic. and Jacob Staphorst, Amsterdam.

"As I shall be in relation with our friends in America, I shall not fail to mention on all occasions the honorable employment and the respect you have attained in your own country, and the great regard you retain for the natives of America, where your character is esteemed, and your name justly beloved for your services."

Jones arrived at Amsterdam on December 18, but waited in vain for a message from Kosciuszko. Impatient, he wrote to him on January 21, 1790:

"I am afraid that the project which you mentioned to me was not accepted, or that my letter did not reach you. I am leaving for the Hague for a few days, and will return here, where I will be glad to receive some news from you."[27]

It is evident from the above letter that, for the moment, Jones was quite willing to consider a Swedish proposition. If Kosciuszko did not answer him earlier, it was only because he still did not know the result of his endeavors. At last Engestrom advised the General that his government was willing to accept Jones' services; Kosciuszko immediately transmitted the welcome news to the Admiral.[28] Several days later, on receiving the above letter from Jones, he wrote to him again, repeating the details:

"I had the honor to write you the 1st or 3rd of February. I do not recollect; but I gave you the information to apply to the Minister of Svede at Hague or at Amsterdam for the propositions, according to what M. D'Engestrom told me they both had order to communicate you. I wish with all my heart that it could answer your expectations. I am totally ignorant what they are; but I could see you to fight against the oppression and tyranny."[29]

---

26 Nov. 2, 1789, Washbourne, *Memoirs*, II, 196.
27 The Polish Academy of Sciences, Kosciuszko Papers, no. 647, as quoted by Korzon, *loc. cit.*, 608.
28 This letter of Kosciuszko, dated Feb. 2, 1790, became evidently lost.
29 Feb. 15, 1790, Washbourne, *loc. cit.*, II, 199.

But, far removed from Kosciuszko's pressure, Jones was unable to shake off the influence of Catherine II. Moreover, he evidently became offended by the way the Swedish Government tried to enlist him for its cause. John Paul Jones always thought very highly of himself. The Empress courted his favor through special couriers and exploited his vanity in other ways in order to entice him to her side. How differently did the Swedes treat him: before them he was one asking a favor, and not one of whom a favor is asked. Jones, therefore, abruptly broke off further negotiations, advising Kosciuszko of it in a rather dry manner:

"The letter you did me the honour to write me the 2nd of February was delivered at my bankers here by a man who demanded from them a receipt. I was then at the Hague and your letter was transmitted to me. On my return here some days ago I found another letter from you of the 15th of February. This letter had by the same man been put in the hands of my bankers. You propose if I am not mistaken that I should apply to a gentleman at the Hague, who has something to communicate to me. But a moments reflection will convince you that consideration of what I owe to myself as well as the delicacy of my situation does not permit me to take such a step. If that gentleman has any thing to communicate to me he can either do it by writing, by desiring a personal conference or by the mediation of a third person. I have shown your letter to my bankers and they have said this much to the gentleman from whom they received it, but this message they say he received with an air of indifference."[30]

This letter closed Jones' correspondence with Kosciuszko. The Admiral returned to Paris in the beginning of March and through Gouverneur Morris, the American Minister to France, made one more effort to induce the Swedish Government to make him a direct offer.[31] No answer came. Broken morally, physically and financially, the Admiral spent the rest of his unhappy days in continuous and degrading efforts to regain the favors of the Russian Empress.[32] Undoubtedly no one in Europe regretted more sincerely Jones' untimely death than his Polish friend.

---

30 Sometime in March, 1790, Washbourne, *Memoirs*, II, 200.
31 Entry of March 8, 1790, Morris, *Diary of the French Revolution*, I, 443.
32 Cf. Russell, *John Paul Jones*, 263-65; also DeKoven, *John Paul Jones*, II, 370 et seq., etc.

II.

THE POLISH-RUSSIAN WAR OF 1792

For a brief time Major General Kosciuszko was stationed in Great Poland, then he was transferred to the Eastern provinces, where the main forces of the Polish army were stationed. There he was most useful to the young and inexperienced Commander-in-Chief, Prince Joseph Poniatowski, whose place he assumed during the Prince's temporary absences. By his devotion to duty, experience and patriotic ardor, Kosciuszko did much to transform gradually the young and ill-equipped army into a fighting force. The Military Commission of the Diet, which performed the duties of the ministry of war, praised his "exemplary" conduct in introducing discipline and order in his brigade and in caring for the welfare of the soldier.[1]

About that time Kosciuszko wrote to one of his friends:

"We must all unite for one purpose: to free our country from the domination of foreigners, from the abasement and destruction of the very name of Pole. Let us only have universal education . . . On ourselves, on our morals, depends the improvement of government. And if we are base, covetous, selfish, careless of our country: it will be just that we shall have chains on our necks, and we shall be worthy of them."[2]

It was this spirit which distinguished his service in the Polish army. When in 1791, the Great Diet enacted the famous Constitution of the Third of May, by which, in the opinion of Washington, "Poland . . . made large and unexpected strides toward Liberty,"[3] he was one of the first to swear allegiance to it together with his troops. It did not fully answer his ideas on needed reforms, but at last he could now confess that he "breathed the spirit of a free citizen and Republican."[4]

The new constitution meant, however, the emancipation of Poland from foreign domination and this provoked the revenge of Catherine II. Considering the aggrandizement of Russia through the destruction of Poland as one of the chief aims of her external politics, she strove to reach that goal with ruthlessness which could be matched

---

[1] Korzon, *Kosciuszko*, 210.

[2] To Michael Zaleski, in 1791, Gardner, *Kosciuszko*, 73.

[3] Washington to David Humphreys, July 20, 1791, Fitzpatrick, *Writings of Washington*, XXXI, 320; hereafter referred to as Fitzpatrick.

[4] Kosciuszko to Michael Zaleski, in 1791, Korzon, *loc. cit.*, 222; the original in Polish.

only by the perversity and cupidity of the Court of Berlin, her faithless ally in the crime of the Partitions of Poland. At her encouragement and under her protection a few Polish magnates, dissatisfied with the new constitution, formed the Confederation of Targowica, so-called from a town in the Polish Ukraine, in an effort to nullify the work of the Great Diet and thus restore the old anarchy so convenient to neighbors looking for constant interference in Polish internal affairs. At the invitation of these traitors Russian armies invaded Poland in the spring of 1792. The nation's effort to amend its errors of old and to recover its independence was to be punished by brutal force. Brazenly betrayed by Prussia, which refused to honor her alliance and all her solemn promises and pledges, Poland was left to fight her battle alone against the overwhelming numbers of the invader. The small Polish army had to retreat and to limit its actions to harassing the progress of the enemy. If there was anything, except patriotism, to inspire the Poles, it was "the example of the Americans who sustained many defeats before they achieved the glorious conquest of liberty."[5]

Usually the most difficult operations were entrusted to Kosciuszko; most frequently his division acted as a rearguard. At Polonne (June 14-15) he saved the army from destruction;[6] at Zielence (June 18) where the Poles were victorious, "he proved very useful not only by his bravery, but also by his extraordinary prudence";[7] Prince Poniatowski praised his "good and cautious disposition" in action at Włodzimierz (July 7);[8] in the most important battle of the campaign at Dubienka (July 18) he repelled the attacks of a threefold stronger enemy for several hours and, inflicting severe losses on him, managed to retreat in "the calmest manner and in perfect order."[9]

According to the testimony of a contemporary, he "taught soldiers and peasants that they are his brothers, his countrymen, that they have a common country for which they were fighting together . . .; he aroused in them love, unbounded enthusiasm and strength which overcame difficulties . . .; he trained them by his example." He was democratic throughout, "without ceremony visiting palaces and huts . . . Recognizing all men as his brothers, he discerned only two kinds among them, good and bad ones . . . he disliked long speeches . . . his good humor was contagious . . .; he was not a terrorist . . . , he was a pupil of Washington and similar to him by his nature. Ladies

---

5 An excerpt from a letter from the Polish camp, June 14, 1792, as quoted in *Dunlap's Amer. Daily Adv.*, Sept. 6, 1792.

6 Wolanski, *Wojna*, 192.

7 Prince Poniatowski to the King, June 18, 1792, Korzon, *loc. cit.*, 230; the original in Polish.

8 Report of Prince Poniatowski, July 8, 1792, Wolanski, *op. cit.*, 297.

9 Gen. Zajączek's *Memoirs*, as quoted by Wolanski, *op. cit.*, 383.

adored him because he told them courtesies and danced with them . . .; he disliked long faces, he considered it one's fortune to risk his life in the service of his country. He went from a ball to a battle and the next day returned to the party without losing the sight of the enemy; he found him again when least expected. He slept equally well on bare soil and in down; he shared the food of the soldier and did not consider himself Spartan enough to refuse a good supper if only his soldiers had something to eat, too . . . He was not very eloquent, his deeds spoke for him, he did not possess that which we call worldly refinement, but he had something more — he had a natural charm which captivated all who approached him without a spirit of partiality."[10]

"Kosciuszko is an unusual man," wrote an eyewitness of the campaign, "under fire he seems to be as on a promenade, he is sensible, brave, beloved and esteemed by his countrymen and by foes as well."[11] The King called him "our excellent Kosciuszko,"[12] decorated him with the Cross of *Virtuti Militari* and advanced him to the rank of Lieutenant General. If success evaded their arms, the Poles at least covered themselves with honor; and historians agree that, in a very large measure, it was the result of Kosciuszko's efforts and leadership.

The unhappy Stanislaus Augustus lacked strength of character which the moment demanded. Yielding to the pressure of Russia, he joined the Targowica and ordered the army to cease further resistance. His step evoked universal indignation among rank and file. Even Prince Joseph, his cousin, condemned him and offered his resignation. Kosciuszko and many officers followed the Prince. In a personal interview the King urged Kosciuszko to reconsider his action, but he remained firm. "With tears in my eyes I answered him (the King) that we would never act against our convictions and honor," he related.[13]

At first Kosciuszko decided to return to America. Interposing with Felix Potocki, one of the chiefs of the Targowica, in behalf of his comrades-in-arms, he wrote: "Watering my native soil with my tears, I am going to the New World, to my second country to which I have acquired a right by fighting for her independence. Once there, I shall beseech Providence for a stable, free and good government in Poland, for the independence of our nation, for virtuous, enlightened and free inhabitants therein."[14]

10 Fiszerowa, "Pamiętnik Damy Polskiej o Kościuszce," ed. by Skałkowski, *Przegląd Historyczny*, ser. 2, vol. XII (1934), p. 249; the original is in French. This source referred to hereafter as Fiszer, "Pamiętnik."

11 A letter by an anonymous Polish officer, *Gazeta Narodowa i Obca*, no. 55, p. 325, as quoted by Wolanski, *op. cit.*, 297.

12 The King to Francis Bukaty, Polish Minister in London, July 14, 1792, *ibid.*, 297.

13 Korzon, *Kosciuszko*, 250.

14 Sept. 6, 1792, Gardner, *Kosciuszko*, 82; the original in Polish.

11

But he changed his mind. Russian troops swarmed over Poland, which has now become virtually a province of Russia. By a new treaty dictated to the last Polish Diet by the Russian Ambassador, Sievers, Catherine II gained unrestricted control over all public life of the nation. The Polish government has been reduced to a status of a puppet; the army subjected to Russian orders, all Polish foreign relations had to be "concerted" with Russian politics. All reforms of the Great Diet were voided.[15] In this situation, the leaders of the patriotic party went into voluntary exile. Against hope, they still hoped for some miracle. "We shall not sink in our hearts," wrote one of them, Hugo Kollontay, who later became one of the most faithful collaborators of Kosciuszko during his Insurrection.[16] "We ought to strive to save our dying country by all means, or at least to muster up courage enough for a magnificent effort which will wipe out the shame from our generation."

The campaign of 1792 won for Kosciuszko great popularity in Poland and abroad. The French Legislative Assembly recognized him as a "defender of the people against despots," bestowing on him, together with Washington and a few other famous contemporaries, the honorary citizenship of France. The fame of his achievements even reached the shores of America. His former Revolutionary colleagues prayed for "a union of all free countries to save Poland from the rapacious hands of all spoilers."[17] Most of the Polish patriots now looked to Kosciuszko as the only man able to raise the falling standard of the White Eagle.

Initiated into their plans, Kosciuszko dropped the project of returning to America. He informed his friend, Zaleski, that he would not go farther than Switzerland or England and assured him that he would observe thence the events in Poland. "If they make for the happiness of the country," he continued, "I shall return; if not — I shall move on further. I shall enter no foreign service, and if I am forced to it by my poverty then I shall enter a service where there is a free state — but with an unchanging attachment to my country which I might serve no longer."[18]

He closed the letter with his usual great modesty: "I do not see — God is my witness — how I, sincerely attached to the country, entering no intrigues, following no side except the public good, could as yet be convinced and shown the necessity of remaining in the country, I who am nothing, poor and whose voice would not be obeyed."

---

15 Konopczynski, *Dzieje Polski*, II, 395.

16 Memorandum in Polish for Thomas Wawrzecki of 1793, Janik, *Kołłątaj*, 347.

17 A toast at the dinner of the State Society of the Cincinnati, Wilmington, Dela., July 6, 1793, *Dunlap's Amer. Daily Adv.*, July 9, 1793.

18 Sept. 30, 1792, Gardner, *Kosciuszko*, 82; the original in Polish.

ITALIAN SCENERY
by Kosciuszko

Archives and Museum of the Polish R. C. Union

Without even a chance to take leave of his relatives he left Poland early in October of 1792. On his way he wrote the following letter to Anna Estko, classic in its simplicity and full of his solicitude for his servants and peasants:

"Permit me, my Sister, to embrace you, and because this may be the last time I shall be given that happiness I desire that you should know my will, that I bequeath to you my Siechnowicze and that you have the right to bequeath it either to one of your sons or to any one, but under one condition: that Susanna and Faustin[19] shall be kept in every comfort until their death; that the peasants from every house in the whole estate shall not do more than two days of forced labor for the men, and for the women none at all. If it were another country where the government could ensure my will, I would free them entirely, but in this country we must do what we are certain of being able to do to relieve humanity in any way, and always remember that by nature we are all equals, that riches and education constitute the only difference; that we ought to have consideration for the poor and instruct ignorance, thus bringing about good morals . . . Embrace Susanna for me. Thank her for the friendship she has shown me. Remember me to Faustin and to your son Stanislaus. Let him give his children a good republican education with the virtues of justice, honesty and honor."[20]

At first he remained in that part of Poland which Austria annexed by the First Partition. While there, a lady admirer offered him her large estate which brought an income of 20,000 Polish zlotys yearly, but he refused "with the assurance that I am satisfied with a little."[21] Soon the Austrian government became alarmed at the manifestations of public enthusiasm for him. Early in December, 1792, Kosciuszko received a police order to leave the country in twelve hours. Under the assumed name of Mr. Bieda, (which means misery in Polish), he passed through Cracow and by the end of December reached Leipzig, in Saxony, where most of the Polish patriotic leaders were already gathered. These were the men "who forgetting themselves, thought of Poland only."[22]

Almost at once he was secretly dispatched to Paris to secure the aid of France for the planned uprising. Only recently the Convention proclaimed "fraternity and succor to all nations desiring to regain their freedom," and it was natural that Polish patriots turned their eyes to France. They were soon to learn the emptiness of these bombastic declarations. In vain Kosciuszko tried to interest French leaders of

---

19 Susanna, his old relation and housekeeper; Faustin, his servant.
20 In 1792, as quoted by Gardner, *Kosciuszko,* 84; the original in Polish.
21 Kosciuszko's deposition made while imprisoned at St. Petersburg, Korzon, *op. cit.,* p. 462; Mazzei, *Memoirs,* 377.
22 Kollontay to Strasser, Jan. 27, 1793, Janik, *op. cit.,* 339; the original in Polish.

different parties in the Polish cause. The Girondists and the Mountain, both alike remained deaf to his pleas. Lebrun, the Foreign Minister, made him some promises, though insincere and delusive; moreover, he and his party were then at the point of being overthrown and under the shadow of the scaffold. Already powerful, but still standing in the background, Robespierre was openly unfriendly. Neither Danton, nor Marat were willing to deal with him. All these men, with high toned maxims on their tongues, cared for Poland only in so far as they could use her as a pawn in their own political collusions. Precisely at the moment when Kosciuszko knocked at their doors only to meet with a rebuff, they made secret preparations to sell France's recognition of the Second Partition of Poland most advantageously.[23]

Most probably Kosciuszko availed himself of his presence in France to pay his respects to Gouverneur Morris and to inquire about arrears of his American pay,[24] which continually failed to reach him. Morris was glad to attest that he was "a man of distinguished talents."[25]

Kosciuszko returned to Saxony empty handed. Equally fruitless was his later visit to Brussels. The patriots had to rely solely on Poland's own resources. Kosciuszko was an optimist in this regard. In his memoir of the campaign of 1792, he had pointed out that lack of funds could not be regarded as a valid reason for Poland's defeat, for the Americans were able to conduct a long war without sufficient monies.[26] In a letter to Engestrom, then Swedish minister in London, he took "a summary view of the vast natural strength of Poland, though the anarchy of more than an age had rendered it a prey to every surrounding despot. He compared the internal resources of his country with those of America, at the time that his love of liberty induced him to fight in the service of those states, where he distinguished himself by exploits of the greatest enterprise and valour; and, though he lamented the want of maritime strength, he was still of the opinion, that Poland, if unanimous, would be able to defend itself against the Russian and Prussian powers."[27]

[23] Askenazy, *Napoleon a Polska,* I, 53-4; *idem, Thaddeus Kosciuszko,* 12; Kukiel, "Kosciuszko and the Third Partition," *Cambridge History of Poland,* 155-6; Eversley, *Partitions of Poland,* 145-172.

[24] Morris to Jefferson, Aug. 17, 1792, Library of Congress, Jefferson Papers.

[25] Oraczewski to Morris, Aug. 15, 1792, *American State Papers,* class I, vol. I, pp. 335-6. Thomas Pinckney, Minister in London, acted in behalf of Kosciuszko and in the summer of 1793 was able to send him a draft for 7,162 florins, representing the arrears till the end of 1792, through bankers at Leipzig and Dresden. This draft never reached Kosciuszko who meanwhile returned to Poland as the leader of the Insurrection (Pinckney to Wilhelm and Jan Willink, Nicolas and Jacob Van Staphorst and Hubbard, Dec. 7, 1797, Mass. Hist. Soc., Jefferson Papers, a copy).

[26] He wrote: "The King frightened by the loss of his crown submitted to conditions dictated by the ambition of Catherine. He excused himself not too properly that there were no funds, but what for? Was there not meat and bread in the country, which citizens would gladly give for receipts? The American revolution provides an example of conducting war for eight years without money, if only the government will take care to supply the soldier with clothes and shoes. Liberty and independence would, as they did there, incite each soldier's heart to bear willingly the temporary lack of comforts." Kosciuszko, *Manuskrypt,* 109).

[27] The original of this letter seems to have been lost. It is quoted here from a summary which appeared in the *Dunlap and Claypoole's American Daily Advertiser,* July 5, 1794.

Working now on the organization of the uprising, Kosciuszko constantly strove to apply his American experiences to conditions in Poland and to inspire his countrymen with the example of the Americans.[28] "Poles! rise and you will win!," ran one of his appeals smuggled to Poland. "Death passes the brave . . . And if anyone of you will die, he will become a hero for freedom and truth . . . When Americans began their fight, the British contemptuously called them scoundrels, now they esteem the liberty of these scoundrels."[29] He returned to his former project of a Polish militia as an auxiliary force, which even in its name imitated the American organization. He insisted that peasants should be prepared for the uprising. "I will not fight for nobles only," he said. "I want freedom for the whole nation and for that only I will risk my life."[30] When on the eve of the rising Kollontay, at his request, wrote an act explaining the purposes of the movement and based it on the principles of the Constitution of the Third of May, he disapproved of it and expressed a wish that Poland should be organized as the American republic was; later, however, he agreed with others that the ultimate arrangement of the future government should be left to the decision of the nation. [31]

To mislead the enemies, Kosciuszko left Saxony for a brief sojourn in Italy early in 1794, but kept in touch with his colleagues and conspirators in Poland.[32] In Pisa he accidentally met Philip Mazzei, now an agent of King Stanislaus Augustus, who, seeing him apparently wandering without aim, suggested "that he go to America, where a large tract of land was due him for his contribution, as a general, to the establishment of independence." In order to throw him off his track, Kosciuszko seemingly agreed and even begged Mazzei to find out from what port he could sail,[33] meanwhile returning secretly to Poland.

With the memories of his American career so strongly inscribed in his mind, he decided at last to strike once more for Poland's freedom. Now was his supreme chance "to be of service to his country." Notwithstanding his optimism, he understood that circumstances favored Poland much less than they favored America a score of years ago. Death or Victory! was his chosen slogan, so oft repeated in his public announcements, and now it was truly a matter of death or life for Poland.

28 Konopczyński, *Dzieje Polski*, II, 399.
29 "To Poles," Janik, *op. cit.,* 333.
30 Konopczyński, *Od Sobieskiego do Kościuszki*, 321; Halecki, *History of Poland*, 206-207.
31 Sobieski, *Dzieje Polski*, II, 92.
32 Tokarz, *Warszawa*, passim.
33 Mazzei, *Memoirs*, 377; also Marraro, "Philip Mazzei," *Bul. of the Polish Institute*, II (1944), 773.

III.

FOR LIBERTY, INTEGRITY, INDEPENDENCE

Meanwhile, amidst the absolute silence and indifference of all Europe, Russia and Prussia concluded the Second Partition of Poland. The Russian Empress, Catherine II, ordered a considerable reduction in the strength of the Polish army. Several times Kosciuszko postponed the outbreak of the uprising because of insufficient preparations. Now the patriots had to act quickly before the disbandment of the army would greatly weaken their forces. On March 16, 1794, Kosciuszko secretly crossed the border of Poland. Taking advantage of the fact that the Russian troops left Cracow to intercept Gen. Joseph Madalinski who had refused to dismiss his brigade, Kosciuszko appeared in that city on March 23. On the next day, amid the ovations of the people gathered in the city square, he solemnly took office as Commander-in-Chief of the Insurrection and swore before "God and the innocent Passion of His Son . . . not to use the power entrusted to him for any personal oppression, but only . . . for the defense of the integrity of the boundaries, the regaining of the independence of the nation and the founding of universal freedom." "Liberty, Integrity and Independence" of the country he proclaimed as the supreme aims of the Insurrection.

Simultaneously he promulgated his famous Act of Insurrection, which is justly considered one of the most important Polish political documents and which deserves to be placed beside the American Declaration of Independence and the French Declaration of the Rights of Man as one of the most notable expressions of 18th century political doctrines.

Most of the subsequent insurrectional proclamations were prepared by Kollontay under Kosciuszko's supervision, but there is no doubt that the Act itself was in the main written by him. For this reason it is also important as an exposition of his political philosophy.

The Act, especially in its opening paragraphs, strongly resembles the Declaration of Independence in general construction and contents. Its definitions of political maxims, its whole tenor, are primarily based on American political literature of the Revolutionary era. Kosciuszko tried to breathe into the organism of dying Poland those animating ideas which he himself had imbibed so long and so fully during his stay in America. But he also tried to interpret them in the light of Poland's situation and needs. He introduced, therefore, some changes in the Act, significant to his way of thinking.

Both documents, the American Declaration and Kosciuszko's Act had identical purposes: externally, to explain the causes and purposes of action; internally, to awake enthusiasm for both movements.

Just like the Declaration, the Act may be divided into three parts, though the order and contents of the divisions differ. The beginning of both documents is strikingly similar: it is an appeal to the sympathies of the world. Just as "decent respect to the opinions of mankind" impelled Jefferson to explain the motives of the American patriots to all the world, so Kosciuszko, too, in the very first sentence turned to all humanity with a tragically brief statement: "The present state of unhappy Poland is known to the world."

Instead of referring next to natural rights, Kosciuszko immediately embarked upon an indictment of Poland's invaders and their hirelings, the Polish Tories. "The indignities suffered by two neighboring powers, and the crimes of traitors, have sunk the country into this abyss of misery," he accused them. "There is no species of falsehood, or perjury, or of treason, which . . . Catherine II and the perjured Frederick William . . . have not hesitated to commit, to satisfy their vengeance and their ambition." This was followed by a long list of wrongs suffered by Poland.

The second part of the Act explained "the sacred objects of our insurrection" which were: "The deliverance of Poland from foreign troops, the recovery of the entire possessions of the state, the extirpation of all oppression and usurpation, external as well as internal, the reestablishment of the national liberties and the independence of the Republic." This part also contained a prayer to God and an appeal to all "Nations which prize liberty above all other worldly goods" to be witness to the pure intentions of the authors of the uprising; though not specifically mentioned, it is clear that the foremost nations to which Kosciuszko addressed this plea were France and, above all, the United States.

The third part of the Act rather resembled the Constitution of the United States. It instituted legislative, executive and judiciary powers, the first two of which Kosciuszko was to share with the Supreme National Council. The functions of that body were modeled after those of the Continental Congress. This consisted of a combination of the legislature and the executive; it differed from the American pattern only in its subjection of all military matters to the authority of Kosciuszko. Undoubtedly, such an arrangement was the result of Kosciuszko's American experiences; he tried to remedy the indecision and slowness of Congress. Later, according to Kosciuszko's wish, the Supreme Council was subdivided into eight different boards, as these existed under the Continental Congress.[1] Moreover, each Palatinate was to have a Commission of Good Order which was to be the local executive body, and territorial Major Generals who were to head the militia. Judicial powers were confided to the Supreme Tribunal and lower courts.

All these powers were to last only till the winning of the basic purposes of the revolution. "Then the nation assembled by its repre-sentatives, . . . will decide on its future prosperity." The transitory character of these Polish revolutionary institutions again demonstrates how Kosciuszko leaned on American precedents.

Like the authors of the American Revolution, Kosciuszko felt the need of explaining the legal foundation of his Insurrection, and in this regard he did not neglect to invoke the American idea of "the right of the people to alter or to abolish governments which become de-structive." He expressed the same thought but in a slightly different manner: "the incontestable right of defending ourselves against tyr-anny and oppression." Neither did he fail to cite natural rights; he mentioned them several times throughout the Act, though there was no separate statement of them. He also deviated from the Jeffersonian definition of "life, liberty and pursuit of happiness," and from the notions of "life, liberty, property," most often advanced by pre-Revolutionary American political writers. Instead, he chose "liberty, security, property." Twice in the Act he repeated this definition, at one point extending it to "liberty, security and property of our per-sons and our possessions." Perhaps in this regard he used as his model Samuel Adams' *Rights of the Colonists* of 1772, in which the Massa-chusetts leader defined "personal security, personal liberty and private property" as the "absolute Rights of . . . all freemen."[2] More probably, however, in this single instance he followed the French Declaration.

What were the causes of these changes? Kosciuszko regarded the natural rights of man as established beyond doubt by the American Revolution. In his eyes, they were truths already accepted by the en-lightened world; he used them to support his claims, but they were not uppermost in his fight for the revindication of Poland's rights. The legal statuses of America and Poland were different. America, aspiring to independence, had to invoke the protection of natural rights from her status as a British dependency. Poland, an independent state for long centuries and still enjoying a waning semblance of in-dependence, could base her claims on her status as a state. The Ameri-

---

1 Appeal to the Citizens of Poland and Lithuania, May 21, 1794, Korzon, *Kosciuszko*, 329.
2 Samuel Adams, *Writings*, II, 356.

cans withdrew their allegiance from an established order; Kosciuszko aimed at restoring an old order, forcibly overturned by aggressors.

In accepting liberty, security and property as better suited to the needs of Poland, Kosciuszko was likewise guided by considerations of her situation. In his eyes, life was "the only good which tyranny as yet did not want to extort from us," so he offered it unrestrictedly on the altar of his country. As to the "pursuit of happiness," there is no doubt that he aimed at making "all inhabitants of Polish provinces truly happy;"[3] he spoke of happiness of the country not only in the Act itself, but used it in several of his later proclamations. However, there were many Polish magnates who made their natural rights to the pursuit of happiness superior to their duties to the country. To speak of happiness to the patriots and the rest of the nation seemed irony. Long files of them were trodding toward the snowy wastes of Siberia under guard of Russian bayonets; their properties were plundered and confiscated, as the partitioning powers like locust beset and devoured everything. Even removal of external oppression was not enough to make Poland happy; she still needed completion of recently inaugurated internal social reforms, and above all, the further improvement of the condition of the peasants, the largest, the most important and at the same time, in all respects, the poorest class of inhabitants. Kosciuszko, therefore, united his war with an attempt at these reforms and in his intentions he far outreached the work of the Great Diet. He had some precedents in the principles and acts of the leaders of contemporary Polish political thought, but it is evident that he strove to raise Poland to the American ideal of social and political equality. It was in this attempt to reform the Polish social structure that he appealed to the nation to "renounce all the prejudices of opinion, which have divided or may still divide the citizens, inhabitants of the same territory, and children of our common country."

Kosciuszko never excelled as a writer. His Act lacks the orderly logic and the classic style of the American Declaration of 1776. However, its dominant tones are a convincing sincerity, an ardent love of country and patriotic despair. The Declaration of Independence preserves its calmness even in those paragraphs which submit the "injuries and usurpations" of George III "to a candid world." "Our despair is full," said Kosciuszko, "and the love of our country is without bounds." When he said that he and the Polish nation were "determined to die or to entomb ourselves in the ruins of our country or to deliver the land of our fathers from a ferocious oppression," he perhaps was echoing Henry's challenge for liberty or death, or the bold Jeffersonian

---

3 Proclamation to the citizens of Brest and Kobryn, May 15, 1794, Mościcki, *Kosciuszko*, 71; he repeated almost the same phrase in his proclamation to the citizens of Warsaw, June 7, 1794, Korzon, *Kościuszko*, 372.

resolution "to die freemen, rather than to live as slaves" of the *Declaration of the Causes for Taking Up Arms* of 1775. With firmness he pledged the nation "to spare no sacrifices whatever, but . . . to use all the means which sacred love of Freedom can inspire in the breast of man; all that despair can suggest for its defence."[4]

The deepest analogy between the American and Polish movements was in their character. There was a strong, though small group among the Polish patriots, inclined to follow blindly French examples. But Kosciuszko refused to make his Insurrection a social upheaval of the French sort, even for the prize of French help. "God sees that we do not start a French revolution," he wrote to Princess Czartoryska.[5] He treated the faint-hearted King with official respect. When the mob at Warsaw hanged a few traitors on June 28, he immediately ordered criminal proceedings against the leaders and most strongly condemned the lynching. "What happened in Warsaw yesterday," he said in his proclamation, "filled my heart with bitterness and sorrow. The wish to punish the culprits was right, but why were they punished without the sentence of a court? Why were the authority and sanctity of laws violated? Know this that those who do not want to obey the laws are not worthy of liberty."[6] It was one of his greatest achievements that he saved Poland from a fratricidal struggle and gave the Polish Revolution the dominant American character of a national war for independence.

At the same time, he steadily, though gradually, broadened the social aspect of his movement. He became the champion of the peasants and of all "who as yet even did not know that they have a country."[7] Recognizing in the peasants the new citizens of the country, he called them to its defense and in his vision he already saw "a mighty mass of free inhabitants . . . fighting . . . against the crowd of . . . frightened slaves . . . for their own happiness."[8] In several proclamations he appealed for justice for peasants, forbade their oppression and interposed with nobles to lighten the burden of their forced labor. In his famous Manifesto of Polaniec he put the peasant under the protection of the government, made him free, recognized his rights to his land, and greatly reduced his socage. Even his most critical biographer acknowledged that this manifesto became "most important to the ideology" of all subsequent Polish generations.[9] In outward appearances he also showed his deep spirit of democracy; he chose the white cloak

---

4 All quotations from the Act of Insurrection are from the contemporary translation in *Dunlap and Claypoole's Am. Daily Advertiser*, Aug. 22, 1794.

5 Sometime in 1794, Korzon, *Kosciuszko*, 331; the original in Polish.

6 Proclamation to the citizens of Warsaw, June 29, 1794, Mościcki, *Kosciuszko*, 80-81.

7 Kosciuszko to Francis Sapieha, May 12, 1794, Korzon, *loc. cit.*, 316.

8 Proclamation of Połaniec, Mościcki, *op. cit.*, 57.

9 Skałkowski, "Finis Poloniae," *Polska, Jej Dzieje i Kultura*, II, 357.

of his peasant scythe-bearers as his uniform; he ordered that their flag bear an eloquent inscription: "They feed and defend."

Forgetting only himself, he embraced with his care all the needs of the country, its army and government, its industry and agriculture, its schools.[10] He had to forego all thoughts of foreign help. "The revolution in Poland won the admiration and prayers of the people . . . of Europe," wrote the imprisoned Lafayette,[11] but the corrupt French Committee of Public Safety stubbornly denied him all support. Saint-Just, speaking on its behalf, said to the Polish envoy: "The republic of France will sacrifice not a single grain of gold, not a single soldier" to aid the Polish cause.[12] "La revolution de Pologne n'en sert pas moins nos vues," wrote Rivals, the French agent at Bale.[13] After the fall of Robespierre in July 1794, the Thermidorists were equally indifferent or even openly unfriendly.[14] Thus Kosciuszko had to rely solely on his country's resources. To Gen. Sapieha he wrote: "Our war has its peculiar character . . . its success depends mostly on spreading enthusiasm and on general arming of the country."[15] Accordingly, he tried constantly to raise the nation to the heights of enthusiasm and heroism. In fiery proclamations, revealing the depth of his noble heart, he spoke to different groups of Poland's inhabitants, trying to win them to the national cause. As political documents they are unique in their lofty idealism in the history of 18th century Europe: "By friendliness, by kindness, we want to attach you, our brethren, to our common country," he said to the clergy of the Greek Orthodox Church.[16] He reminded others that "no Pole can honestly look for personal good, except in common good; none can think of saving honors and estates, except in saving the country."[17] He was one of the first statesmen to recognize the modern idea of self-determination and in another proclamation assured the inhabitants of Courland: "Poland will make no decisions concerning you without you. She will ask you what will be pleasant and useful to you."[18] "Let us lift our country out of slavedom," he wrote in his proclamation to the Polish and Lithuanian armies,[19] "let us restore its lustre to the name of Pole, to the Nation its independence, let us merit the gratitude of our country and the

---

10 Konopczyński, *Od Sobieskiego do Kościuszki*, 325.

11 "Kosciuszko and La Fayette," an essay by Lafayette, written in 1796, University of Chicago, Lafayette Papers, vol. II.

12 Askenazy, *Napoleon a Polska*, I, 63.

13 To Buchot, the Commissary of Foreign Relations, 2 Messidor (June 20), 1794, *Papiers de Barthelemy*, IV, 152.

14 Askenazy, *loc. cit.*, I, 67. See also: Tacitus, "Characteristic Sketch—General Kosciuszko," *Claypoole's Am. Daily Advertiser*, Philadelphia, April 12, 1797.

15 May 12, 1794, Korzon, *loc. cit.*, 316; the original in Polish.

16 Undated, Mościcki, *op. cit.*, 65.

17 Appeal to the Roman Catholic clergy of March 24, 1794, Nabielak, *Kościuszko*, 45.

18 The Supreme National Council to the citizens of Courland and Semigalia, July 8, 1794, *ib.*, 293.

19 March 24, 1794, Mościcki, *Kościuszko*, 45.

glory dear to a soldier." Sometimes his appeals reached poetic heights; in his first proclamation to the citizens he said: "The first step to throw off the yoke is to dare to believe ourselves free — and the first step to victory is confidence in our strength."[20] After the victory of Racławice (April 4), where he personally led the attack of his peasant battalion armed with scythes, he said: "Nation! . . . Feel at last thy strength, put it wholly forth; set thy will on being free and independent!"[21] When he suffered defeat at Szczekociny (June 6) because of an unexpected appearance of Prussian troops supporting the Russians, he openly explained the circumstances to the nation and closed his proclamation: "Nation! Your soil will be free, only let thy spirit be high above all."[22]

In all his actions he perhaps came nearest to the ideal of Jefferson, who said that "the whole art of government consists in the art of being honest."[23] At the height of his career, though already famous all over the civilized world, and now clothed with dictatorial power, Kosciuszko dreamed of a moment when, after freeing his country, he would "throw his sword at the feet of the Nation,"[24] and again "enjoy peace in a little house and play with his garden."[25] The burden of public duties weighed heavily upon him. "Let no virtuous man desire power," he wrote to Gen. Sapieha. "It was placed in my hands for this critical moment. I do not know whether I have deserved this trust, but I know that to me this power is only an instrument for the efficacious defense of my country and I confess that I desire its end as sincerely as the salvation of the nation itself."[26]

According to an eyewitness who visited Kosciuszko's camp and admired its "fine order, great subordination and discipline," he was "a simple man and . . . one most modest in conversation, manners, dress. He unites with the greatest resolution and enthusiasm for the undertaken cause much composure and judgment. It seems as though in all that he is doing there is nothing temerarious except the enterprise itself. In practical details he leaves nothing to chance: everything is thought out and combined. His may not be a transcendental mind, or one sufficiently elastic for politics. His inborn good sense is enough for him to estimate affairs correctly and to make the best choice at the first glance. The love of his country is the only thing which animates him. No other passion has dominion over him."[27]

---

20 March 24, 1794, contemp. translation from *Dunlap and Claypoole's Amer. Daily Advertiser*, Aug. 22, 1794.

21 "Report to the Nation" of April 5, 1794, Mościcki, *loc. cit.*, 52.

22 June 9, 1794, Gardner, *loc. cit.*, 136.

23 "A Summary View of the Rights of British in America," Lipscomb, I, 210.

24 Proclamation to the citizens of Poland and Lithuania, May 21, 1794, Korzon, *op. cit.*, 329.

25 To Princess Czartoryska, sometime in 1794, Korzon, *loc. cit.*, p. 650, note 593; the original in Polish.

26 May 12, 1794, Korzon, *loc. cit.*, 300; the original in Polish.

27 Joseph Ossolinski to Thugut, May 1, 1794, Gardner, *loc. cit.*, 131.

Once he said: "We have sinned by forbearance and this is the cause why Poland is perishing"[28] but, according to his most important biographer, "he had severity on his tongue . . . , his heart overflowed with love and mildness."[29] During all his tenure of office as Commander-in-Chief he signed not a single sentence of death. His love of justice is well illustrated by an episode in which Lewis Littlepage of Virginia was involved.[30] This American Secretary to the King found himself on the list of persons suspected of treason; he was considered an agent of Russia and there was incriminating evidence against him. Littlepage became frightened and appealed for protection directly to Kosciuszko. Introducing himself as an American citizen and reminding Kosciuszko of his former title of an American General, he protested his innocence and conjured him in the name of America, "his second country," to do him justice and appoint a commission to investigate the accusation. Kosciuszko answered him in a letter which revealed again the beauty of his soul and his attachment to America:

"I do not know what opinion you have in Poland, but I know that in your case I have given no orders; however, to get an answer to your questions directed to me you will do best by addressing the

---

28 Proclamation to the citizens, March 24, 1794, Mościcki, *loc. cit.*, 44.

29 Korzon, *loc. cit.*, 419.

30 Lewis Littlepage of Virginia (1762-1802) was sent by his guardian, Benjamin Lewis, to Madrid in 1780, to complete his education and to make a start towards a diplomatic career under his relative, John Jay, the American Minister to Spain. Instead he became an adventurer, an highly objectionable character. In 1781, he took part in the Spanish expeditions against Minorca and Gibraltar. In 1782-3, he lived in Paris, and visited London. On his scandalous behavior in France see Mazzei to the King of Poland, Jan 30, 1789, Marraro, "Philip Mazzei," *Bulletin of the Polish Institute*, II (1944), 786-790. Together with Prince Charles de Nassau-Siegen, another notorious adventurer, he made a journey to Turkey through Poland in 1784. Introduced to Stanislaus Augustus he received a proposition to become his secretary. Littlepage accepted it gladly, but before entering his new duties in Poland, he returned to the United States to put his affairs in order. On this occasion the King gave him a letter of introduction to George Washington. While in America Littlepage entered into a scandalous dispute with Jay which produced two pamphlets revealing their private affairs and almost resulted in a duel between both relatives. (Jay was the first to publish: *Letters Being the Whole of the Correspondence between the Hon. John Jay and Mr. Lewis Littlepage, a Young Man whom Mr. Jay when in Spain Patronized and Took into his Family*, New York, 1786; Littlepage retorted with: *Answer to a Pamphlet Containing the Correspondence between the Hon. John Jay, Secretary for Foreign Affairs, and Lewis Littlepage, Esquire, of Virginia, Chamberlain and Secretary of the Cabinet of His Majesty the King of Poland*. Philadelphia, 1786). In 1786, Littlepage returned to Poland and remained in the employ of the King till his abdication in 1795, meanwhile serving also as a volunteer with the Russian army in the war with Turkey in 1778-9. It was he who induced John Paul Jones to enter the Russian service to the latter's detriment. Stanislaus Augustus made him his chamberlain and bestowed other favors on him, which did not prevent him from shamelessly exploiting the lavishness of the King and from betraying Poland (see Jefferson's letter to Madison, July 31, 1788, Lipscomb, VII, 94-5). Gen. Igelstrom, Commander-in-Chief of the Russian forces in Poland, recommending Littlepage to Sievers, the new Russian Ambassador, on March 27, 1793, assured him that Littlepage is "completely of our system. He has all the power over the mind of the King." (Sievers, *Drugi Rozbiór Polski*, I, 69). It was he who extracted from the unhappy King the promise to sign the Second Partition of Poland (*ibid.*, I, 105), for which service Sievers promised Littlepage to cash the King's notes in his possession; in 1793, these notes amounted to nearly one million Polish zlotys (Korzon, *Wewnętrzne Dzieje*, III. 90) and were coaxed out of the King by Littlepage for services of dubious character. The Russian Ambassador contemptuously called him "an Anglo-American spy." After the Third Partition Littlepage remained in Poland waiting for the payment of his Judas' pieces of silver, meanwhile "dividing his time between Venus and Bacchus" (J. U. Niemcewicz to Jefferson, Aug. 7, 1800, Hayden, *Virginia Genealogies*, 412). Broken in health as a consequence of his dissolute life, he returned to America in 1801, and the next year died in Spotsylvania, Va. A Polish historian branded him as "one of the most abominable figures" in the history of Poland's partitions (Krzeminski, *Stanisław August*, I, 155). A brief biography of Littlepage given by Hayden, *loc. cit.*, is without value, except for a handful of original letters quoted in full. On his relations with John Jay cf. Jay, *Life of John Jay*, I, 204 ff.

Supreme National Council which most assuredly will not fail to render justice and which is better informed in this matter than myself You may be sure that a despotic act never would receive my approbation. The title of an American will always be sacred to me. You do not need to remind me of it to find justice among us. Can a nation fighting to gain it from its oppressors, deny it to others?

"I venture, therefore, to be an interpreter of principles which are and always will be inspiring the revolution in Poland."[31]

By his untiring efforts, Kosciuszko succeeded in spreading the insurrection to all parts of Poland. In answer to his appeals, Warsaw and Wilno rose spontaneously and rid themselves of the Russians. The flame of Insurrection involved Great Poland and all Lithuania; they even reached Dantzig and Courland.[32] All the best elements of the nation flocked to Kosciuszko's support. His army grew to 90,000 men at one time, the largest armed force old Poland was ever able to muster. His greatest triumph was the repulse of a two-months long siege of Warsaw by the combined Russian and Prussian armies, the last force personally commanded by King Frederick William II (July 13 — September 6). But the days of the Insurrection already were numbered. On October 10, overwhelming Russian forces crushed Kosciuszko's army in the bloody battle of Maciejowice. With utmost bravery he personally led his soldiers and, seriously wounded, was taken prisoner. This was almost the end of the Insurrection. Warsaw still tried to resist the armies of Field Marshal Suvorov, but succumbed after the bloody slaughter of almost all the inhabitants of Praga, its suburb, ordered by the ruthless Russian commander. There was no one to take Kosciuszko's place and all resistance was soon crushed. The Third Partition followed (1795) and Poland disappeared from the map of Europe.

Kosciuszko was carried off to St. Petersburg and placed in strict confinement. The best sons of Poland shared his fate. Kollontay, one of his most ardent collaborators, now brooding over the tragic past in an Austrian prison, aptly defined Kosciuszko's role in history of Poland in the simple words of this patriotic elegy:

"Bless the knight who, though perishing himself,
Saved you from a dishonorable death; you have died with honor."[33]

But is was only as a political entity that Poland died on the battlefield of Maciejowice. "Not by the strength of a genius, but by the wisdom of his heart,"[34] Kosciuszko saved the life of the nation.

31 Dubiecki, "Tytuł Amerykanina Jest Święty." *Dziennik Chicagoski*, Aug. 13, 1926, p. 5; the original letter in French.
32 Konopczynski, *Dzieje Polski*, II, 400 and 405; Halecki, *History of Poland*, 207.
33 Janik, *Kołłątaj*, 405.
34 Askenazy, *Napoleon a Polska*, III, 29.

What was more, the Insurrection inspired it most strongly, as no other factor, with an indestructible will to survive and with the determination to regain its rights. Kosciuszko became the symbol of the most sublime national virtues and his name a watchword for all patriotic endeavors of succeeding generations. "Out of nonentity," said an eminent Polish historian, "he extracted an immense force; he demonstrated what the nation, even without foreign help, can accomplish; by his single achievement, notwithstanding immediate defeat, he opened a source of lasting hope for the future. From a leader of a lost insurrection, he became forever a symbol of national resurrection."[35]

Undoubtedly Kosciuszko had his shortcomings as a military leader. One fact speaks out for him most eloquently: he was handicapped by the numerical inferiority of his forces, their lack of equipment and experience, and by the devastation of the country by partitions and long foreign military occupations; abandoned and disregarded by all Europe, he succeeded in opposing singlehanded three great military powers of the continent for over six months. His political acts as chief of the nation sometimes lacked an indisputable legal basis, but they all were aimed at the highest good of the nation and no one ever questioned his motives.

A shortsighted Polish historian criticized him for following American examples too often and too closely.[36] As a matter of fact, Kosciuszko became the foremost standard bearer of American ideals in Europe. His Insurrection was so closely associated with and patterned after the American Revolution as no other movement in European history.[37] From among the host of foreign officers who heeded the call of 1776, none, not excepting Lafayette, could compare with him in the audacity of his undertaking, none in purity of his motives and none learned better the lesson of democracy. Revolutionary France disgraced her rapture for freedom with injustice and crimes. Transplanting American ideals into Poland — the farthest point on the globe reached by the immediate influence of the American Revolution — Kosciuszko succeeded in preserving them unstained. He did not attain for his country the blessings of freedom which he saw and tasted in the New World. But, though knowing well from the very beginning all the difficulties of his task, he at least dared to try to wrench the stolen rights of his people out of the bloody hands of tyrants.

Even contemporaries recognized the American influence in the Kosciuszko Insurrection. "The revolution in Poland, conducted by the gallant Kosciuszko, the pupil of the immortal Washington, was a con-

---

35 *Ibid.*, III, 30.
36 Skałkowski, "Finis Poloniae," *Polska, Jej Dzieje i Kultura*, II, 346.
37 Sister M. Liguori, "The Ideal Cultural Link," *Polish-American Studies*, II (1945), 68.

sequence flowing from the struggles of America," said the Rev. George Richards of New Hampshire in his Fourth of July oration of 1795.[38]

Since 1791, events in Poland absorbed the attention of Americans. It was the Constitution of the Third of May that started a wave of popular enthusiasm for Poland in the United States. But while the French frenzy, the Whisky Rebellion, the hotly contested election of a new Congress in 1794, Washington's attack on the Democratic societies, the Jay Treaty and other events successively shook and divided American public opinion more and more sharply, Poland escaped the fate of becoming a subject of strife between two warring camps of American political thought. Republicans and Federalists remained unanimous throughout in extolling her struggle for freedom. Sentiment for Poland contained no elements which might have caused any divergence of opinion.[39]

The Insurrection intensified this enthusiasm. Kosciuszko still was well remembered by many of his former comrades-in-arms. At once he became the "Washington of Poland," acclaimed in verse and in innumerable toasts, in sermons and in orations, and in the press. His "bold enterprises, his patient endurance, his invincible courage, his unyielding firmness and his ardent patriotism, were the daily theme of private circles and public journals."[40]

The progress of the Insurrection was followed by Americans with deep interest. The press printed long accounts of events, mostly reprints from the English press. Another proof of this interest is found in contemporary letters touching on the subject. "There is great reason to hope he (Kosciuszko) will be successful, and prove the Washington of Poland, and I am sure there is no harm in saying, *God grant it,*" wrote a "gentleman" of Boston residing at Rotterdam, to his home city.[41] "Kosciusko is by the last accounts going on well," Humphreys informed Washington. "I dread, however, the result from the formidable force that will be opposed to the Poles. Unanimity is everything. If they hold out this Campaign, I trust the Insurrection will terminate in Independence."[42] Rev. William Gordon, historian of the American Revolution, was full of enthusiasm and nearly agreed with Humphreys as to the possible success of the movement. He wrote to Washington: "You was raised up by the Lord of Hosts to be an instrument of saving the United States from slavery. I most sincerely wish, that the same Omnipotent Power may have commissioned Kosciusko to deliver the Poles from under slavery. If he and his coadjutors can just weather the

---

38 Richards, *Oration,* 30-31.
39 Cf. Haiman, *Fall of Poland, passim.*
40 Goodrich, *Token,* 346.
41 May 30, 1794, *Dunlap and Claypoole's Am. Daily Advertiser,* Aug. 26, 1794.
42 June 28, 1794, Humphreys, *Life and Times of David Humphreys,* II, 213.

present year, I shall scarce doubt of his succeeding in his glorious attempt."[43] The strength of the Insurrection seemed to surprise Monroe who reported to Jefferson from Paris: "The spirit of liberty begins to shew itself in other regions . . . in Poland under the direction of Kosciuszko who acted with us in America, a formidable head has been raised against Prussia and Russia."[44]

According to the testimony of a contemporary, Noah Webster, a Federalist, "the minds of Americans . . ." were "extremely agitated with respect" to Poland at that period. Extolling the "glorious . . . enterprize" of Kosciuszko, he continued in one of his editorials in the *American Minerva:* "With what emotions of joy did we hear the intelligence of *Poland in arms!* Kosciusko was hailed as the deliverer of his country and numbered with the Washingtons of the Age! What pleasure was inspired in our bosoms, when he was successful . . . How short the delusion! No sooner did the irresistible veterans of the savage North appear in Poland, than Kosciusko is defeated, his troops dispersed and the hero himself a prisoner in chains . . . Unfortunate Poland! Freemen will never erase the sigh for thy deliverance! . . . the hearts of Americans, with one consent, will exult in the triumphs which must ultimately crown your exertions."[45]

Rev. Jedidiah Morse, pitying Kosciuszko for his wounds, stressed in one of his sermons that his "fate interests the feelings of *the friends of liberty* through Europe and America."[46] William Loughton Smith of South Carolina, another Federalist, assured Kosciuszko and Poland of "fervent prayers" of a "united America" for their delivery[47] and John Dickinson, the Republican "Fabius," deplored the unhappy outcome of the Insurrection "by which a noble nation was despoiled of liberty, at the very moment when they were most sensible of its value;" he branded the destruction of Poland as "a deed, as base and as cruel, as any of the records ancient or modern, of tyrannical hostilities against human race, can supply."[48] Jefferson and John Adams agreed that partition of Poland was a "wound" inflicted upon the "character of honor" of European governments and that it destroyed that old "respect to faith" and "dignity" which heretofore was considered their inseparable attribute.[49] Washington himself was no less indifferent toward the sad fate of Poland. Assuring a veteran of the Kosciuszko Insurrection that he prayed for Poland during that "arduous contest,"

43 Sept. 12, 1794, Gordon, "Letters," *Mass. Hist. Soc. Proceedings,* LXIII (1931), 573.
44 Sept. 7, 1794, Hamilton, *Writings of Monroe,* II, 53.
45 *Minerva,* as reprinted in *Dunlap and Claypoole's Am. Daily Advertiser,* Feb. 26, 1795.
46 Morse, *The Present Situation,* 24.
47 Smith, *Oration,* 28.
48 Letter IV, "The Letters of Fabius," *Political Writings,* II, 188; also many other references to Poland, *passim.*
49 Jefferson to Adams, Jan. 11, 1816, and Adams to Jefferson, Feb. 2, 1816, Lipscomb, XIV, 394 and 424.

he wrote: "That your country is not as happy as your struggle to make it so, was Patriotic and Noble, is a matter which all lovers of national Liberty and the Rights of Man, have sorely lamented."[50]

The only gesture made by Kosciuszko intended for the United States during his brief rule in Poland were his instructions to Francis Barss, his envoy in Paris, to deliver a copy of the Act of Insurrection to the American Minister.[51] Well he understood what Webster said in the above quoted editorial: "Your distance places you beyond the reach of our assistance." His move had only one purpose: to win the sympathy of the country whose memory was sacred to him. In that he succeeded entirely.

---

[50] To Niemcewicz, June 18, 1798, Fitzpatrick, XXXVI, 297.
[51] This copy, in French, is still preserved in the National Archives, Division of State Department Archives, Miscellaneous Letters.

IV.

ON HIS SECOND TRIP TO AMERICA

"M. de St. Priest tells me his news from Petersburg. The Emperor took his son to the apartment where Kosciusko lay ill. He told the prisoner that he saw in him a man of honor who had done his duty, and from whom he asked no other security but his word that he would never act against him. Kosciuszko attempted to rise, but the Emperor forbade him; sat half an hour and conversed with him, told his son to esteem the unhappy prisoner, who was immediately released — the guard taken away. At the same time expresses were sent off into Siberia, and ten thousand Poles confined there received passports and money to bring them home. This story is afterwards told me by M. Laskoren-ski,[1] a Pole, who can scarcely restrain his tears as he relates it. They are all of them in ecstasy . . ."[2]

Thus under the date of December 19, 1796, Gouverneur Morris, then residing in Vienna, recorded in his diary the unexpected release of Kosciuszko from Russian imprisonment. At first the General was confined in the dungeons of the Petropavlosk fortress, but, when his physical resistance failed and he became mortally sick, he was transferred to more comfortable quarters at the Orloff Palace at St. Petersburg. "Overwhelm'd with the flood of Despair"[3] over the fate of Poland, tortured by cross-examinations, he became a physical and nervous wreck. His unhealed and badly attended wounds deprived him of the use of his legs. And only the almost sudden death of Catherine II brought him freedom after two years of tortures.

One of the first official acts of the new Tsar, Paul I, was to visit Kosciuszko and to pronounce him free. The General requested that, above all, his compatriots, the prisoners of the Insurrection, should also be freed. To gain their release he had to take an oath of allegiance to the Russian Emperor and this was the greatest sacrifice of his life. The memory of this self-imposed subjugation forever weighed heavily on his mind. As to himself he had only one wish: that he might be allowed to depart for America.

The Tsar, the Tsarina, and the Grand Dukes, showered him with courtesies and costly gifts. The Emperor also gave him twelve thousand

---

1 Lanckoronski, a Polish magnate family.

2 Gouverneur Morris, *Diary and Letters*, II, 238.

3 "Lamentation of Kosciuszko," a poem, *Columbian Centinel*, March 30, 1796.

roubles for his traveling expenses, but this Kosciuszko refused.[4] He was entertained at the imperial palace with highest distinctions. All this was like a most fantastic tale! But Kosciuszko had no illusions. He, whom the slightest act of kindness on the part of his friends moved deeply, accepted all Russian graces courteously and with dignity, but with inner aversion and suspicion. Julian Ursyn Niemcewicz, his secretary during the Insurrection, was one of the first to visit him after the liberation. He found Kosciuszko very much changed, but what he noticed above all, was his fear of spies; he was afraid to speak aloud even in private.[5]

On December 19, the same day Morris received the news of his liberation at Vienna, Kosciuszko left St. Petersburg for the long voyage across the Atlantic. He was accompanied not only by Niemcewicz, but also by one Libiszewski, a former Polish officer of considerable strength, whose duty was to carry Kosciuszko from his bed or couch to his carriage.

Slowly passing through Finland, the Aland Islands and Sweden, during the heavy snows of midwinter, the travelers reached Stockholm on January 26, 1797. Their journey was like a triumphal procession. Highest officials and plain people welcomed them everywhere with enthusiasm and deepest esteem. "Our doors never closed," wrote Niemcewicz in his diary; "everybody strove to see the man who so bravely defended his dying country."[6]

On February 23, Kosciuszko left for Gothenburg to await a vessel for England. Here again the same scenes were repeated. "The principal inhabitants of the city go to see him, and keep him company, as he cannot stir from his house," wrote an anonymous correspondent. "The ladies of the place take instruments of music with them, and strive by chorus of melody to assuage his misfortunes. The Americans, I am sure, will love him, like us, to adoration. He is a man of great information, amiable to the extreme . . ."[7]

Kosciuszko was not able to leave Gothenburg until May 10. It took him nearly three weeks on a Swedish vessel to reach England.

His arrival in London on May 29 was rather inconvenient to the government of Pitt. The former American "rebel," now an impotent

---

4 So says Zeltner, "Personal Reminiscences," *U. S. Service Mag.*, IV (1865), 138. When Kosciuszko reached England, he continues, he was informed by the bankers of the Emperor of Russia, Messrs. Thompson, Bonard & Co., that the sum of money presented to him by Paul had been placed in their hands, and was at his disposal. According to Madame Fiszer, Kosciuszko accepted the money for fear of compromising the fate of his former soldiers, but on reaching London he left it in that bank. ("Pamiętnik," 253); opinions of Polish historians on this point differ. Justice Wayne, in deciding the case of his American estate in 1852, said however, that he declined to accept all presents from the Tsar (Howard, *Reports*, XIV, 424).

5 Niemcewicz, *Pamiętniki*, 292.

6 *Ibid*, 312.

7 An excerpt from a letter from Gothenburg, April 5, 1797, in *Carey's Daily Advertiser*, July 8, 1797.

invalid, but still politically dangerous, came like a reminder of the crime of the Partitions perpetrated on Poland with the tacit approval of England; his presence might disturb those guilty powers, their hands still covered with the blood of Poland, which Pitt now expected to win for a coalition to destroy revolutionary France. Still the Tory papers did not dare to attack the guest, and enthusiasm carried the people. He was greeted by throngs with the "greatest excitement."[8] People besieged his hotel[9] to pay him a visit, or at least, to catch a sight of the famous man. Some could not restrain their tears on seeing him.[10] Foremost Whigs like Fox, Wilberforce, Cartwright and Grey, men of letters like Sheridan, Wolcott and Landor, prominent ladies like Lady Oxford and Duchess of Devonshire, paid him homage. Sir John Sinclair, president of the Board of Agriculture, availed himself of his announced early departure to entrust him with notes and packages for Washington and President Adams. The artist Cosway mixed with the crowd and clandestinely sketched Kosciuszko's features. The Whig Club of England, at a numerous and distinguished meeting, unanimously accepted a motion of Gen. Tarleton, seconded by Fox, to present Kosciuszko with a costly sword "as a public testimony of their sense of his exalted virtues and of his gallant, generous and exemplary efforts to defend and save his country."[11] Others heaped presents on him, though he tried to avoid them. His sojourn in London lasted only two weeks, but it was long enough to impress his features "worn by horrid suffrance — mightily forlorn,"[12] his emaciated figure as he leaned against a sofa, with bandaged head, on the imagination of a whole generation of English romantic poets. Keats, Tennyson, Byron, Hunt, Campbell, all sung his virtues in unforgettable stanzas.[13] Jane Porter wrote her famous romance *Thaddeus of Warsaw,* which, notwithstanding its mediocrity, became one of the most popular novels of the century on both sides of the Atlantic.

On the express order of the Emperor, Count Semen Vorontsov, the Russian Minister, was another frequent visitor of Kosciuszko. In letters full of admiration for the Pole, Dr. Rogerson, the Russian court physician, begged him to do everything in his power to restore his health.[14] Vorontsov called a consultation of the most prominent Eng-

8 Niemcewicz, *Pamiętniki,* 317; on the stand of Pitt's government see also: *Carey's Daily Advertiser,* August 9, 1797, and a letter from London in the *Nouvelles Politiques,* Paris, July 3, 1797, as quoted by Skałkowski, *O Kokardę Legionów,* 181-2. For excerpts from the London press pertaining to Kosciuszko's sojourn in the British capital see M. Tuleja, "Z Pobytu T. Kościuszki," *Prawda,* Oct. 15, 1917.

9 It was La Sablonniere, at Leicester Square, "a good and cheap but not fashionable" hotel kept by a French emigrant (Engestrom, *Pamiętniki,* 184).

10 Warner, *Literary Recollections,* II, 135.

11 *Carey's Daily Advertiser,* August 12, 1797.

12 Keats, *"Sleep and Poetry,"* verses 387-8.

13 Kosznicki, "Sonet Keats'a do Kościuszki," *Tygodnik Polski,* August 8, 1943.

14 Korzon, *Kosciuszko,* 478 and note 709.

lish physicians to examine Kosciuszko and to prescribe a cure for the use of American physicians, who would take care of the distinguished patient. The consultation took place on June 3, and among its participants were Sir George B. Baker, the King's own physician and president of the College of Physicians; John H. Hunter, William Saunders and Sir Gilbert B. Blane, all three Physicians Extraordinary to the Prince of Wales, the last mentioned famed as an authority on naval medicine; David Pitcairn, a very popular physician, renowned for his charity; Henry C. Cline, a surgeon; Matthew Baillie, the famous Scottish anatomist, and some others, no less prominent.[15] They found that Kosciuszko's "considerable pains in the head" were caused by a stroke of "a blunt sabre" which severed a nerve "at the lower part of the hind head"; similarly "the Paralytic state of Thigh and Leg" was "owing to another wound he received . . . in the Hip, with a Cossack pike" which injured "the Sciatic nerve." Their verdict as to the curability of these injuries was hopeful to Kosciuszko. The physicians came to the conclusion that "he will probably recover in a considerable degree." They closed their report: "It gives us the most heartfelt satisfaction to think, that we may probably contribute to the comfort of a man, whose Character and exertions in behalf of his country, have called forth the admiration of the whole civilized World."[16]

Dr. Thomas Beddoes, known for his work on pulmonary consumption and founder of the "pneumatic" hospital at Clifton,[17] also examined Kosciuszko and wrote a separate report, supporting the above opinion.[18] All these medical papers were handed to Kosciuszko for the use of Dr. Benjamin Rush of Philadelphia whom the British physicians unanimously recommended as the ablest physician in America. Still another British physician, Dr. Benjamin M. Moseley, who served overseas with the British army during the Revolution, wrote to Dr. Rush:

"As the virtuous and renowned general Kosciusko, is now here, on his way to Philadelphia, and as his health is such, as will require great care and attention when he arrives in your country, I have recommended him through the means of friends, and have given him this letter, to you. I was the more anxious that he should be under your care, lest so valuable a man should fall into ignorant hands; which would be a great grief to the friends of freedom in England. Not only your country, but the world owes him great obligations; and I most sincerely hope that the remainder of his life will be happy."[19]

---

15 Hubotten, *Biographisches Lexikon, passim.*
16 Ridgway Library, Rush Papers, 7246 F. 39.
17 Hubotten, *loc. cit.,* I, 419.
18 June 17, 1797, Ridgway Libr., Rush Papers, 7246 F. 40.
19 June 11, 1797, Ridgway Libr., Rush Papers, 7241 F. 101.

Among other visitors of Kosciuszko in London there also was Rufus King, the American Minister, who in his official capacity and out of his personal friendship, extended all possible courtesies to the traveler. He related to Kosciuszko all the latest events in America and the changeable fortunes of his old comrades. He arranged passage for him to America,[20] and tried to make easy his way by letters of introduction. He recommended him most warmly to Col. Timothy Pickering, Secretary of State:

"I have the honor to introduce to you General Kosciuszko who seeks in America that Repose, which he has long desired, as necessary to restore and confirm his Health.

"The General is accompanied by two of his Friends one of whom Julian Niemcewicz is likewise his Relation;[21] these Gentlemen merit esteem and Respect, and will I am persuaded share in those Demonstrations of affectionate attachment with which General Kosciuszko will be welcomed in every Part of our Country."[22]

A similar letter was addressed by King to John Jay,[23] the governor of New York, where Kosciuszko expected to visit Gen. Gates.

"The virtuous patriot, and gallant general"[24] left London on June 12, and after a night spent in Bath, reached Bristol the next day. Again followed familiar scenes of welcome by officials and private citizens. Col. John Trumbull, his colleague of the Ticonderoga campaign, now in the American diplomatic service, took part in the procession in his honor. While at Bristol, Kosciuszko availed himself of the hospitality of Elias Vanderhorst of South Carolina, the American Consul and his old friend, and accepted lodgings at his house.[25] "Great numbers waited on him,"[26] among them a deputation of citizens who presented him with silver plate of one hundred guineas value, together with an address extolling his "exalted genius, . . . intrepid valour, and unshaken constancy in defense of the freedom," and expressing a wish "that in the bosom of a country, whose subjugation you virtuously resisted, and whose glorious independence your heroism contributed to establish, you may experience its warmest gratitude . . ."[27]

Not only visitors, but also correspondents took up Kosciuszko's time. Despite his bad health he made a "Point of answering every

20 Kosciuszko to King, London, June 3, 1797, King, ed., *Life and Correspondence of Rufus King*, II, 188.

21 King was mistaken; Niemcewicz was no relation to Kosciuszko.

22 June 10, 1797, Mass. Hist. Soc, Pickering Papers, XXI, 143.

23 June 10, 1797, Johnston, ed., *Correspondence and Public Papers of John Jay*, IV, 228.

24 *The Time Piece*, Sept. 18, 1797.

25 This house is still preserved. Its present address is 37 Queen Square. It bears a memorial tablet commemorating Kosciuszko's stay, Bristol Development Board, *Birthplace of America, Bristol—England*, 29.

26 *The Time Piece*, Sept. 18, 1797.

27 *Claypoole's American Daily Advertiser*, Aug. 22, 1797.

letter."[28] Before leaving London he thanked King for his courtesies, then from Bristol he again wrote him a letter overflowing with gratitude for favors:

"Your generous heart," he wrote,[29] "has found no limits, and you have continued your kind care at Bristol and America. I am under the greatest obligation to you, and more forcibly not having deserved it . . .

"I have been particularly desired by Mr. Vander-Horst, American Consul, and his amiable Family to accept a Lodging at their house, where I am more tenderly treated than if I had been a Member of their Family. You can not conceive what Cares and friendly attentions are shown to me. It grieves me much that I am not able to shew them a degree of Gratitude equal to my feelings . . ."

On Monday, June 19, the Adriana, with Kosciuszko aboard, left Bristol amid manifestations of greatest public emotion. Thousands of people lined the banks of the Avon River and bade him adieu with shouts and waving of hats and kerchiefs. Some followed the Adriana in boats, notwithstanding the rough sea, to offer fruits and flowers to the hero and to catch a last glimpse of him. Among these was the family of Vanderhorst, whom he did not neglect to rebuke in a friendly way for so endangering their lives. "When separation took place," he wrote, "our hearts were melted in tears. And we were frightened at their return, with fears of what might happen to them upon a high sea in so small a boat. Every rising wave gave the greatest pain to our anxiety, and the extreme painfulness of our alarm, even increased when we were so far off that we could not see them more."[30]

A local editor wrote him a farewell: "May God of heaven, earth and sea protect him on his voyage! May the gentlest gales waft him over the mighty ocean, and conduct him safe to America, the chief, if not the ONLY asylum for the persecuted sons of freedom! He carries with him the prayers of thousands . . ."[31]

The Adriana had a rough passage amid "winds adverse and obstinate storms."[32] Once the ocean almost became the grave of the hero. At 40th degree latitude[33] "a vessel belonging to a fleet of merchantmen, returning from Jamaica, was separated from her company in a dark night, and whilst sailing with the greatest rapidity, struck the American ship. Masts, rigging and sails were instantly entangled. Two large vessels lay beating forcibly against each other. Great was the

28 Kosciuszko to Joseph Cattle, Bristol, June 17, 1797, The University of Chicago Libraries.
29 June 16, 1797, King, Life of Rufus King, II, 189.
30 Dated "At sea," Porter, Thaddeus of Warsaw, 531.
31 Reprinted in The Time Piece, Sept. 18, 1797.
32 Niemcewicz, Pamiętniki, 319.
33 Ibid, 321.

CABIN BOY OF THE ADRIANA
by Kosciuszko

tumult, noise and disorder upon deck — death stared us in the face."
Frightened passengers, crying women and children, all thronged into
the cabin of Kosciuszko as if expecting help from him. "Kosciusco
viewed the scene, at this dismaying and terrifying moment, with his
usual serenity and composure." The danger lasted for an hour till
sailors, armed with axes, at last cut the entangled riggings and sails.
Happily the ship did not spring a leak. The accident was caused by
the helmsman of the Anna, the eastward sailing vessel; he had fallen
asleep at the wheel after too many drinks.[34]

The trip was also otherwise unpleasant. The ship was crowded
with Welsh and Irish immigrants. Kosciuszko had to share his cabin
not only with his companions, but also with a stranger, Mr. Joshua
Sutcliffe of Philadelphia. [35] Provisions became low and passengers had
to be satisfied with salt pork and crackers, though Captain Lee had
fresh poultry for Kosciuszko alone. Drinking water became spoiled.
Amid all these inconveniences the General found pleasure in drawing
sketches of the persons around him.

It is almost certain that immediately after his liberation, Kosciuszko was seriously inclined to make America his home for the rest
of his life, "if only the memory of his country would not follow
him."[36] For two years he had been almost cut off from the outside
world, yet undoubtedly some news of world events had reached his
ears through the walls of his prison. On his way through Northern
Europe, he had become acquainted with the European and Polish political situation more detailedly. The news that had been most startling
to him was of a Polish armed force being organized under French
orders by Gen. John Henry Dombrowski, who had served under him
with distinction in the Insurrection. It seems that Kosciuszko had even
protracted his stay at Gothenburg purposely to enter into his first contact with leading Polish exiles. But the news of the armistice of Leoben,
so chilling to Polish hopes, fear for the fate of his countrymen just
liberated from Russian prisons by the amnesty bought by his sub-
mission, and "all too fresh memories of St. Petersburg,"[37] had
impelled him to continue his journey.

Europe was now entering the Napoleonic era and important
political repercussions seemed to be imminent. Without revealing his
heart to anyone, Kosciuszko decided to wait and observe. Meanwhile
his thoughts turned to the other side of the Atlantic where he expected soon to meet his American friends and to revisit familiar
places of his American career.

34 Niemcewicz's eulogy of Kosciuszko, Warsaw, Nov. 14, 1817, Niles, *Principles and Acts of the Revolution,* 475.
35 *Carey's Daily Advertiser,* Aug. 19, 1797.
36 Fiszer, "Pamiętnik," 253.
37 Askenazy, *Thaddeus Kosciuszko,* 18.

V.

AT PHILADELPHIA

The America of 1797 was much different from the America which Kosciuszko had left thirteen years before. "When I returned from France, after an absence of six or seven years, I was astonished at the change which I found had taken place in the United States in that time," wrote Jefferson to William Short.[1] "No more like the same people; their notions, their habits and manners, the course of their commerce so totally changed, that I, who stood in those of 1784, found myself not at all qualified to speak their sentiments, or forward their views in 1790." If Jefferson found such radical changes in 1790, what of the last decade of the eighteenth century, which still more profoundly inscribed its path across the pages of the country's history.

Time had removed the destruction and healed the wounds caused by the Revolutionary War. The country had prospered. It had doubled in population. It had made quick progress in all fields of public life. But it was still very young. Only ten years had passed since the adoption of the new federal constitution. The new order of the land was gradually and painfully consolidating and transforming the country into a nation. Not only the most important and still unclarified constitutional questions, not only far reaching national and international problems, but also, what would appear today, the simplest, sometimes the silliest questions, provoked the most vehement disputes.[2]

Out of the patriotism of the Revolutionary era two schools of political thought arose, ruthlessly fighting each other. The Republicans proclaimed the sovereignty of the people. The Federalists thought that people should be governed, considering only themselves capable of constituting this governing power. The Republicans were strongly convinced that the Federalists were aristocrats, monocrats, even monarchists. The Federalists hated the Republicans as Jacobins bent on destruction of everything held sacred by man. If not the most heroic, it was perhaps the noisiest period in the history of the United States.

No internal issue divided the nation so strongly, as America's attitude toward revolutionary France and toward England. With impunity both powers had been for a long time trampling upon the

---

1 Oct. 3, 1801, Lipscomb, X, 284.
2 Fay, *The Revolutionary Spirit*, passim; Hazen, *Contemporary American Opinion*, passim; McMaster, *A History of the People of the United States*, II, 329, and passim; etc.

rights of the United States, especially on the seas. In the opinion of Washington, "the conduct of France towards the United States," was "outrageous beyond conception;"[3] but for the sake of peace the country had "to acquiesce in silence to the capturing of" its "Vessels; impressing" its "Seamen; or to the misconduct of the Naval, or other Officers of the British government."[4] "We are low indeed with the belligerents," wrote Jefferson to Edward Rutledge of South Carolina. "Their kicks and cuffs prove their contempt."[5] The only way to remedy this was to go to war. But even if the country were prepared for war — which of the two powers should it choose as her enemy? The Jay Treaty disappointed everybody and did not solve the dilemma even in part. The Federalists became "Anglomaniacs," and, forgetful of what France had done to make America free, now pressed for a war against her. The Republicans, blind to all the stupid and brutal excesses of the French Revolution, strove to imitate it, at least verbally, and wanted peace with France at all costs. From month to month, as the events progressed, the chasm between the two parties grew deeper and deeper.

"The passions are too high at present, to be cooled in our day," hopelessly wrote Jefferson. "You and I have formerly seen warm debates and high political passions. But gentlemen of different politics would then speak to each other, and separate the business of the Senate from that of society. It is not so now. Men who have been intimate all their lives, cross the streets to avoid meeting, and turn their heads another way, lest they should be obliged to touch their hats."[6] Personally Jefferson complained of "the floodgates of calumny . . . opened upon him."[7] President Washington was constantly attacked "in such exaggerated and indecent terms as could scarcely be applied to a Nero; a notorious defaulter; or even to a pickpocket."[8]

Such was the difference between the America which Kosciuszko remembered and the America to which he now approached. He had left her still in ecstasy over her newly-won freedom, and it was now a country where "politics and party hatreds" destroyed "the happiness of every being."[9] It was the "moment when the storm is about to burst, which has been conjuring up for four years past."[10] The ill-feeling between the parties was now at a culminating point. It was certainly the most inopportune moment for the return of Kosciuszko.

---

3 To Timothy Pickering, Jan 9, 1797, Fitzpatrick, XXXV, 361.
4 Washington to Alexander Hamilton, Jan. 22, 1797, *ibid.,* 372.
5 June 24, 1797, Lipscomb, IX, 410.
6 To Edward Rutledge, June 24, 1797, *ibid.,* IX, 411.
7 To Uriah McGregory, Aug. 13, 1800, *ibid.,* X, 171.
8 Washington to Jefferson, July 6, 1796, Fitzpatrick, XXXV, 120.
9 Jefferson to Martha Jefferson Randolph, May 17, 1798, Washington, ed., *Writings of Jefferson,* IV, 191.
10 Jefferson to Benjamin Rush, Jan. 22, 1797, Lipscomb, IX, 374.

However, his liberation from prison had been generally greeted in America with joy. When the Republican Philip Freneau of the *Time-Piece* had written that "Paul immortal honor gains in breaking Kosciusko's chains," Major Benjamin Russell of the Federalist *Columbian Centinel* had thought the epigram so much to the point that he reprinted it with commendations for the author.[11] At the Hay Market Theatre in Boston *Zorinski or, Freedom to the Slaves*, by Thomas Morton, had been staged.[12] At Philadelphia "capital" portraits of Kosciuszko had appeared for sale. At public dinners toasts for Kosciuszko and Poland had again been raised. One of the toasts at the Feast of Reason at New York, in honor of James Monroe, who had just returned from a "tedious and unthankful Embassy" in France, had run: "A speedy arrival of Kosciusco; — May the air of Freedom cure the wounds he received in her defence." Gen. Horatio Gates presided at this function.[13]

But the occasion had also provoked some dissonance. The arch-libeller, William Cobbett, had raised a discordant note immediately after the receipt of the news of Kosciuszko's liberation. In his opinion, the Tsar had acted "very inadvisedly"[14] in freeing Kosciuszko; Cobbett attacked Benjamin Franklin Bache of the *Aurora* for praising Paul and his liberal ideas. The presentation of Kosciuszko with a sword by the British Whigs also scandalized Cobbett. The Whigs, he said, were "the very offal of both Houses of Parliament," and he scoffed at Tarleton: "You present the Polander with a sword, as a token of your approbation of his labours in the cause of what you call *liberty*, when it is well known that you owe your present rank and pay to your having fought against him, having sought his destruction, when he was engaged in that very cause."[15]

So even before his landing and quite innocently, Kosciuszko became embroiled in the American party strife.

The Adriana entered the Philadelphia harbor on Friday, August 18, at 4 P. M., after sixty-one days of rather rough sailing. Lieut. Henry M. Muhlenberg, commander of Fort Mifflin,[16] was the first to greet Kosciuszko with a federal salute of thirteen guns. At the boom of the salvos citizens forgot their shops and labors, their troubles and quarrels, and poured en masse on the wharf and adjoining streets; not even the dread of yellow fever which had just reappeared and was

11 *Columbian Centinel*, April 3, 1797.
12 *Independent Chronicle*, May 8, 1797.
13 *Argus*, July 14, 1797.
14 "Eulogium on the Emperor of Russia by the Sans-Culottes," *Porcupine's Works*, V, 118.
15 "Porcupine to General Tarleton," *ibid.*, VII, 5.
16 Hiltzheimer, *Extracts from the Diary*, 255.

mercilessly destroying human lives in the city,[17] could deter them from welcoming the "illustrious Defender of the Rights of Mankind."[18] When the vessel came to anchor, John Lockwood, the sailing master of the renowned frigate United States[19] which was just being fitted out in the harbor, had his barge manned with eight masters of vessels, and waited upon the General to take him ashore. A delegation of citizens also reached the Adriana, and Henry H. Heins, an officer of the Philadelphia Society for the Information and Assistance of Persons Emigrating from Foreign Countries,[20] gave a speech to which Kosciuszko briefly replied, assuring: "I consider America my second country and feel very happy on returning to her."

In a chair he was lowered into the boat. The crew of the Adriana bade him adieu with a triple: "Long live Kosciuszko!", which was echoed by cheers of the people on the shore. In a brief moment the General found himself in the midst of his old companions-in-arms, his friends and acquaintances. The citizens hailed his arrival with unaffected pleasure. Thomas Lloyd, Revolutionary Captain, now the official stenographer to Congress, renowned as "the Father of American Shorthand," became the leader of the enthusiastic throng.[21] "The editor of the Aurora and his coadjutors" also "were conspicuous on that occasion."[22] In their ardor the citizens unharnessed the horses from Kosciuszko's carriage and dragged it to his lodgings, which again provoked some caustic remarks not only from Cobbett[23] but from other Federalist writers. John Fenno of the *Gazette of the United States* openly condemned the crowd as "cattle."[24] Even the more poised Maj. Russell and Noah Webster were shocked. The first one considered honors paid to Kosciuszko as "bordering on adoration."[25] In the opinion of Webster the act was "debasing," though it was meant to honor "brave Kosciusko." "Men who can decline a common mark of genteel civility to the President," he wrote alluding to the Republican insults against Washington and Adams, "can become beasts to a patriot. But the bait will not ensnare the HERO of Poland," he rightly added: "He will never be a sport of party."[26]

The people of Philadelphia, however, sought not to embroil the hero in party politics at the moment. Even Kosciuszko's eminent serv-

17 First victims of the fever fell on August 17, 1797, *ibid.* 246.

18 *Carey's Daily Advertiser,* August 19, 1797.

19 Lockwood was to die of yellow fever on September 12, 1797 (Clark, *Gallant John Barry,* 387).

20 Scharf, *History of Philadelphia,* I, 480.

21 For his brief biography see Griffin's, "Thomas Lloyd," *Am. Catholic Hist. Researches.* VII (1890), 19, and XX (1903), 19-26.

22 *U. S. Gazette.* Aug. 23, 1798.

23 *Porcupine's Works,* VII, 113.

24 *U. S. Gazette,* Aug. 23, 1798.

25 *Columbian Centinel,* Sept. 6, 1797.

26 *Herald,* Aug. 23, 1797.

ices in the Revolution played a secondary part in their spontaneous welcome. Above all, the popular greeting was the tribute of a free people to the tragic leader of a people who had lost their freedom; it was one of the earliest outbursts of American public enthusiasm for foreign national causes. Niemcewicz, a witness to the scene, rightly comprehended its meaning: "Oh! it was greatful to the heart of a Polander to perceive in the honor and respect with which his chief was received, esteem and consideration for the fate of an unjustly destroyed nation."[27]

Everywhere the news of Kosciuszko's arrival spread as quickly as the means of communication then allowed. The details of the welcome, first appearing in the *Claypoole's American Daily Advertiser,* were reprinted by the press all over the country. Even the unfriendly Cobbett had to acknowledge that "an almost universal infatuation prevailed in favor of this mutilated rebel."[28] Articles extolling Kosciuszko's virtues and describing his personal misfortunes and those of Poland appeared in the press.[29] Poets lamented that his wounds "call forth from ev'ry eye a tear,"[30] and assured him that

> "Columbia's ports their bosom wide expand,
> Inviting thee to seats of joy and rest;
> The sons of freedom hail thee to their land,
> And blooming virgins sing thee ever blest."[31]

In prose, though in no less affectionate words, John Armstrong,[32] with whom Kosciuszko had shared the ventures of war longer perhaps than with anyone else, welcomed him to America in a letter to Gates, evidently written under the fresh impression of the news of his arrival;

"I am much interested in Kusciusko's future fortunes. He ought to have a bed of roses amongst us — I hope Philadelphia will not entirely engross him, and if his object be (as I suppose it is) retired life I know no place so well fitted for his purpose as the banks of this river. He would find amongst us friends that love him, a people that admire him, — a pleasant country — and an easy access to the stores

27 Niemcewicz's eulogy, *loc. cit.,* 476. The description of Kosciuszko's welcome in Philadelphia given here is based on: *Carey's Daily Advertiser,* August 19, 1797; *Claypoole's American Daily Advertiser,* August 19, 1797; Niemcewicz's eulogy and *Pamiętniki,* 323; de Saint-Mery, *Voyage,* 254, entry of January 20, 1798, and *Dziennik Patryotycznych Polityków,* 1797, no, 243, as quoted by Korzon, *Kosciuszko,* 489 and note 741.

28 *Porcupine's Works,* X, 13-14.

29 See "Kosciuszko," *Claypoole's American Daily Advertiser,* October 3, 1797; *The Independent Chronicle,* October 5, 1797; *The* (Washington, Ky.) *Mirror,* November 25, 1797.

30 Anonymous "Lines on the Arrival of General Kosciusko at Philadelphia," *Kentucky Gazette,* December 6, 1797.

31 Della Euranadda, "Address to Kosciusko, Late Commander in Chief of the Armies of Poland and Defender of the Rights of Man," *The Herald of Times,* Wilkes-Barre, Oct. 31, 1797, as reprinted by Harvey, "Wilkes-Barre's Earliest Newspapers," *Proceedings and Collections of the Wyoming Hist. and Geological Soc.,* XVIII (1922), 67; also in *The Independent Chronicle,* Nov. 16, 1797.

32 At that time Armstrong, married to a sister of Robert R. Livingston, lived on a farm at Red Hook, on the Hudson, Dutchess County, New York.

of literature, the conveniences of life and the pleasures of the city if his wishes ever lead him thither. You have no doubt already written to him & will write to him again: Mention me to him as warmly as you do yourself. Tell him how delighted I would be to see him anywhere but particularly on the banks of my Euphrates where like Candid I sit and philosophize without a Pangloss & where I sometimes think it the best & sometimes the worst of all possible worlds. When I heard of his captivity & wounds and recollected his virtues and his courage and found that neither would protect him against the rage & malevolence of fortune I really thought that we had all along mistaken the business & that it was for us as well as for Cato to discover our error at the last gasp — (but now these very wounds & calamities have restored him to us), I begin to be selfish enough to regard them in a new light & to think less ill of any circumstance that tended to produce the effect of bringing us together once more."[33]

But amid the popular rejoicing there were also some thorns which painfully hurt Kosciuszko's feelings. The American political turmoil could not leave untouched his oversensitive nature. He accepted Cobbett's provocations with silence; but it seems, he had suffered some personal affront from those whom he remembered as friends, who years ago "were Samsons in the field and Solomons in the council,"[34] but who now had become "changelings and apostates," as Jefferson characterized them.[35] What was worse, even here in America Kosciuszko felt himself trailed and spied upon. To some extent his suspicion was undoubtedly of a neuro-psychiatric nature, the result of the treatment he had been subjected to in the Russian prison. But, on the other hand, it cannot be denied that his complaint may not have been entirely groundless. At that time Jefferson constantly complained to his trusted friends that all his "motions . . . are watched and recorded," that even his mail is being intercepted at the post offices[36] manned by the Federalists. The latter sniffed treachery everywhere and organized committees for the purpose of spying on Republican leaders.[37] In this atmosphere of mutual distrust, Kosciuszko might have appeared to some as a Jacobin agent and "a French emissary,"[38] and evidently their whispered scoffs were not discreet enough to escape his attention.

Gradually the more fanatical Federalists drew away from Kosciuszko. Their press began either to ignore him, or to treat him lightly;

---

33 N. Y. Hist. Soc., Gates Papers, box 18, no. 49.
34 Jefferson to Mazzei, April 24, 1796, Lipscomb, IX, 336.
35 Jefferson to Kosciuszko, June 1, 1798, Lipscomb, X, 49.
36 Jefferson to Madison, April 5, 1798, Lipscomb, X, 22; to Samuel Smith, Sept. 26, 1798, ibid., X, 56; to A. H. Rowan, Sept. 26, 1798, ibid., X, 59; to Elbridge Gerry, Jan. 26, 1799. ibid., X, 74, etc.
37 Logan, Memoir, 54.
38 Carpenter, Memoirs of Jefferson, II, 26.

in the rare moments it spoke of him, it referred to him with indifference, or sometimes with a snear. Cobbett, however, alone dared to attack Kosciuszko openly, and even he acknowledged that this was disapproved by many men of his party.

Kosciuszko occupied a modest apartment at the hotel of a Mrs. Lawson on Fourth street.[39] There he decided to divulge his plans, at least partly, to some trustworthy friends. Ignoring the honest, but loquacious Niemcewicz, he secretly summoned the local French Consul, Letombe, who since the revocation of Adet in 1796, performed the functions of charge-des-affaires. On the 3rd Fructidor,[40] the Consul advised Charles Delacroix, the French Minister of Foreign Affairs, that a member of the committee of the House of Representatives entrusted with the investigation of William Blount's conspiracy had made public the result of its labors; and continuing, Letombe added:

"The same Member of Congress came to tell me that General Kosciusko desired to speak to me, therefore I went to the general last night. He wants to go to France. He will go there immediately by a safe way. He is observed here. This Martyr of liberty cannot speak or act, but only with the greatest precaution. He is here only to mislead his enemies. He asked me, Citizen Minister, to inform you of these facts without delay."[41]

Who was the Member of Congress that served as Kosciuszko's intermediary? The committee consisted of five members, of whom only one, John L. Dawson of Virginia, was a Republican. He later sponsored Congressional action in regard to Kosciuszko's arrears in pay. Jefferson considered him "worthy of entire confidence."[42] Undoubtedly it was he who had summoned Letombe. The only other person before whom Kosciuszko fully opened his soul at that time was Dr. Rush. They had known each other since the days when Rush served as Surgeon General of the Middle Department of the Revolutionary army. Kosciuszko handed him the letters of the British physicians, but what he needed was, above all, a cure for his perturbed soul.

What was in Kosciuszko's mind? The very thought of being indebted for his freedom to the Russians who had destroyed his country was utterly painful to him. The Tsar succeeded in extorting from him the oath of allegiance, but no power on earth was strong enough to wrest the love of Poland out of his breast. He wanted to break with the Tsar soon after reaching America, but Niemcewicz, to whom he had confided his design, had dissuaded him by warning him

---

39 *Aurora,* August 19, 1797.
40 August 20, 1797.
41 Turner, ed., "Correspondence," II, 1069; the original in French.
42 Jefferson to Joel Barlow, March 14, 1801, Lipscomb, X, 223.

of the consequences.[43] Personally Kosciuszko undoubtedly would have preferred to cling to his original intention of settling in America. Even though there were some "who do not like either you or me," as Jefferson wrote him,[44] yet there were hosts of friends among whom he might gladly spend the rest of his life in peace. But the weight of responsibility for his country's fate lay heavy upon his shoulders. The solemn vows of his Cracow oath still rang in his ears. As long as there was the slightest ray of hope for Poland, he would follow it. Forgetting the base treatment he had received from France, he still considered her the only country affording some hope of succor for Poland and the only republic strong enough to defy the autocratic and despotic governments of Europe.

Kosciuszko's deep suffering, his utmost precaution is visible in the following letter, which he wrote to Dr. Rush on leaving Philadelphia:

"before I write I most beg you would be so kind after reading the contents of this Letter to burne. I would not chose that any body besides you should know any thing even your Lady for whiche I have soche veneration and Esteeme, —

"Inclos'd it is a letter for Clarkson in which is the Bank note you know for what porpose. for god sake press him that he should not loose time and do fast as he can you cannot concive how inHappy I am in mind and how distress me moche my situation, help him do as you can, I shall write you from new Brunswick . . ."[45]

The Clarkson alluded to in the letter was Matthew Clarkson, former mayor of Philadelphia and an eminent merchant and philanthropist. The exact substance of Kosciuszko's request is unknown, but it seems that it pertained in some way to his intended secret and hurried departure for France.

His almost feverish haste is visible also in another matter which, besides confusing his enemies as to his true intentions, was the purpose for his coming to America. He felt that he had honestly earned by his blood and sweat whatever America owed him for his services in the Revolution. He wanted to arrange his financial affairs in this country in such a way as to assure himself a steady, though modest, income. Evidently he was under the impression that to reclaim the money would be a simple matter. Within a few days after landing he had appealed to Col. Pickering for help in finding means of profitably locating some twelve thousand dollars. That was roughly the sum he expected to receive as his arrears. The leader of the Essex Junto was

43 Niemcewicz, *Pamiętniki,* 327.
44 Feb. 21, 1799, Libr. of Congress, Jefferson Papers.
45 Undated, Ridgway Libr., Rush Papers, 7246 F. 35. Kosciuszko wrote again to Rush in this matter, but in a calmer tone, from Rose Hill, undated, *ibid.,* 7246 F. 36.

honest and kind enough not to turn his back on the exile; in several other instances he also served Kosciuszko in a friendly capacity. Writing to Col. Clement Biddle, prominent Philadelphia merchant, for further advice in this regard, Pickering remarked: "Your knowledge of the subject and respect & friendship for him, induce me to request your opinion on the subject . . . The sooner you can favor me with answer, the more acceptable to the General, who wishes to remove a little into the Country."[46]

Before yielding to the entreaties of Dr. Rush, who wanted Kosciuszko to leave the infested city, the General wished first to settle some urgent matters. There still remained errands entrusted to him by Sinclair. Pickering had already informed Washington of Kosciuszko's arrival.[47] In those few lines which Kosciuszko penned with difficulty to his former Commander-in-Chief, one cannot fail to perceive a note of deep sympathy and respect for the retired President, who, after having "spent five and forty years, *All the prime of his life,* in serving his country"[48] at last felt free to spend the remainder of his days "in rural amusements," without "those cares (from) which public responsibility is never exempt."[49]

"By sending a Packet delivered to me by John Sinclair for you," wrote Kosciuszko, "I have the honor to pay my respects not only to my Chief Commander, but to a great man whose eminent virtues to his country rendered him dear to every feeling breast."[50]

Kosciuszko entrusted the letter, together with the package, to Pickering. As Charles Lee, the Attorney General, was just leaving Philadelphia for his native Virginia, Pickering gave him the package for delivery. The letter reached the hands of Washington before the package and he immediately sent back a reply, again using Pickering as an intermediary. "Not knowing where Genl Kosciuszko may be," he wrote to the Secretary, "I pray your care of the enclosed to him as it is probable his movements will be known to you."[51]

The haste of Washington's reply to Kosciuszko was eloquent in itself. It disproves the assertion of some historians that different political attitudes in the post-revolutionary period caused a division between the two men. The old Washington became slow in his correspondence even with his intimate friends,[52] but evidently he did not

---

46 Aug. 24, 1797, Mass. Hist. Soc., Pickering Papers, vol. VII, fol. 119.

47 Aug. 19, 1797, Mass. Hist. Soc., Pickering Papers, VII, 106.

48 Washington's Farewell Address, First Draft, May 15, 1796, Fitzpatrick, XXXV, 60.

49 Washington to Sarah Cary Fairfax, May 16, 1798, Fitzpatrick, XXXVI, 263.

50 August 23, 1797, Library of Congress, Washington Papers.

51 August 31, 1797, Fitzpatrick, XXXVI, 23. The package contained Sinclair's papers on agriculture (Washington to Sinclair, Nov. 6, 1797, ibid., XXXVI, 66).

52 Excusing himself for having left several letters without answer and describing the order of his day, Washington wrote to James McHenry, the Secretary of War, on May 29,

want to keep Kosciuszko waiting for an acknowledgment. His answer was couched in most cordial terms:

Mount-Vernon, 31 August 1797

"Dear Sir,

"Having just been informed of your safe arrival in America, I was on the point of writing you a congratulatory letter on the occasion, welcoming you to the land, whose liberties you had been so instrumental in establishing, when I received your favour of the 23 instant from Philadelphia; for which and the Packet, that you had the goodness to bear from Sir John Sinclair, I offer you my thanks.

"I beg you to be assured, that no one has a higher respect, and veneration for your character than I have and no one more sincerely wished, during your arduous struggle in the cause of liberty and your country, that it might be crowned with Success. But the ways of Providence are inscrutable, and Mortals must submit.

"I pray you to believe, that at all times, and under any circumstances, it would make me happy to see you at my last retreat, from which I never expect to be more than twenty miles again . . ."[53]

Acknowledging the receipt of his package, President Adams wrote to Kosciuszko:

"Quincy, the 4 September 1797.

"I have received a letter You did me honour to write me on the 24 of last month and thank you for your care of my Packet from the worthy John Sinclair, whose benevolent labours promise so much advancement to Mankind.— Give me leave, Sir, to congratulate you on your arrival in America, where, I hope, You will find all the consolation, tranquility and satisfaction you desire after the glorious efforts you have made on a greater Theatre. On my arrival in Philadelphia I hope to have pleasure to receive you . . ."[54]

Meanwhile already "half ye City" became "deserted."[55] "During our whole stay in Philadelphia," says Niemcewicz, "the yellow fever, the debates about its cause, the disputes of physicians over the means of cure, the manifestos of the government,[56] and the brutal arguments

---

1797: (in the evening) "a walk, and Tea, brings me within the dawn of Candlelight; previous to which, if not prevented by company, I resolve, that, as soon as the glimmering taper, supplies the place of the great luminary, I will retire to my writing Table and acknowledge the letters I have received; but when the lights are brought, I feel tired, and disinclined to engage in this work, conceiving that the next night will do as well: the next comes and with it the same causes for postponement, and effect, and so on" (Fitzpatrick, XXXV, 455-6).

53 Fitzpatrick, XXXVI, 22.

54 Princes Czartoryski Museum, MS 2791.

55 Edward Burd to Jasper Yates, Philadelphia, August 30, 1797, *The Burd Papers*, 194.

56 Proclamation of Gov. Mifflin ordering barricading of streets, hanging yellow flags from infected houses, carrying the sick out of town and providing heavy penalties for infractions.

of newspapers greatly vexed the inhabitants. The ado was greater than the evil itself. Thirty six thousand inhabitants left the city. The streets were deserted and only funerals interrupted this solitude. Dr. Rush persuaded Kosciuszko to depart and Generals White and Gates, his old friends, urged him by frequent letters that he come to stay with them. We decided then to leave the city."[57]

Happily married for the second time to the former Mary Vallance of Maryland, Gates now lived at his estate Rose Hill, near New York. Gen. Anthony Walton White, with whom Kosciuszko had struck a friendship during the Southern Campaign, lived at New Brunswick, very conveniently on the way to New York. There were others in that part of the country, whom Kosciuszko might embrace again with delight. But some of his dearest friends, like Greene and Williams, were no more among the living. Others, like Lewis Morris, lived too far away.

On Wednesday, August 30, at six in the morning, accompanied by Niemcewicz and his Polish servant, Stanisław Dombrowski, Kosciuszko left Philadelphia for the North in a hired two-horse carriage.

It seems that his departure was rather hurried, as he left without notifying even Gates of his intentions in advance. Dr. Rush, however, helped him out in this regard and on September 3, he wrote to the General:

"Our illustrious friend Kusiosco left this city a few days ago & is now pleasantly & hospitably accommodated at General White's at Brunswick. His wounds are all healed. One of them on his hip has left his thigh & leg in a paralytic State. Time has done a little towards restoring it. I do not despair of his being yet able to walk. He will always limp — but what then? To use an ancient play upon words, 'every Step he takes will remind him of his patriotism and bravery' —

"I take it for granted, you will pay your respects to him at Brunswick. How gladly would I witness your first interview! His Soul is tremblingly alive to friendship. He loves your very name . . ."[58]

---

[57] Another diary of Niemcewicz, W. M. Kozłowski, ed., "Pobyt Kościuszki i Niemcewicza w Ameryce," *Biblioteka Warszawska,* IV (1906), 249; hereafter referred to as Kozłowski, "Pobyt."

[58] N. Y. Hist. Soc., Gates Papers, box 18, no. 52.

VI.

WITH THE WHITES AND THE GATESES

"Through a flat country covered with farms . . . with cornfields and fruit-trees shutting off the view on every side," the travelers reached Frankford, where they briefly rested at Washington Tavern, and at noon arrived in Bristol. Here they met a Spanish Consul, "an excellent prattler," and lunched with a former purveyor for the Revolutionary army who now drove a large herd of oxen for the market. At Trenton they crossed the Delaware and, passing through Princeton, where Elias Boudinot, the Director of the Mint, entertained them lavishly,[1] they reached Kingston where they spent the night at an inn. The next morning they set out on their way and at ten reached the Ellis House, standing "on a hill a little distant from the city,"[2] where Gen. White lived.

The Revolutionary War had ruined the General financially. According to Washington, he was formerly "celebrated for frivolity, dress, empty shew,"[3] but surely that seems to be a traditional fault of all young and handsome cavalry officers. After the war he tried to recoup his losses by speculation, like so many other well-known figures of the post-revolutionary era, but was unsuccessful. Niemcewicz records that the bad state of his finances made him "a gloomy melancholiac." "Grief poisons his family life," he adds. "His farm is neglected . . . Everywhere may be seen the spirit of dissatisfaction and discontent."[4]

The generosity of Miss Mary Ellis, his sister-in-law, saved him from extreme poverty. During his service in the South he married Margaret Vanderhorst Ellis, a fifteen year old Charleston belle. After the war, when the Whites settled in New Brunswick, Mary followed them there. The spinster was the owner of the farm on which the Whites lived, and, it seems, she also was one of their chief supporters.[5]

Despite these disagreeable conditions, Kosciuszko seemed to feel happy among his hosts. Most probably both women were known to

---

1 Kosciuszko to Boudinot, undated, but endorsed as received Sept. 1797, Polish R. C. U. Museum, Kosciuszko Papers, No. 46.

2 All quotations from Kozłowski, "Pobyt," 250-2.

3 Washington to James McHenry, Sept. 14, 1798, Fitzpatrick, XXXVI, 443.

4 Kozłowski, "Pobyt," 252.

5 Benedict, *New Brunswick,* 130. The Ellis House stood on Livingston avenue, where the Y.M.C.A. now stands.

him before. If the General was morose, the southern vivacity of the ladies, their charm and hospitality, the warmth of family life, whatever was left of it in the circumstances, and, finally, their common reminiscences of the proverbial old and better times, brought comfort to his heart. There was also the sweet and happy voice of Eliza, the five year old daughter of the General, and Kosciuszko loved children, especially in the later years of his life.

Mrs. White idolized him; in her eyes, he was second only to Washington.[6] He tried to repay her kindness with presents and letters, which give a little glimpse of his life under the roof of the Whites.

"I am not at rest Madame," so he wrote,[7] "before I obtain your Pardon in full extend and force, for the trouble I gave you during my stay at your house. The uneasinesse hangs on my mind, and my feelings suffer greatly. — I was perhaps the cause of depriving you a passtime, more suited to your inclination and satisfaction than wyth me; you never was out on a visite; you was pleased to inquire every day, what I like or dislike every wysh was complied, every thought was prevented, to make my sytuation more comfortable and agreeable — let me read in your enswer of forgiveness and I beg Elisa to solicite for me.

"I am too much indebted to you to express in words coresponding to my obligation and gratitude lit suffice that I will never forget neither the memory will cease for a moment in my breast."

Answering some lines of Mrs. White, Kosciuszko repeated his warm gratitude in another letter and, teasing her, continued: "You were pleased to write me that you were happy in my company, and in doing everythink for me, but this only shows the good heart of yours; and you do not grant pardon for the trouble I gave you . . . Send me a pardon madame, in a formal lawyer's parchment, and signed by yourself."[8]

He also kindly mentioned Miss Ellis and sent Mrs. White copies of his portraits — an exceptional token of his gratitude, as he had an aversion for all attempts at copying his features. Generations of the White family retained him in their reminiscences immobilized by his lameness, "sketching with pencil, and painting in water-colors and India-ink, fancy pieces, which when finished he threw on the floor to be gathered by Mrs. General White who gave them to friends."[9] The little Eliza, as a grown-up woman, told a Polish exile familiar details of his life among her family. "He was simple," she said, "and

<hr />

6 Evans, *Memoir,* 3.

7 *Ib.,* facsimile appendix D, pp. 47-8; most probably the date of the letter, Philadelphia, April, 1798, given by Evans, is wrong. Allen, *Autocrasy,* 128, reproduces the "doctored" text of the letter with a more likely date of January 26, 1798.

8 Undated, Evans, *loc. cit.,* 49.

9 Evans, *loc. cit.,* 23.

unostentatious in his habits, unwilling to be made the object of special attention . . . He pertinaciously resisted any attempt to obtain his likeness, and one day perceiving a lady stealthily endeavoring to sketch his features whilst he was lying upon a sofa, he immediately threw a handkerchief over his face."[10] According to another lady admirer, "his manners and conversation were as little imposing as his person and countenance."[11]

Eliza White remembered that he "carefully avoided neighborhood notoriety,"[12] still undoubtedly he was only too glad to renew his acquaintances with Col. John B. Bayard, with William Paterson, Justice of the Supreme Court of the United States, and with his other local friends. Among his newest pleasant acquaintances was John Garnett,[13] the owner of the historic Buccleuch House, a mathematician of some renown and a personal friend of Gen. Gates; Kosciuszko considered him a man of "many amiable good qualities."[14] The General's infirmity prevented him from leaving the house, but Niemcewicz, full of curiosity for the strange country and its people, gladly performed many social duties as his proxy, being entertained by town celebrities.[15]

Immediately after having made himself at home with the Whites, Kosciuszko wrote to Gates, advising him of his being on the way to Rose Hill.

"I am at Mr. White's house now away from Philadelphia," he wrote on September 1. "I propose to see you and before hand I feell great Satisfaction in Embracing you once more, that I never expectet that happines.

"Be pleased to present my respects to your Lady she aught to be of very amiable disposition because she is beloved by every person who know here do not forget of my old friends and acquietence."[16]

A few days later, seemingly in answer to a letter from Gates, Kosciuszko wrote him again with a dose of his old good humor:

"If you know well my Heart, you ought to expect that I would pay invoidably my respects to you at your House, and for that purpose I came out from Philadelphia this way.— I propose to set out in three days, from General White's to go at your's and to stay their one Weak; onless you will set your dogs at me, and by force throw me

10 Allen, *Autocrasy*, 127.

11 Goodrich, *Token*, 348. Most probably to Kosciuszko's stay with the Whites pertain the reminiscences of Elizabeth Ryer, published anonymously under the title "The Fur Coat," by Goodrich, *loc. cit.*, and republished by Gaffney, "Kosciuszko's Gift to Jefferson," *Poland-America*, XIII (1932), 176-8. They are full of naive sentimentality, but seem to be historically true.

12 Allen, *loc. cit.*

13 Benedict, *New Brunswick*, 53 and 135.

14 Kosciuszko to Gates, Feb. 22, 1798, N. Y. Hist. Soc., Gates Papers, box 18, no 62.

15 Kozłowski, "Pobyt," 254.

16 N. Y. Hist. Soc., Gates Papers, box 18, no. 50.

out from your House.— I recolect perfectly well the obligation I ow
to you; and respect Esteem, Veneration and afection, too strongly
imprented in my breast, not to Listened to the call of Sentyments and
to pay the common gratitude with all Cytizens of this Country for
your great exertions during the War.— I have only one Friend and
one Servant wyth me — and with suche army I will attack your house,
but will surrender imidiatly to your good, hospitable and Friendly
Heart my best respects to your Lady. Hear I stop for fear you should
not be Jeaulous of me."[17]

In fact, three days after this letter, Kosciuszko left Ellis House
with his modest retinue. "We left New Brunswick on Saturday, September 9, to visit General Gates," narrates Niemcewicz. "We traveled
through a flat country, cultivated and peopled in the same manner
as that we saw on our way from Philadelphia. Springfield, Elizabethtown and Newark are the little towns through which we passed · · ·
After crossing salt marshes and a dam several miles long, we came to
Hoboken very late in the evening. We found the inn full of sailors and
tramps; all were merry with drink and in the most hilarious mood;
they danced in the room downstairs . . . We had to dispense with
dinner because everything was consumed; we slept in uncomfortable
beds and paid very dearly for our lodging the next morning.

"Sunday morning, September 10, the view of the beautiful North
River and the towers of New York recompensed me somewhat for the
bad shelter. We crossed the river in a sail-boat with favorable wind
and tide. The transportation costs us ten shillings. It is rather much,
but at least, the people who put our carriage and baggage on the boat
(a task which demands not a little labor), do not ask tips as in Europe."

Kosciuszko wished to escape the ovations of the inhabitants. "We
landed near the new prison,"[18] continued Niemcewicz, "avoiding in
this way the burdensome passage through the town. At last we were
shown the gate of the house of General Gates and soon found ourselves
before a beautiful house, decorated with Corynthian columns which
form the peristyle of General's dwelling.[19]

"We were met at the threshold by the victor of Saratoga. He is
an old man, seventy-five years of age,[20] still quite lively, kind and
very cheerful for his age." There was also Mrs. Gates to greet the
guests. "Such a wife is a real treasure for this old man," opinioned
Niemcewicz. "She is fifty years of age, still beautiful and of the hap-

---

17 September 6, 1797, *ibid.,* box 18, no. 51.

18 It was Greenwich Prison, erected in 1797, on the Hudson and the present 10th St.
(Bonner, *New York,* 225).

19 Gates' house, then, according to Niemcewicz, three miles distant from New York,
stood near the present corner of 22nd Street and 2nd Avenue (Lossing, *History of New York
City,* I, 52).

20 In fact, at that time, Gates was 70 years old.

piest temper. Only she could render agreeable the indispositions and griefs of such an old age. When one sees how they live together . . . it seems that it is the first year of the marriage of a twenty year old couple . . .

"During our whole stay with General Gates we had innumerable visits in the afternoon hours. It is impossible to remember all persons . . . ," recorded Niemcewicz.[21] Half-complainingly, half joyfully Gates wrote to a friend: "General Kosciuszko is . . . hourly visited by all the best company, which finds me in constant and unremitted employment."[22] Still the old General himself invited guests from all around, especially Kosciuszko's former companions. To George Clinton, who then lived in temporary retirement from his numerous public duties, he penned a note immediately after Kosciuszko's arrival, in such a haste that he hopelessly misspelled his name: "Your old Friend Gen. Kosiuisko is Just arrived. If you wish to see him, come to Dinner."[23] Not content with his duties as host, he himself, to the astonishment of Niemcewicz, went around the shops, buying groceries and everything necessary for the entertainment of the constant stream of guests. As far as Niemcewicz remembered, there came "a dozen Livingstons, men and women, among them Edward[24] and John[25] whose wives are very beautiful," and who arrived with all the aristocratic splendor, in "nice carriages," with "magnificent horses, servants in livery"; "the numerous family of the Stevenses," rich New York merchants, among whom there undoubtedly was the former Major Ebenezer Stevens, chief of artillery in the Ticonderoga and Saratoga campaign; Misses Sarah and Julia Broome, daughters of John Broome, another prominent merchant;[26] a Miss Johnson, the niece of Robert Smith of Maryland, later Secretary of the Navy and Secretary of State; Mrs. Vining of Delaware, wife of a United States Senator, "young, comely, very interesting, a good singer and painter," and a Miss Nicholson, daughter of the "Commodore" James Nicholson, whose magnificent house in New York served as headquarters for local Republicans. A very frequent guest was Marinus Willett, another veteran of the Northern Campaign of 1777, a merchant of means and a neighbor of the Gateses. Niemcewicz describes him as "very good, much attached to his wife and also to his garden;" Mrs. Willett, nee Susan-

---

21 Kozłowski, "Pobyt," 257-60.

22 Date unknown, quoted by Griffin, "Gen. T. Kosciuszko," *Am. Cath. Hist. Researches,* new series, VI, 191.

23 Polish R. C. U. Museum, Kosciuszko Papers, no. 77A.

24 The famous jurist, then member of Congress.

25 John Livingston was aide-de-camp to Governor Clinton in 1778. Brockholst and James L. Livingstons fought with Kosciuszko in the Northern Campaign of 1777, and most probably were also among his visitors, though not mentioned by name by Niemcewicz.

26 They were Sarah, who married James Bogg, president of the Phoenix Bank, and Julia, later wife of Col. John Livingston, great-grandson of the second Lord of the Manor (Lamb, *History of the City of New York,* II, 384, note).

nah Nicoll of New York, was "a famous chess-player, bright and well-educated, but she" liked "the city more than it becomes the wife of a Quaker."[27] She even tried her coquetry on Kosciuszko and, inviting him to give her a lesson of chess, wrote him temptingly: "the men may haunt me for my attachment to you."[28]

Still another familiar guest was the Duke de La Rochefoucauld-Liancourt, "one of the principal noblemen of France . . .", who "was President of the National Assembly of France in its earliest stage, and forced to fly from the proscriptions of Marat."[29] He paid Kosciuszko a very warm tribute in his diary: "There is no heart friendly to liberty, or an admirer of virtue and talent, in whom the name of Kosciusko does not excite sentiments of interest and respect. The purity and liberality of his intentions, the boldness of his undertakings, the able manner in which he conducted them, and the misfortunes and atrocious captivity which have been their consequence, are too well known to require repetition . . . The consequences of his wounds, which still prevent him from the free use of one of his legs, and his rigorous confinement, have impaired his health, but it now begins to be reestablished. Simple and modest, he even sheds tears of gratitude, and seems astonished at the homage he receives. He sees in every man who is the friend of liberty and of man, a brother. His countenance, sparkling with fire, discovers a soul which no circumstances can render dependent, and expresses the language of his heart, *Shall I never then fight more for my country?* He speaks little, particularly on the misfortunes of his country, although the thoughts of these occupy his whole soul. In a word, elevation and sentiment, grandeur, sweetness, force, goodness, all that commands respect and homage, appear to me to be concentrated in this celebrated and interesting victim of misfortune and despotism. I have met few men whose appearance so much excited in me that effect."[30]

Kosciuszko's friends in the vicinity wanted to share with Gates the honor of entertaining him. Janet Montgomery, nee Livingston, the widow of the brave Richard Montgomery, even accused Gates of selfishness in keeping the "Martyr to liberty" all to himself. "I pray you to offer him my respects & wishes," she wrote, "surely there is another world where virtue and the love of our Country will meet other rewards than wounds and death — else why did a Montgomery die or the Polish *Hero* bleed —"[31]

---

27 Quotations from Kozlowski, "Pobyt."
28 Mrs. Willett to Kosciuszko, Sept. 1797, *Penna. Mag. of History,* XXIII (1899), 122. The marriage of Willett's was an unhappy one and ended in a divorce in 1799 (Willett in the *Dictionary of Amer. Biography,* XX, 245).
29 Jefferson to Col. Hite, June 29, 1796, Lipscomb, IX, 345.
30 La Rochefoucauld, *Travels,* II, 468-9.
31 To Gates, Oct. 7, 1797, N. Y. Public Libr., Emmett Collection.

If there was another among his old comrades living in that part of the country, besides Gates, whom Kosciuszko would gladly embrace, it was certainly John Armstrong. Writing to Gates on August 26, Armstrong promised to see him "in a fort-night,"[32] but to his great regret, "one unlooked-for occurrence and another was perpetually breaking in upon" his plans. "I the more regret this," he wrote, "as it has kept me from seeing and embracing our very interesting and muttual friend Kusciusko and (should he mean to winter south of the Potowmack as I am told he does), will defeat my wishes on that score for some months to come."[33]

Despite all these visits, Kosciuszko found time enough to turn snuff-boxes and other trifles as souvenirs for his friends.[34] Undoubtedly most pleasant to him were the hours of conversation with his host. Some passages in his later correspondence suggest that he revealed his plans to Gates. With his usual courtesy he acknowledged all letters and gifts sent by admirers. He thanked David Longworth, the New York printer: "You lay me under great Obligation by sending a book of Telemacus; a testimony of your Friendship for me."[35] Jesse & Robert Waln, shippers of Philadelphia, informed him of the arrival of his baggage from Europe in one of their ships; advising them to leave it in the hands of the custom officers, he wrote: "Be pleased to receive my warmest thanks for the trouble I gave you with this baggage."[36] Similar notes of acknowledgments of favors are comparatively common in manuscript collections.

Letters of Washington and Adams[37] reached him at Rose Hill. Pickering took care of transmitting his mail, including also a welcoming letter from Col. Michael Jackson of Massachusetts. "I hope they will find you," the Secretary added, "and as well and as happy, as your wounds, mental and corporeal, will possibly admit."[38]

On September 29, "with great regret," narrates Niemcewicz, "we left the house of General Gates and his kind wife. We placed General Kosciuszko in a boat with great difficulty, and once more embracing Gen. Gates who accompanied us to the bank of the North River we crossed it."[39]

---

32 N. Y. Hist. Soc., Gates Papers, box 18, no. 49.

33 Armstrong to Gates, Nov. 13, 1797, *ibid.*, box 18, no. 54.

34 Kosciuszko to Henry Gahn, counting merchant of New York, Sept. 1797: "Be so good to order your Servants for delivering my two boxes wyth turning instruments to Mr. Niemcewicz" (Mass. Hist. Soc., Jefferson Collection, the letter wrongly endorsed as of Sept. 1798).

35 Sept. 20, 1797, Polish R. C. U. Museum, Kosciuszko Papers, no. 7A.

36 Sept. 20, 1797, Polish R. C. U. Museum, Kosciuszko Papers, no. 45.

37 See *supra.*

38 Sept. 12, 1797, Mass. Hist. Soc., Pickering Papers, VII, 179. Kosciuszko thanked Pickering for his exertions in a letter dated Rose Hill, Sept. 17, 1797, *ibid.*, XXI, 242.

39 Kozłowski, "Pobyt," 261.

The old warrior forever preserved a warm heart for his Polish friend. Long after Kosciuszko's departure, he often spoke of him with his friends and extolled his virtues. Once in a conversation with William Dunlap, the artist and author, he said that "Kosciuszko is the only pure republican he ever knew." "He is without any dross," he added.[40] It was undoubtedly as a reminiscence of Kosciuszko's visit that Dunlap staged *Zorinsky* in his Park Theatre in March 1798, "with care and expense."[41]

Passing through Newark, "a cheerful town, having several nice houses," the travelers reached Elizabeth on the same day at noon. Here for three weeks Kosciuszko stayed at the famous Indian Queen Tavern.[42] One of the first things he did was to write to Gates:

"I cannot be at rest till I desharge part of the obligation that I ow to your kindness and hospitality I received in your house — if my wishes would correspond with the feelings of my heart, you would be the most happy person upon the Glob — believe me that my gratitude never will stop upon any occasion to show you, as well to convince you of my perfect respect, Esteem and afection."[43]

Again old friends surrounded the hero during his stay at Elizabeth. "All Citizens of the town and its vicinity began to visit Kosciuszko."[44] There came Mrs. Susan Kean, the widow of John Kean of South Carolina whom Kosciuszko had befriended during the Revolution; the visit marked the beginning of a romance; a few years later she married Niemcewicz. Another visitor was Capt. Shepard Kollock, publisher of the *New Jersey Journal* and such an ardent admirer of the Pole that he named his son Shepard Kosciusko. This pleased the General so much that, meeting the youngster, he took him up in his arms, kissed him and fastened to his coat his own cross of the *Virtuti Militari.*[45]

On October 20, the travelers left for New Brunswick where they again put up with General White[46] "whose family," according to Niemcewicz, "was hospitable and considerate as before. The Bayards and the Patersons were as corteous as before, and the city also was as gloomy, as during our first stay."

The monotony of town life, however, was soon interrupted by preparations for a visit of President and Mrs. Adams. They were re-

40 Dunlap, *Diary,* I, 338-9, entry of Sept. 14, 1798; cf. also I, 202, 338.

41 *Ib.,* I, 222, 232, 233, 234, 237; cf. also Dunlap, *History of the American Theatre,* 222.

42 Sesquicentennial Committee, *Revolutionary History of Elizabeth,* 33. This tavern, also called Red Lion Inn, stood on corner of Broad street and Rahway avenue, now occupied by the Public Library. See also: Mills, *Historic Houses of New Jersey,* 119.

43 Oct. 3, 1797, N. Y. Hist. Soc., Gates Papers, box 18, no. 53.

44 Niemcewicz, *Pamiętniki,* 325.

45 Alden, *Collection of American Epitaphs,* I, 139; also W. H., "Kosciusko," *Mag. of American History,* VI, (1881), 383.

46 *Aurora,* Oct. 26, 1797.

turning from Braintree for a new session of Congress by way of New York, where a few days earlier citizens, under the chairmanship of Mayor Richard Varick, entertained the distinguished guests at a public dinner, never yet equalled in the city "for elegance and taste," at the New City Assembly Room. This was preeminently a Federalist affair though Gen. Gates, because of his old friendship (now considerably cooled by politics) for Adams, was, too, on the committee.[47] Among the toasts there was one for Kosciuszko, too: "May private Friendship and public Honor sooth the wounds he has received in the cause of Freedom."[48]

Another series of receptions awaited the Adamses at New Brunswick. Niemcewicz was full of excitement and activity. The suffering and quiet Kosciuszko preferred to retire "near the chimney corner with the book."[49] On November 8, repeating his thanks for hospitality, he advised Gates: "The Presydent dining here to-day and as write this, the Canons give notice by their little noise of his aproching near the town, I expect see him at Gen. White's where he will drinck tea."[50] Niemcewicz, so exact in his description of the reception at New Brunswick, passed in silence over the meeting of Adams and Kosciuszko; there is no evidence that it ever took place.[51]

The literature which absorbed Kosciuszko's mind at that time consisted of the writings of John Dickinson, most probably the new series of his *Letters of Fabius*. Especially pleasant to the General's heart were those passages in which the venerable author most strongly condemned the Partitions of Poland. But Dickinson's eloquent arguments on the political situation of the United States also appealed to Kosciuszko's opinions and made a deep impression upon him. He wrote to Dickinson on November 24:

"The language of truth is the same in any shape whatsoever is dresed, I have not accustomate to express my Ideas in so simple and comformable maner to every man's understanding; yet I am of the same opinion, and if the exterior not correspond, in my heart I am a kwaker too, will do anything for the hapiness of Human kind —

"Your Enswer to my letter came to my hands at New Brunswick the 20 of November, when it was solong I cannot tell, otherwise you should have sooner my thanks. It grieves me very much to hear your bad state of health, but I hope my wishes and of the others friends in

---

47 *U. S. Gazette,* Oct. 20, 1797.

48 *Mass. Mercury,* Oct. 27, 1797.

49 Kosciuszko to an unknown addressee, Nov. 3, 1797, Polish R. C. U. Museum, Kosciuszko Papers no. 47.

50 N. Y. Hist. Soc., Gates Papers, box 21, no. 71.

51 According to Fenno and Cobbett, Kosciuszko did not meet President Adams at that time (*Porcupine Works,* X, 12), but this information cannot be considered as absolutely reliable.

Poland where you have many, amongst whom your Character is in very high estymation: will restore you to the Comfort of all — if my health will permit me no doubt I shall not be deprivate of so desird satisfaction to shake you by the hand, and convers wyth you; whoes habilities and good heart rendered so many services to the Public — you Improved Sir their Mind to virtue, love of the Country and Humanity — I shall stay two days under your roof if you will allow me, that I may reap the advantage of your instruction, and fashion my own Mind by yours —"[52]

About this time Major Evan Edwards of South Carolina also remembered himself to Kosciuszko in an "obliging and friendly letter," evidently touching on some financial affairs. Answering him, Kosciuszko expressed "the highest aprobation of" his "conduct in the matter of Dollars. your Character," he assured him, "never put me in doubt that you will acte otherwise by which you acquired Esteem and lowe of Your fellow Cytysens, as the others hatred wyth contempt — . . . as to your Lady . . . you will kiss her 20 times for me wyth my respects — . . . if I was their I should take wilingly that charge for you."[53]

Colder weather brought the epidemic of yellow fever in Philadelphia to an end and Kosciuszko began preparations for his return to the city. Sent in advance, Niemcewicz, with the help of Dr. Rush,[54] found him "a dwelling as small, as secluded and as cheap," as instructed by the General.

One of Kosciuszko's last acts before leaving the hospitable home of Gen. White was to write again to Gen. Gates on November 27:

"It would Hurt my feelings had I not write you leaving this place — and not send you my warmest thanks for your friendship shown me under your roof, as well as to Mrs. Gates to her I send my respectfull Kisses. To-morrow I set out for Philadelphia . . ."[55]

About that time young John Quincy Adams, the American Minister at Berlin, spent a pleasant evening in the home of Prince Anthony Radziwill, who had recently married Princess Louise, daughter of Prince Ferdinand of Prussia, mentioned in some circles as the future king of a rebuilt Poland. The hosts "talked much of Kosciuszko, with great apparent regard and respect — of America, of General Washington, and asked a great number of questions relative to the United States."[56] Lafayette, recently released from his long imprisonment,

52 Hist. Soc. of Pa., Gratz Collection, case 14, box 4.
53 Nov. 5, 1797, Hist. Soc. of Pa., Etting Papers.
54 Kosciuszko to Rush, Nov. 11, and another letter undated, Ridgway Libr., Rush Papers, 7246 F. 37 and 38.
55 N. Y. Hist. Soc., Gates Papers, box 18, no. 55.
56 Adams, *Memoirs of John Quincy Adams,* I, 209, entry of Dec. 6, 1797.

wrote to James McHenry, the Secretary of War: "Remember me also to Gen'l Kosciusko. I Hope His Health is Better. My Great Regard for Him Makes me More affectionately Partake in every thing that Concerns Him."[57] On the dark firmament of Europe, now turned into "one Golgotha" by "contaminating principles and abominations,"[58] Kosciuszko's name shone like a star and the eyes of many of those who longed for a better world unconsciously turned along after him to the happier American shores.

[57] Dec. 26, 1797, Steiner, *Life of James McHenry,* 288.
[58] Abigail Adams to Mrs. Mercy Warren, June 17, 1798, Mass. Hist. Soc., *Warren-Adams Letters,* II, 339:

VII.

BACK IN PHILADELPHIA

Kosciuszko's return to Philadelphia brought almost the entire city to the door of his modest apartment at No. 172 Third Street South. It was a small boarding house kept by a Mrs. Relfe, occupied mostly by students of medicine and young artisans; the rent was cheap, and this was important to Kosciuszko. He had a small room for his own use, where he could receive not more than four persons at one time. Another room, still smaller, was occupied by Niemcewicz, but, because it was not heated, he used it only as a sleeping-room.[1] When more visitors came than could be accommodated, they had to divide into groups and take their turns.[2] The General received his visitors lying in bed, or sitting in a large chair, always with bandaged head, "with a posture of sickness."[3] He could not even move "from one place to the other without the support and help of his Crutches and a Servant."[4] According to Fenno,[5] he was "politely attended by every distinguished member of the federal government; by most of the ladies, as well as the gentlemen of this city."[6] Niemcewicz says "it was customary for young girls to visit Kosciuszko, he drew portraits of some of them."[7] "The young misses . . . accepted these *devoirs* with avidity."[8]

Fenno, who watched Kosciuszko with an Argus eye, enumerates the following among "the most intimate and frequent" visitors of the General: Dr. George Logan, Judge Thomas McKean, Governor Mifflin, Senator Stevens Thomson Mason of Virginia and other Republican members of both houses of Congress.[9] Matthew Carey, the publisher, evidently also belonged to the inner circle of Kosciuszko's friends.[10] The French Consul Letombe came often with European political news. Visitors from among the French emigres included General Victor Collot, Moreau de Saint-Mery[11] and the Orleanist

---

1 Kozłowski, "Pobyt," 265.
2 Moreau de Saint-Mery, *Voyage,* 256.
3 *Ibid.*
4 Kosciuszko to Charles Pettit, Jan. 10, 1798, N. Y. Public Libr., Misc. MSS.
5 John Ward Fenno who succeeded his father in editing the *Gazette of the United States.*
6 *U. S. Gazette,* Nov. 6, 1798.
7 Niemcewicz, *Pamiętniki,* 331.
8 *U. S. Gazette,* Nov. 9, 1798.
9 *Ibid.,* Nov. 6, 1798.
10 Kosciuszko to Carey, undated, Polish R. C. U. Museum, Kosciuszko Papers, no. 52.
11 Moreau de Saint-Mery, *Voyage,* 256.

princes, the Duke of Orleans, the future King of the French, with his brothers, the Duke of Montpensier and Comte de Beaujolais. The younger princes often spent their evenings at the bedside of Kosciuszko. When they left Philadelphia in the spring for a trip to other parts of the country, Kosciuszko presented Comte de Beaujolais with a pair of fur-boots, which the lad accepted with joy and gratitude.[12]

An unusual guest of Kosciuszko was Me-She-Kun-Nogh-Quah, the Little Turtle, chief of the Miamis, who happened to be in Philadelphia to negotiate with the government about some matters pertaining to his nation. On paying a visit to Kosciuszko, the Indian, dressed in a uniform of an American General with large epaulets, presented the host with a tomahawk. Kosciuszko reciprocated with a felt-cloak. The chieftain saw a pair of spectacles and seemed to be eager to acquire them. Nothing could equal his joy when Kosciuszko presented them to him. He could not comprehend how glasses enlarged objects. "You have given me new eyes," he exclaimed with joy and astonishment.[13]

But the most frequent and the most welcome visitor of Kosciuszko was the Vice-President of the United States, Thomas Jefferson. Both men agreed almost unanimously in their political convictions, in their general opinions, even in their fancies. During the Revolutionary War they met only occasionally; Kosciuszko, then a young officer was as yet little known outside army circles, notwithstanding his distinguished service record; Jefferson, a political leader of growing importance, was almost exclusively occupied with civil affairs. Undoubtedly it was sympathy for the unhappy champion of common ideals that brought Jefferson to Kosciuszko's door for the first time. A sincere and lasting friendship ensued, interrupted only by their deaths. Niemcewicz said that "Kosciuszko completely adhered to Jefferson."[14] The latter wrote to Gates: "I see him (Kosciuszko) often, and with great pleasure mixed with commiseration."[15]

It may be surmised that conversations between the two new friends centered mostly around American and European political events. The genius of Napoleon had just begun its meteoric rise in the brilliant Italian campaign, which forced Francis II to sue for peace. The news of the treaty of Campo Formio fell heavily on Kosciuszko's heart. "Kosciuszko," wrote Jefferson, "has been disappointed by the sudden peace between France and Austria. A ray of hope seemed to gleam

12 Niemcewicz, *Pamiętniki,* 330-31.
13 Kozłowski, "Pobyt," 266; cf. also Love, "Me-She-Kun-Nogh-Quah," *Ohio Archael. and Hist. Publ.,* XVIII (1909), 125; according to Love, it was a pair of pistols which Kosciuszko donated to the Little Turtle.
14 Niemcewicz, *Pamiętniki,* 327.
15 Feb. 21, 1798, Lipscomb, IX, 441.

on his mind for a moment, that the extension of the revolutionary spirit through Italy and Germany, might so have occupied the remnants of monarchy there, as that his country might have risen again."[16]

Kosciuszko read in American newspapers of the final ratification of the treaties which sealed the end of Poland, of there "not remaining the least shadow of probability that that Country will ever be restored to its former political existence";[17] but he also read of the insurrectionist movement in southeastern Poland, of the Polish Legions in action, even of plans to convoke the Polish Diet in exile. Perhaps the echo of the famous Dombrowski Mazurka, in which the soldier, shedding his blood for his country on the banks of the Tiber and Po, yearningly sang: "Poland is not yet lost . . . God will give us Kosciuszko," reached his ears over the breadth of the Atlantic. The terms of the treaty threatened the whole existence of the Polish Legions, which had rendered important services to Napoleon and remained the only visible symbol of Poland's aspirations to national life. Nevertheless, Kosciuszko "hoped that the successful struggle of France against the enemies of Poland might open possibilities of renewing, defending and reclaiming her rights to independence." With rising conviction, he felt "that his presence and his intercession might add weight to her cause."[18] Dombrowski and other Polish exiled leaders urged him to join them and to lead them. Members of the French Directory invited him to come to Paris, especially since a renewal of the war was expected. The Poles needed Kosciuszko's moral authority, the Frenchmen thought that his presence might be used as a political trump.[19] It seems that as late as early March Kosciuszko was still hesitating as to whether he should follow these entreaties or not. He even wrote of "going to the country very soon."[20] Only recently he had been considering several propositions of acquiring a country seat. Declining an offer of a farm in Pennsylvania, he accepted, however,

---

16 To Gates, Feb. 21, 1798, Lipscomb, IX, 441.

17 *Mass. Mercury*, Sept. 2, 1797.

18 Paszkowski, *Dzieje Kościuszki*, 193.

19 Such is the opinion of the brilliant historian Askenazy, *Napoleon a Polska*, III, 33. Unhappily, no documents are known to exist which would throw more light on this question. Kosciuszko, who, by the way, was most careless with his papers, undoubtedly destroyed the French invitation for secrecy's sake. The character of the invitation must have been private, so as to keep the government free of any responsibility. Madame Fiszer, however, heard Kosciuszko say explicitly that he had been invited by the French government. Her explanation sounds very reasonable: "Had he (Kosciuszko) not been called by something connected with his patriotic views, I do not doubt that a man so reluctant to renown, so tired as he was, would ever have moved without important reasons; but on the other hand I have been informed by a most reliable source . . . that Kosciuszko had been misled by taking a personal invitation for a general one. The events were so fresh that everything which was reported to him, made a great impression on his mind; at that time he might easily have been deceived." (Fiszerowa, "Pamiętnik," 253). Evans (*Memoir*, 25) says that some mail received by Kosciuszko in the spring of 1798, made such an impression on him that he, an invalid though he was, suddenly "sprang from his couch into the middle of the room." Korzon wrongly accepted this tale as a sudden recovery (*Kosciuszko*, 495, and "Kwestja Wyjazdu," *Biblioteka Warszawska*, CCLXV, 399), later explained by Kozłowski ("Rozstanie się," *Kwartalnik Hist.*, XX, 225-252, and "Pobyt Kościuszki," *Biblioteka Warszawska*, CCLXI, 241-284).

20 Kosciuszko to an unknown addressee, but most probably Thomas Pinckney, March 3, 1798, Polish R. C. U. Museum, Kosciuszko Papers, no. 49.

MISS LUCETTA A. POLLOCK
by Kosciuszko

an invitation to visit Armstrong in the Hudson Valley in the spring and "then decide for or against" that neighborhood.[21] Jefferson later revealed that he had endeavoured to induce Kosciuszko to settle in Virginia, assuring him that his State "would have peculiar sensibility if he had thought proper to make his residence."[22] With this indecision evident, Kosciuszko wrote to Gates on February 22:

"Had I been informed that my letters would afford you a satisfaction: I would certainly write you often and express what a feeling heart wyth Friendship and Esteem, could sugest in my Mind. Genl. Armstrong wrote me of a Farme in his neighborhood, I enswered him, that in my way to Saratoga Spring I would be glad to see it—;" he added significantly: "but you know in this world we are not Sure of anything."[23]

To be prepared for any contingency Kosciuszko wished to put his financial affairs in order. Congress was in session since November, so he could hope for some action on his Revolutionary account. The importance of the matter to him may be surmised from his letter to Washington, written while he was still in Elizabeth, October 8:

"I return You my warmest thanks for the Honour You have done me — If the situation of my health would admit my travelling so far, I would immediatly pay you my Respects and my personal Homage—; it was my first intention, and I hope I shall at last accomplish it —

"Your High Character, Reputation and the Goodness of Your Heart, may give me the liberty to mention a circumstance concerning me and is this — From the United States, I have not received neither the procent for Fourteen years nor the Sum due to me; formerly I was independent, but now my only resource is in the Justice of Congress, having lost my Certificate and wyth my Country lost my All — I must Request Sir, You will be so kind to mention my situation to that August Body and entreat, that I may be paid my Just demand; without the trouble of making other Application—"[24]

Washington replied on October 15:

"I am sorry that the state of your health should deprive me of the pleasure of your company at this place — and I regret still more that the pain you feel from the wounds you have received — though glorious for your reputation — is the occasion of it. —

"Whatever I can do as a private citizen (and in no other capacity I can now act) consistently with the plan I have laid down for my future government, you may freely Command. — You will find how-

---

21 Armstrong to Gates, Feb. 18, 1798, N. Y. Hist. Soc., Gates Papers, box 18, no. 61.
22 Jefferson to Niemcewicz, Nov. 30, 1798, Libr. of Congress, Jefferson Papers.
23 N. Y. Hist. Soc., Gates Papers, box 18, no. 62.
24 Libr. of Congress, Washington Papers.

ever, contrary as it may be to your expectation or wishes, that all pecuniary matters must flow from the Legislature and in a form which cannot be dispensed with — I may add I am sure, that your claim upon the justice & feelings of this country will meet with no delay — Nor do I suppose that the loss of your certificate will be any impediment.— Your work and services in the American Army are too well known to require that testimony of your claim and the Books of the Treasury will show that you have received nothing in discharge of it — or if any part, to what amount.—"[25]

The above letters closed the mutual relations between the two men. Kosciuszko left America without meeting Washington. A score of months later "The Father of His Country" died. Kosciuszko's neglect in visiting Mount Vernon and Washington's refusal to mediate the General's claim before Congress have been taken by some historians as additional proofs of allegedly cool relations between the two Revolutionary veterans, chilled still more by their opposite political leanings in the American crisis of 1797-8. The facts, however, do not support such a theory.

If Kosciuszko, who was so reluctant to ask favors for himself, turned to Washington for help in the matter of his pay, was it not an act of confidence in his old chief? Foreseeing no difficulties in the settling of the matter by Congress, Washington declined to interfere; in fact, since his retirement from the presidency, he lived in comparative seclusion. Except for a time when war with France appeared imminent, his correspondence of that period was almost completely devoted to agricultural subjects and to the small affairs of his home and estate. He kept strictly to his decision not "to mix again in the great world, or to partake in its politics," but to "seclude myself as much as possible from the noisy and bustling crowd."[26] He stressed that desire many times to different persons.

Those few letters, which Washington and Kosciuszko exchanged in 1797, are marked by the same straightforwardness and sincerity that characterized their Revolutionary correspondence. The last letter of Kosciuszko clearly shows his desire to personally pay his respects to his former Commander-in-Chief. Though now he leaned visibly and decisively toward the Republican point of view, he wisely kept himself aloof from any active participation in the stormy American politics. There is no reason to attach any political meaning to Kosciuszko's

25 N. Y. Public Libr., Washington Press — Copies, no. 97.

26 Washington to Henry Knox, March 2, 1797, Fitzpatrick, XXXV, 409. The objection of some of Kosciuszko's biographers that notwithstanding his refusal to interpose in behalf of Kosciuszko, Washington tried to effect the liberation of Lafayette, does not stand criticism. Though stressing the private character of his request, Washington asked the Austrian Emperor to free the Marquis while he still was President. (Washington to the Emperor of Germany, May 15, 1796, Fitzpatrick, XXXV, 45).

neglect in fulfilling his promise of visiting Washington. The distance of the journey;[27] an early and severe winter,[28] which made travel most difficult for a person in a bad state of health; Kosciuszko's desire to settle his financial affairs; and finally, his hurried and secret preparations for his departure — these were the reasons why he did not undertake the journey to Mount Vernon. There should be no doubt that the expressions of mutual esteem between the two Generals were not only empty courtesies. Even after Kosciuszko's departure, Washington "with compassion" inquired of Niemcewicz as to the health of his chief.[29] Kosciuszko sent his compliments to Washington by Dr. Logan even from France;[30] if his choice of the envoy was not very diplomatic, undoubtedly the message was sincere.

That Kosciuszko at first actually planned a southern excursion is best proved by his promise to visit ailing John Dickinson at his home at Wilmington. At that time he repeatedly talked of going to Virginia, which would also give him a chance to take mineral baths for his health.[31] On his departure, he used his announced plans as an innocent subterfuge to cover his movements, but this in itself does not deny the truth of his original plans. If he disappointed Washington, he equally disappointed Dickinson, with whose political views he certainly agreed in full. He wrote to the latter on January 4, 1798:

"I have spend my time few days in the must agreable manner by the perusal of your books — It is wrot wyth great force, energy, perspicuity and the knowledge of the human Nature.

"I cannot tell you precisely now, what time I shall have the honour to see you, but I will give you notice before hand."[32]

Some time later, while extolling the merits of Dickinson's works and assuring him that "what Come's from your pen, I must have in my library of Choice," Kosciuszko could only write: "My health not permit me yet to have the pleasure of shaking the hand a respectable friend at Wilmington, I leave to time my wyshes and enxious hope."[33]

There is no record of any meeting between Kosciuszko and Dickinson, though Wilmington is not far away from Philadelphia. Meanwhile a letter from Alexander Garden of Charleston vividly brought to Kosciuszko's mind all the recollections of his Southern Campaign of 1781-2. Years later Garden, in his Revolutionary reminiscences,

---

27 Mount Vernon is about 150 miles from Philadelphia, while New York only about 90.
28 Washington to John Marshall, Dec. 4, and to George Washington Motier Lafayette, Dec. 5, 1797, Fitzpatrick XXXVI, 94 and 96.
29 Niemcewicz to Jefferson, May 27, 1797, Libr. of Congress, Jefferson Papers.
30 U. S. Gazette, Nov. 15, 1798; Columbian Centinel, Nov. 24, 1798.
31 Porcupine's Works, X, 12.
32 Hist. Soc. of Pa., Gratz Collection, case 14, box 4.
33 Undated, ibid.

was to criticize the Polish commander in none too gentlemanly a manner, but now his lines seemed full of the old friendship, and Kosciuszko answered him:

"I am very sinsible of the honour you do me, and send you in return my warmest thanks, as well to your amiable handsome Lady, wyth my respects; I am sorry to hear that the time was so ungenerous to dymnishe the number of my acquientences, however to thos steal in life be pleased to present my Compliments, more particularly to Cls Grimke,[34] Shoubrick,[35] Mr. Scott in James Island, or to his Wife, where i was treated wyth afection, friendship and nursed like their one Child.—" He also enclosed his regards to Major Edwards, Col. William Washington, and, above all, to his former bosom friend, Major Lewis Morris, and his beautiful wife. Jestingly he begged Mrs. Morris to send him "a dish of Coffe and such as I tasted at Accabie."[36]

Just as Washington foresaw, the settlement of Kosciuszko's accounts did not meet with much difficulty. On December 22, 1797, Dawson called the attention of the House to Kosciuszko's situation; recalling his services to America and his struggle for Poland's independence, Dawson offered a resolution providing for the appointment of a Committee which would inquire into the provisions necessary to obtain the payment of Kosciuszko's claim; "as it was justice only which he sought for this brave man, he doubted not that a spirit of justice would insure its adoption."[37] Josiah Parker of Virginia seconded the motion. Joshua Coit, a Federalist of Connecticut, demanded that the resolution be referred to the Committee of Claims; his motion, however, was defeated by an overwhelming vote, many Federalists voting with Republicans to kill it. Whereupon Thomas Pinckney of South Carolina in a lengthy speech explained how in 1793, as Minister to Great Britain, he had tried to remit the interest due to Kosciuszko up to the end of 1792.[38] He had never heard any more on the subject until he saw the General in Philadelphia and was informed by him that the draft had never reached his hands; it was just before the outbreak of the Insurrection and, absorbed by its preparations, Kosciuszko moved from place to place. He had, therefore, written immediately to the American bankers at Amsterdam[39] requesting them to

---

34 Lt. Col. John F. Grimke of South Carolina Artillery.

35 Capt. Thomas Shubrick of the Second South Carolina Continental Regiment.

36 Accabee, a plantation near Charleston which belonged to the Elliott family; Morris married Nancy Elliott. The original of this letter, dated Dec. 17, 1797, in the So. Caro. Hist. Soc.; reprinted in *The So. Caro. Hist. and Geneal. Magazine*, II, 126.

37 *Aurora*, Dec. 26, 1797.

38 For the years 1789-1792 inclusively, as it was supposed by the Treasury that all officers of the Continental Army had received their interest to the 1st of January 1789. The interest for 1785 to 1788, however, did not reach Kosciuszko (*Aurora*, Dec. 30, 1797).

39 Pinckney to Wilhelm & Jan Willink, Nicholas & Jacob Van Staphorst and Hubbard, Dec. 7, 1797, Mass. Hist. Soc., Jefferson Papers, a copy. Oliver Wolcott, the Secretary of the Treasury, also wrote to the above firms on the same subject. March 13, 1798, *ibid*.

redraw the money still in the banks in Leipzig or Dresden and to transmit it to this country for the General's use. "But, as he might, in the mean time stand in need of it, it might be proper in the United States to anticipate its return, by settling the account with the General. He hoped in whatever way this business was effected, it would be in such a way as not to wound the feelings of a man who had deserved so well of this country."

The House eventually set aside Dawson's motion, directing instead the Secretary of the Treasury to prepare a report on what legislative provision was necessary to meet Kosciuszko's demands. "Whatever difference of opinion there was in the House, as to the mode of doing the business, there seemed to be but one sentiment, as to the propriety of complying with the spirit of the resolution."[40]

On December 28, Oliver Wolcott, the Secretary of the Treasury, submitted his report,[41] according to which Kosciuszko was entitled to receive without any further action of Congress, the principal of $12,280.54, the sum of his lost certificate, and $2,947.33 as interest for the years 1785 to 1788. Wolcott claimed that the Treasury had no power to advance the interest supposed to have been remitted to Leipzig or Dresden in 1793 and that, according to a regulation of 1792, the certificates of foreign officers ceased to bear interest since December last of that year, when provision had also been made for paying the principal due on them.

Consequently, Dawson reported a bill providing for the payment of the interest on the claim of Kosciuszko for the years 1789-1792 and in addition for the years 1793-1797, inclusive. The bill was passed by the House on January 5, 1798,[42] but the Senate attached an amendment, suspending the payment of the first four years' interest which, it was said, Kosciuszko could claim directly from European banks. For some time the bill became a subject of seesaw tactics between the two houses. Again taking up the matter in the House, Dawson pointed out that the money remitted to Europe could more easily be withdrawn by the government, that the regulation of 1792 was not based on any law, but had been made by the Treasury of its own accord, and that Kosciuszko had never heard of the regulation until he arrived in America. His motion to repass the bill "was finally agreed to without division."[43] Twice the House rejected the Senate amendment, and twice the Senate insisted upon it.[44] The deadlock was broken by

---

40 Rives, *Abridgement of the Debates,* II, 191.
41 Wolcott, *Report.*
42 *Aurora,* Jan. 10, 1798.
43 Rives, *Abridgement of the Debates,* II, 191.
44 *Aurora,* Jan. 17, 1798.

a request to recommit the matter to a conference.[45] The House finally receded from its position when Pinckney, one of the conferees, informed it that a settlement at the Treasury could take place to accommodate the General.[46] The bill, with the Senate amendment, passed both houses on January 17th. It became a law on January 23, 1798.[47] It simply provided for the payment of interest from January 1, 1793, to the end of 1797, which amounted to $3,684.16, a very small sum even in proportion to the state of the American Treasury at the time. That was the gift which Congress saw fit to present Kosciuszko above what was due to him by law and without his solicitation. The significance of the measure lay in its exceptional character. In the opinion of Justice Wayne, given half a century later, however, "it was not a gratuity, but a simple act of justice, graduated then by the inability of our country to do more."[48] To some extent it was a compensation for the negligent treatment Kosciuszko had received from the Continental Congress. It is to the honor of the Fifth Congress that at a time of great political dissension it not only saw the justice of Kosciuszko's claim, but, moreover, made a gesture of magnanimity toward the invalid Polish exile.

Altogether Kosciuszko received $18,912.03, besides the interest for four years which was sent to Europe in 1793 to the amount of $2,947.33. It seems that Peter Porcupine was the only malcontent. "Disinterested, generous Kosciuszko!" he bantered. He "received *in cash* his full proportion of what American soldiers received *in paper.*"[49]

It is interesting to add, that the assertion of the Treasury about the interest supposedly dormant in German banks was inaccurate, as Kosciuszko found out on his return to Europe.[50] The money had been returned to the Treasury years ago. Kosciuszko was so affected by what he supposed was a trick played on him by the Federalists, that he urged Jefferson "to publishe thos letters that the public should now (know) their Characters."[51]

---

45 The Committee of Conference was composed of Senators Uriah Tracey of Connecticut and James Ross of Pennsylvania, both Federalists, and Representatives Pinckney, Federalist, Dawson and Gallatin, Republicans. (*U. S. Gazette*, Jan. 16, 1798).

46 *Aurora*, Jan. 19, 1798.

47 *Laws of the U. S.*, III, 25. The original act is in the National Archives.

48 Howard, *Reports*, XIV, 412.

49 *Porcupine's Works*, X, 82.

50 I. C. Hottinguer to Kosciuszko, 7 Fructidor an. VI, Mass. Hist. Soc., Jefferson Coll.

51 Kosciuszko to Jefferson, undated, but written sometime in the late summer of 1798, *ibid.*

VIII.

DEPARTURE FOR FRANCE

Meanwhile the situation in America was becoming discouraging. Relations with "intoxicated and lawless France"[1] grew worse from day to day. American envoys, Charles C. Pinckney, Marshall and Gerry, waited long for an understanding with the Directory, and waited in vain. In a message to Congress in March President Adams recommended large armaments on land and sea. A faction of the Federalists pressed hard and vociferously for a break with France. Early in April, into the strained American atmosphere there burst the XYZ affair which "produced such a shock . . . as had never been since our independence."[2] It brought the whole indignant nation to its feet. "Awe and ridicule arose . . . in both houses of Congress," recorded Niemcewicz; "for a long time one could hear in Philadelphia constantly repeated words: beaucoup d'argent."[3] War now seemed inevitable. Simultaneously "all the passions were boiling over";[4] the reign of terror against the Republicans became intensified and the Alien and Sedition Bills, which Jefferson considered a "libel on legislation,"[5] were introduced. Some later historians have thought that the first of these bills was also directed against Kosciuszko; but Jefferson who undoubtedly knew well the trend of public opinion, disagrees with this view. He acknowledges that there were "some . . . cold to . . . his pure and republican zeal," but "the mass of our countrymen have the highest veneration and attachment to his character."[6]

Under the influence of these events, Kosciuszko accepted Jefferson's suggestion of bringing the two nations, after Poland, most dear to his heart, to a peaceful settlement of their differences. "Jefferson considered that I would be the most effective intermediary in bringing an accord with France, so I accepted the mission even if without any

---

1 Washington to Alexander Martin, Feb. 22, 1798, Fitzpatrick, XXXVI, 168-9.
2 Jefferson to Madison, April 6, 1798, Lipscomb, X, 26.
3 Niemcewicz, *Pamiętniki*, 330.
4 Jefferson to James Lewis, Jr., May 9, 1798, Lipscomb, X, 37.
5 Jefferson to Joseph Priestley, March 21, 1801, *ibid.*, X, 229.

6 Jefferson to Niemcewicz Nov. 30, 1798, Libr. of Congress, Jefferson Papers, vol. 104. According to Jefferson, the bill was mainly aimed at Volney, attacked most vehemently by pastors for his deism, and Gen. Collot, suspected of acting clandestinely to regain Louisiana for France (Jefferson to Madison, April 26, and May 3, 1798, Lipscomb, X, 32, and 35.) Some considered the Alien Bill as meant more against the Irish than against the French; Gallatin was also mentioned as one of its intended victims (Bowers, *Jefferson and Hamilton*, 374-6). A correspondent of the *Aurora* mentioned Kosciuszko as an example of the injustice of the Alien Bill (Dec. 11, 1798).

official authorization," Kosciuszko himself said some years later.[7] Now he saw clearly the necessity for his quick departure. Two purposes inspired him with growing intensity: a peace mission for America and a new service for Poland.

He began hasty preparations in utmost secrecy. In that he succeeded much better than did Dr. Logan, who, notwithstanding all precautions,[8] exposed himself to being branded as a traitor and drew much persecution on his wife and friends. In Kosciuszko's case the secrecy was most important not only because of the excitement in America, but also because of the danger of his being seized on the sea by some British cruiser. Jefferson undertook to secure passage and to procure passports for the General

For greater safety and secrecy, Kosciuszko decided to use an assumed name and chose that of Mr. Kann. Jefferson changed it to Thomas Kannberg. In order to mislead further his eventual pursuers Kosciuszko was to sail via Lisbon, where he expected to stay for a few days. He wrote to Jefferson in this regard:

"You had the goodnes to take me under your care and protection. I beseech to continue to the end.—

". . . I must know six or ten days before I go to prepare the things and in the maner that nobody should know it. — it is requisit that I should have passports on the name of Mr. Kann[9] from Ministers English, Portugal, Span, French . . . recomend me I beg you to your friend at Lisbon to help me in every thing and as I am a Stranger and will stay few days I would wish if possible that he should take me to his house upon any Condition — not forget to recomend me to the care of the Capitain in whose Ship I will go . . ."[10]

Jefferson promptly and personally applied to the ministers, assuring them that the passports were intended for "his friend Thomas Kanberg, . . . a native of the north of Europe (perhaps of Germany)," who "has been known to Thomas Jefferson these twenty years in America, is of a most excellent character, stands in no relation whatever to any of the belligerent powers, as to whom Thomas Jefferson is not afraid to be responsible for his political innocence, as he goes merely for his private affairs. He will sail from Baltimore, if he finds there a good opportunity for France; and if not he will come on here."[11]

---

[7] Drzewiecki's memoir, as quoted by Skałkowski, *O Kokardę Legionów,* 28 n.; cf. also Paszkowski, *Dzieje Kościuszki,* 196.

[8] Logan, *Memoir,* 57-61.

[9] Jefferson in his own hand added "Thomas" above the line and "berg" after Kann.

[10] Undated, Maine Historical Society, Fogg Collection.

[11] Jefferson to Liston, March 27, 1798, Lipscomb, X, 48.

Kosciuszko then turned his attention to the final settling of his financial affairs. He changed a considerable sum of cash into drafts for Amsterdam banks,[12] and with Jefferson's help tried now to locate the rest of his American money in some safe investments. Besides Biddle's advice, he also asked Charles Pettit, former Assistant Quartermaster General under Greene, and now an importing merchant in Philadelphia, how to "lay Money upon interest but in the surest way, not subject to Changes, and other Circumstances, and that I may draw regularly procent due from this Sume."[13] Jefferson, however, suggested his own private banker, John Barnes, then living in Philadelphia, but soon to become a distinguished resident of Georgetown, with the history of which city he became closely connected for the rest of his life.[14] A man of sterling character, Barnes not only gladly agreed to take care of Kosciuszko's finances, but kept it up till the end of his life in a most honest and disinterested manner. It was a service dictated by his noble nature and by friendship for Kosciuszko, whom he learned to revere from the depth of his heart. Years after Kosciuszko's death, he spoke of him with enthusiasm.[15] Jefferson's choice was the best possible.

With impatience Kosciuszko now awaited the day of his departure. Some time in April he wrote to Jefferson:

"I afraid to hurt your feelings by my reiterated importunities, but I am so enxious of going away, that not one moment in a day I have a rest, if this occasion fall of going to Bourdeau, I should prefer to Lisbon to avoided of bieng taking by the English. The Season far advenced and rumour of this Country is very desigreable to a feeling heart as we cannot talk fully upon this Subject, I beg you was kind to put me a paper like this for information how and when I expect to go.—"[16]

In the first days of May Kosciuszko conferred more frequently with Jefferson, Niemcewicz recorded many years later.[17] Most probably his remark referred to the whole period, when Kosciuszko ultimately decided to depart. One more noble thought occupied the General's mind. He planned to leave his well-earned capital to America

---

12 In the Jefferson Collection, Mass. Hist. Soc., there are two drafts on two different banks in Amsterdam, one dated April 14, for 6,315 guilders and 16 stivers, ($2,400 at the current exchange value of 38 cents), the other dated April 19, 1798, for 3,157 guilders and 18 stivers ($1200). Kosciuszko wrote to Jefferson about that time: "I send inclosed a Varrant for the letters of Exchange. I live to your jugement in what maner to be done that I may receive without trouble or loss of time. Six hundred eighty four out of the whole money will serve to pay my passage the rest out of this I would wish to have by me in hard Cash..." (Undated, Maine Hist. Soc., Fogg Coll.)

13 Date illegible, perhaps Jan. 10, 1798, N. Y. Public Libr., Misc. MSS.

14 Cf. Jackson, "John Barnes," *Records of the Columbian Hist. Soc.*, VII (1904), 39-48.

15 Benjamin L. Lear to Jefferson, Sept. 19, 1821, Libr. of Congress, Jefferson Papers.

16 Undated, Mass. Hist. Soc., Jefferson Coll.

17 Niemcewicz, *Pamiętniki,* 331.

and to dedicate it to a great social purpose. The misery of the Negroes always excited the deepest sympathy of his good heart. He devoted his last moments on American soil to composing a will, bequeathing all his funds in this country to the cause of freedom and education of slaves. Little versed in the legal terms of a language which he never was able to master, Kosciuszko called on Jefferson for help: "When ever you will have a time in the daytime for a quarter of hour I beg you would grante me to finish what I have begone . . ."[18]

The well known and often reproduced text of this American will of Kosciuszko[19] is not the original one. Though written in Kosciuszko's hand, it was only his transcript from a copy undoubtedly prepared by Jefferson; preserving Kosciuszko's idea and some of his phrases, the Vice-President completely rewrote the testament, giving it the required legal form and terms. The original will, written by Kosciuszko sometime before April 30, has all the simplicity and crudeness of his style, all the imperfection of his English pen, but it reflects much better and more vividly all the goodness of his heart and his ideas of raising the social position of the Negroes.

The text of this original will, published here for the first time, is as follows:

"I beg Mr. Jefferson that in case I should die without will or testament he should bye out of my money so many Negroes and free them, that the restant Sum should be Sufficient to give them education and provide for their maintenance. That is to say each should know before, the duty of a Cytyzen in the free Government, that he must defend his Country against foreign as well internal Enemis who would wish to change the Constitution for the vorst to inslave them by degree afterwards, to have good and human heart sensible for the sufferings of others, each must be maried and have 100 ackres of land, wyth instruments, Cattle for tillage and know how to manage and Gouvern it as well to know how behave to neybourghs, always wyth kindness and ready to help them — to them selves frugal to their Children give good education I mean as to the heart and the duty to ther Country, in gratitude to me to make themselves happy as possible. T Kosciuszko."[20]

On April 30 this will was attested to by John Dawson and John Barnes. With the exception of these witnesses and of Jefferson, nobody,

---

18 Undated, Mass. Hist. Soc., Jefferson Coll.

19 The original in the Albermarle County, Virginia, Circuit Court, Will Book No. 1, p. 42.

20 This will is in the Mass. Hist. Soc., Jefferson Coll., together with "Gen. Kosciuszko's Power of Attorney to Mr. Jefferson dated Philadelphia, 20 April, 1798" (the power of attorney itself is dated April 30, and is entirely in Jefferson's handwriting) and an affidavit signed by John Dawson and sworn at Philadelphia, June 15, 1798, as to the identity of documents.

I beg Mr. Jefferson that in case I should die without will or testament he should bize out of my money So many Negroes and frie them. that the restante Summ should be Suficient to give them aducation and provide for thier maintenance. that is to say. should know before; the duty of a cityzen in the free Government. and that he must defend his Country. against foreign as well internal Enemis who wanted wish to change the Constitution for the vorst. to inslave them by degrée afterwards. to save good and human heart. sensible for the Sufferings of

THE ORIGINAL FIRST DRAFT OF KOSCIUSZKO'S AMERICAN WILL
Page One

others. he must be maried and
have 100. aikres of land. wyth
instruments. Catle for tillage
and know how to manage and
Gouvern it as well to know behave to
neybourghs. always wyth kindnes. and ready to help them
to them selves frugal. to ther
Children give good aducation
jmean as to the heart. and the
duty to ther Country. in gratitude to me to make themselves
hapy as possible. Kosciuszko

THE ORIGINAL FIRST DRAFT OF KOSCIUSZKO'S AMERICAN WILL
Page Two

not even Niemcewicz, knew of the document. During the last months of their sojourn in America, relations between Kosciuszko and his former aide-de-camp cooled somewhat. Niemcewicz offended the General's reserved nature by his loquacity and his curiosity, which was but natural in a writer travelling, for the first time, in a new and interesting country. It was only on the evening of his departure that Kosciuszko disclosed to Niemcewicz that he was about to leave alone that night, but not even then did he tell him his destination and the purpose of his trip. To preserve complete secrecy, he directed Niemcewicz to tell everybody only that he was leaving for a health resort in Virginia, and to go South three days after his departure as if to follow him there.

There remained yet some items of his personal property which Kosciuszko wanted to dispose of. He gave Jefferson a "Bear Skin as a Token of my veneration, respect and Esteem for you ever."[21] He also presented Jefferson with a costly sable fur, the gift of the Tsar, begging him delicately to use it just "for experiment Sake to try whither the hops in this Country will have the same effect as it is in mine." He was careful enough to add full directions for the use of hops.[22] He sent the Vice-President some other items by Niemcewicz with the request that Jefferson would "turn in money thos things";[23] eventually Barnes sold them cheaply at vendue, among them table linens, a carpet, articles of apparel etc.[24] The plate presented him by the citizens of Bristol and some other items he left as a gift to Niemcewicz, who, however, "much affected"[25] by the treatment at Kosciuszko's departure, refused to accept it,[26] just as he refused to accept some cash which Kosciuszko left for him and for his servant Dombrowski.

"I took leave," narrates Niemcewicz, "too excited by all I heard to be able to sleep. At one after midnight I left and roamed through the streets thinking of my grief . . . , at four in the morning Mr. J(efferson) approached in a covered coach. K(osciuszko) took

---

21 Undated, Maine Hist. Soc., Fogg Coll.

22 No date, Mass. Hist. Soc., Jefferson Coll. This is the fur which several artists used in portraying Jefferson. It is shown on the well-known portrait of him by Rembrandt Peale, the original of which hangs over the mantelpiece in the central hall of the Jefferson Memorial Home, Monticello (Patton and Doswell, *Monticello*, 47). It is also on the portrait by Thomas Scully which now hangs in the U. S. Military Academy at West Point. The sculptor, Rudolph Evans, also uses the Kosciuszko coat in the statue of Jefferson for the Jefferson Memorial at Washington.

23 Undated, Mass. Hist. Soc., Jefferson Coll. Jefferson met Niemcewicz for the first time in France while he was Minister at Paris (Jefferson to Mrs. Church, July 1798, Randolph *Domestic Life*, 253).

24 Gen. Kosciuszko in account with John Barnes, Nov. 15, 1799, and April, 1800, Mass. Hist. Soc., Jefferson Coll.

25 Jefferson to Kosciuszko, June 1, 1798, Lipscomb, X, 47.

26 Jefferson to Kosciuszko, Feb. 21, 1799, Libr. of Congress, Jefferson Papers, vol. 105. The inventory of the plate is in the Mass. Hist. Soc., Jefferson Coll.

a seat beside him[27] without embracing me . . . The thought of dangers to which he exposed himself, especially in his situation and without help, brought tears to my eyes . . . I followed the coach with my eyes as far as I could. They chose a road which led in the opposite direction from the port. I do not know why they underwent all these precautions as everybody still slept. Later I learned that they went by land to Newcastle where a ship lay waiting."[28]

Carrying out his instructions, Niemcewicz left Philadelphia a few days after Kosciuszko's departure and turned south, as if to follow the General. On his way, he wrote to Jefferson: "I visited Baltimore and for the last fifteen days I am at Federal City, at the house of Mr. Law.[29] Everywhere I have been overwhelmed with questions, I do not know how I have acquitted myself; I only know that the profession of a liar (to him who is not used to it) is as difficult as it is humiliating. You may be sure, however, that the secret is strictly kept, nobody guesses the truth; some think that he, in fact, is on his way to the baths, others imagine that we have quarrelled and separated. At last someone wrote from Philadelphia that you have kidnapped and concealed him at Monticello. You are then accused of rapture and violence, try to clear yourself as well as you can."[30]

Taking advantage of Volney's return to France, Jefferson wrote by him to Kosciuszko a few days later:

"Your departure is not yet known, or even suspected . . . The times do not permit an indulgence in political disquisitions. But they forbid not the effusion of friendship, and not my warmest toward you, which no time shall alter."[31]

Still, on June 18, writing again to Kosciuszko and advising him that Captain Lee of the Adriana brought him the sabre from the Whig Club of England,[32] Jefferson was able to assure him: "Not a doubt is entertained here but that you are gone to the springs."[33] In fact, the secret of his departure was kept so well that Republicans continued to toast him at their dinners[34] as if he were still present in America.

Gradually, however, gossip began to rise. Again Bache, the editor of the *Aurora,* considered himself obliged to defend the General

---

27 Of course, carried down by the servant, Niemcewicz to Jefferson, Sept. 3, 1798, Libr. of Congress, Jefferson Papers, vol. 104.

28 Kozłowski, "Pobyt," 270-2.

29 Thomas Law who married Elizabeth Parke Custis, granddaughter of Mrs. Washington.

30 May 27, 1798, Libr. of Congress, Jefferson Papers; the original in French.

31 June 1, 1798, Lipscomb, X, 47.

32 Cobbett repeatedly alluded to the sabre with sarcasm. This caused Bache to ask: "Were the London Whigs, or the American Federalists under greater obligation to treat the brave Kosciousko with politeness and hospitality?" (*Aurora,* June 11, 1798)).

33 Libr. of Congress, Jefferson Papers.

34 *Aurora,* May 5 and 14, and July 12, 1798.

CAPTAIN FREDERICK LEE OF THE ADRIANA
by Kosciuszko

against "the aspersion of certain persons."[35] The troubles of Niemcewicz, who meanwhile visited Washington at Mount Vernon[36] and
spent his time in traveling around the country, grew more and more
unpleasant. On September 3, he wrote to Jefferson from Elizabethtown:

"I spent a few days with Chancellor Livingston and General
Armstrong. Mr. Dawson preceded me there and I found these gentlemen informed of the departure and of the destination of G(eneral)
K(osciuszko). The secret is in good hands, I am not uneasy on that
account; but what was my surprise when having arrived at Elizabethtown I found that place filled with most absurd tales. I was told that
Major Touzard[37] passed through here ten days ago and while staying
with Mr. Dayton, the speaker, assured the whole world that he saw
a letter written from Virginia which announced that G.(eneral)
K.(osciuszko) left this country alone and in the strictest secrecy for
Ireland to take command of the insurgents.[38] Be that as it may, but
what was my indignation and my astonishment when I was informed
that Major Touzard had the impertinence to say that the wounds and
the terrible state of an invalid and a cripple, in which the General
was, were only a farce, a dissimulation, and that he was seen marching
in New Castle. I rejected this calumny as absurd and injurious to the
character of the Gl., assuring all these gentlemen that on the day of
his departure for the sea I had seen the Gl. carried as usual to the
carriage by his servant.

"It is no less true that these absurd tales caused gossip and guesses
here which are hurting and humiliating me. I am afraid that it is even
worse in the large cities."[39]

At last the secret came out. Early in September the American
press received news of Kosciuszko's landing in France.[40] A little later
copies of the Paris *Moniteur* reached America, containing an interview of its Bayonne correspondent with Kosciuszko; some of his reported remarks on conditions in this country were rather critical,[41]
but the distorted facts made it clear that the interview, at least in
some parts, was fabricated to suit excited French opinion. The more
rabid Federalists were indignant. In their eyes Kosciuszko at once
became "an object of detestation."[42] Now Cobbett could triumphantly

35 *Ibid.*, Aug. 25, 1798.
36 He spent two weeks as guest of Washington. For an interesting diary of his stay at
Mount Vernon see Kozłowski, "A Visit," *Century Mag.*, XLI, 510; also Haiman, *Poland and
the American Revolutionary War*, 166-176.
37 Louis Tousard, one of the French volunteers in the Continental Army, aide to Lafayette.
38 The United Irishmen rebellion of 1798; the insurgents appealed to France for help.
39 Libr. of Congress, Jefferson Papers; the original in French.
40 *Aurora*, Sept. 10, 1798.
41 *U. S. Gazette*, Nov. 6, 1798; *Porcupine's Works*, X, 12.
42 *Aurora*, Nov. 30, 1798.

boasts that he had foreseen the purpose of Kosciuszko's visit to America: it was "merely for the money; and . . . the moment it was in his pocket, he would go to France, and become the open enemy of those who relieved him."[43] If we might believe Fenno, even the "amiable daughters of Columbia" who not so long ago swarmed to Kosciuszko's dwelling to be portrayed by him, now were "determined with a spirit as patriotic as they are amiable to consign to the flames these mementos of a man who has practised upon them as well as their country the lowest deceptions."[44]

The tongues and pens of gossipers were now doubly busy. Some persons intimated that Kosciuszko had left America in the same vessel with Dr. Logan[45] and Volney, each of this "contraband cargo" having departed clandestinely and separately, meeting below New Castle.[46] Fenno expressed malignant surprise that Kosciuszko had not been accompanied to Europe "by his very courteous and distinguished companion," Thomas Jefferson.[47]

---

43 *Porcupine's Works*, X, 83.

44 *U. S. Gazette*, Nov. 9, 1798.

45 Logan left America after Kosciuszko, most probably ignorant of his plans. Kosciuszko could know of Logan's mission from Jefferson. From Hamburg, Logan wrote to his wife on July 6, 1798: "I am informed that General Koskiuszko is arrived in Paris he will cooperate with us" (Logan, *Memoir*, 71).

46 *U. S. Gazette*, Nov. 6, 1798.

47 *Ibid.*, Nov. 6, 1798.

IX.

LABORS AND PLANS FOR AMERICA

The long rest in America and the sea voyage had a most beneficial influence on Kosciuszko's health. He landed and walked on French soil without the help of a servant and crutches.[1] Niemcewicz considered his recovery "mysterious & wonderful."[2] No doubt it was hastened by the regenerating strength of Kosciuszko's will, now absorbed with plans of a new service to the cause of peace and freedom. Immediately after landing, Kosciuszko began working to mitigate the bellicose attitude of the French government. He had frequent and secret talks with the members of the Directory.[3] Notwithstanding the lack of official documents in this connection,[4] there is not the slightest doubt, that the General intervened with the members of the Directory, counselling them most strongly to avoid war with America. Nathaniel Cutting, American diplomatic agent, then in Paris, reported to Jefferson: "General Kosciuszko . . . has, I am persuaded, improved every opportunity of pleading our cause at the Fountain-head of Power in this Country."[5] Simultaneously Kosciuszko supported the efforts of others, aimed at the same purpose. He met Gerry and undoubtedly they agreed in their sentiments and views.[6] Then, too, he supported wholeheartedly the self-assumed mission of Dr. Logan. The "brave man received him with the most distinguished kindness, warmly appreciated his motives, and approved of his design, which he promised to support with all his interest, but cautioned him at the same time not to repose any confidence in the promises of the French government of what they would do in future unless they would immediately give a pledge of their sincerity by a removal of embargo."[7] Finally their efforts, the remonstrances of others, and the decided stand of America seemed to bring results. The Directory relinquished its demands for

---

1 Jefferson to Niemcewicz, Jan. 16, 1799, Libr. of Congress, Jefferson Papers.

2 Niemcewicz to Jefferson, Jan. 19, 1799, Libr. of Congress, Jefferson Papers.

3 Paszkowski, *Dzieje Kościuszki*, 196.

4 Archives du Ministere des Affaires Etrangeres, Correspondance Politique, Etats-Unis (photostats in Library of Congress) contain no references to this action of Kosciuszko. Cf. Fay, *Revolutionary Spirit*, 427.

5 Aug. 27, 1798, Libr. of Congress, Jefferson Papers.

6 Gerry on his return to America carried Kosciuszko's letters to Jefferson and Niemcewicz (Jefferson to Niemcewicz, Jan. 16, and Feb. 21, 1799, and Niemcewicz to Jefferson, Jan. 19, 1799, Libr. of Congress, Jefferson Papers).

7 Logan, *Memoir*, 65, note. On Kosciuszko's efforts to help Logan see also: *Journal des Francs*, 8 Fructidor VI, as quoted by Skałkowski, *O Kokardę*, 119, and Ingersoll, *Recollections*, I, 172, 179 and 189.

"money in any shape," recalled its discriminatory edicts, released imprisoned American seamen and promised to receive an American envoy. Some Federalists were skeptical; George Cabot, a leader of the Essex Junto, considered that Kosciuszko by his uninvited intervention rather aggravated the situation.[8] Richard Codman, another Federalist, an eyewitness to the events in Paris, thought otherwise. In a letter to his co-partisan, Harrison Gray Otis of Boston, he acknowledged: "The Directory have been induced to make this essential alteration in their conduct from representations made to them by Dupont, Kosciusko, Volney & others lately from America."[9] Cutting expressly assured Jefferson that Kosciuszko's intervention had a "good effect."[10] According to Gen. Paszkowski, Kosciuszko became "the first link" of rapproachment between the two nations.[11] Antoine Jullien, a contemporary French author, said that Kosciuszko's remonstrances and friendly steps in the Executive Directory contributed much to bringing France and the United States closer."[12]

Without mentioning in detail his steps in Paris, Kosciuszko wrote to Jefferson about the results obtained, sending the letter perhaps by Logan when he returned to America:

"The Amicable disposition of the Gouvernement of France are realy favorable to the interest of the United States, by the recent prouves they give, you ought not to doubt that they choose to be in peace and in perfect harmonie with America. before it was misrepresented by some the facts relative to your Contry, but now they are perfectly acquiented wyth yours and their interests and Mr. Logan eyewitness of the Sentyment they have towards the Nation of the United States. At present it is a duty of every true American as you, to publishe and propagate their friendship, and to Compele your Gouvernment by the Opinion of the Nation to the pacifique Measures with Republique of France, otherwise you cannot but to loose every thing even your Liberty by a conexion so intimet wyth England which increasing son influence can easily subdue and exercise son despotique pouver as before. write me soon as possible of the effects which the news by Logan's arrival will produce in America, as well as by the Election of the members for Congress, you may rely upon my indevours here but you most work in America wyth your friends and Republicans and state their reall interest."[13]

---

8 Cabot to Oliver Wolcott, Oct. 5, 1800, Wolcott, *Memoirs*, II, 432.
9 Aug. 26, 1798, Morison, *Life and Letters of Harrison Gray Otis*, I, 168.
10 Cutting to Jefferson, Aug. 27, 1798, Libr. of Congress, Jefferson Papers.
11 Paszkowski, *Dzieje Kościuszki*, 196.
12 Jullien, *Rys Życia*, 30.
13 Undated, Mass. Hist. Soc., Jefferson Coll.

The passing of the danger of war between the two countries did not diminish Kosciuszko's interest in America. His home became a mecca for Americans living in France or visiting the country. After the Poles, he felt best among them. Madame Fiszer says that "he did not make any difference between them," treating both "with fatherly tenderness and brotherly love."[14] He was always ready to render them whatever help they needed and that "with all his heart." In turn, the Americans paid him the respect "due to a patriarch of their revolution," and nobody ever dared to question his eminent position.[15] Often he visited them and "they welcomed him affectionately."[16]

While in France, Kosciuszko's help was eagerly sought by many who had any dealings with the United States or intended to settle here. If he considered their requests worthy enough, the General wrote letters of recommendation to his American friends. Among such was Thomas Addis Emmet, the Irish patriot and a "great sufferer for his opinion to liberty," whom he recommended to George Clinton,[17] thus helping Emmet to start a most successful law career in New York. He concerned himself with supplying America with books.[18] Becoming deeply interested in the Pestalozzi educational system, he made a contribution to American education by helping Francis J. N. Neef to come to the United States and to establish here the first such school in Philadelphia.[19]

In order to acquaint his countrymen with American ideas, Kosciuszko tried to introduce them into the small American circle in Paris. He did this in his usual good-natured manner. Madame Fiszer tells of the following incident: he invited her to accompany him to Mr. Livingston, the American Minister; when they arrived at the gate of the Minister's residence, she discovered that a ball was in progress; she was not dressed properly and, notwithstanding Kosciuszko's solicitations, she insisted that he should make his visit alone and she would wait for him in the carriage; he pretended to agree, but in a while he returned with a group of young men and an ultimatum that she join the ball voluntarily or be carried in by force. When she yielded and entered the hall, but still refused to dance, Kosciuszko said to her: "They are not Frenchmen, they are Americans, honest people; put away your ceremoniousness and be a good girl." She acknowledged that seldom had she enjoyed a more happy company.[20]

---

14 *"Pamiętnik,"* 256 and 260.
15 *Ibid.,* 248 and 256.
16 *Ibid.,* 260.
17 July 29, 1802(?), Polish R. C. U. Museum, Kosciuszko Papers, no. 60.
18 Kosciuszko to Jefferson, undated, Boston Public Library, and a letter of Charles Pougens to Kosciuszko, July 28, 1802, Libr. of Congress, Jefferson Papers.
19 Kosciuszko to Jefferson, March 10, 1806, Mass. Hist. Soc., Jefferson Coll.
20 Fiszer, *"Pamiętnik,"* 261.

Kosciuszko continued to maintain most friendly relations with Livingston's successor, John Armstrong, one of his most beloved former companions-in-arms. In 1806, he acted as godfather for Armstrong's son who was christened Kosciuszko in his honor. His bequest of a small sum for the godson is a further proof of their ever cordial relations.[21] Joel Barlow, who succeeded Armstrong, lived on very intimate terms with Kosciuszko till the poet's tragic death in Poland in 1812.[22] On the election of Jefferson to the presidency, Kosciuszko warmly recommended Barlow's appointment to the vacant post of American Minister in Paris. He "has so many qualities that were he your personal Enemy . . . still I would recommend him for that Place," wrote Kosciuszko.[23]

Outstanding among Kosciuszko's relations with America during this period was his irregular, but continuous, correspondence with Jefferson, his "old and good friend,"[24] interrupted only by his death. The Polish exile was always glad "to receive a letter from my dear and respectable Mr. Jefferson whom all love in Europe."[25] The sage of Monticello, whom Kosciuszko so amiably called "Mon cher Aristide,"[26] was, in his opinion, the acme of every civic virtue and the greatest of contemporaries. Once, in an excess of friendly rapture, Kosciuszko divulged: "I love you, you are the only hope of all humanity and I should like you to be an example to posterity."[27] He did not, however, let his feelings carry him off blindly. By Robert Fulton, returning to America in 1806, Kosciuszko sent Jefferson the usual friendly greetings and expressions of admiration, but with a stipulation:

"From the depth of my heart I express to you my esteem, respect and Sincere friendship, these Sentiments of Conviction will last as long as you will be useful to humanity and behave as at present amid universal admiration."[28]

In turn, Jefferson was always "anxious to hear of" Kosciuszko[29] and often assured him of his "constant and affectionate friendship."[30]

21 Armstrong to Jefferson, Jan. 4, 1818, White, "The Truth About General Kosciuszko," *Conn. Mag.,* XII (1908), 380. In 1818 Armstrong's claim amounted to $3,704 (Jefferson to Wirt, June 27, 1819, Libr. of Congress, Jefferson Papers). For a copy of this will see Peters, *Reports,* VIII, 56.

22 Barlow to his wife, Aug. 22, 1800; a note on one of Barlow's books, Houghton Libr., Barlow Papers, MS Am 507; see also: Todd, *Life and Letters of Joel Barlow,* 199.

23 Kosciuszko to Jefferson, 18 Vendemiaire (Oct. 10, 1800), Mass. Hist. Soc., Jefferson Coll.; the original in French.

24 Kosciuszko to John Barnes, Dec. 1, 1808, Mass. Hist. Soc., Norcross Coll.

25 Kosciuszko to Barnes, Nov. 26, 1815, Polish R. C. U. Museum, Kosciuszko Papers, no. 68; the original in French.

26 Kosciuszko to Jefferson, Feb. 1, 1812, Mass. Hist. Soc., Jefferson Coll.

27 Kosciuszko to Jefferson, Nov. 15, 1805, *ibid.;* the original in French.

28 Kosciuszko to Jefferson, April 24 (1806), *ibid.;* the original in French.

29 Jefferson to Kosciuszko, June 18, 1798, Libr. of Congress, Jefferson Papers.

30 Jefferson to Kosciuszko, March 14, 1801, Lipscomb, XIX, 122.

"He has so many titles to my affectionate esteem," averred the Virginian to one of his correspondents.[31] To Kosciuszko he openly confessed: "Your principles . . . were made to be honored, revered and loved."[32]

Turbulent political conditions obliged the friends to restrain their pens. Both were careful enough to exchange letters "but by safe conveyances,"[33] usually by friends crossing the ocean. Such were, besides Volney, Gerry and Fulton, Dupont de Nemours, Dawson, Monroe, Barlow, George Ticknor and a few others less prominent. During Madison's presidency, Jefferson mailed several letters through the Department of State with diplomatic mail. As an additional precaution, the friends arranged for the use of a cipher[34] before their parting, but, it seems, they never made use of it.

In one regard the letters of Kosciuszko are very characteristic: they are so devoid of personal details that even Jefferson complained: "Your letters are too barren of what I wish most to hear, I mean things relating to yourself."[35] But Kosciuszko usually ignored this plea and this clearly reflected his modesty and reserved nature.

At first, the mutual exchange of letters was quite lively. Besides the efforts of Kosciuszko in maintaining peaceful relations between the United States and France, other less important matters pertaining to the settling of his estate in America, also occupied their correspondence.

The turn-about of American public opinion at the end of John Adams' administration and Jefferson's election to the presidency on the crest of the Republican tide elated Kosciuszko. Soon after the surprising defeat of the Federalists in New York and before the actual election, the General hurried with his congratulations: "I most before hand pay you the first my respects as to the President of the United States. I hope you will be the same in that new station always good, true Americane a Philosopher and my Friend."[36] Some time later he again commented on the event:

"At last Virtue is triumphing if not yet in the old, then at least in the new World. The people of decency and solid judgment became aware that they must nominate you for the sake of their happiness and independence and they do not err. I add my wishes to the General voice. Meanwhile remember," he continued with friendly admoni-

31 Jefferson to Jacob Van Staphorst, May 8, 1800; Libr. of Congress, Jefferson Papers.
32 Jefferson to Kosciuszko, June 1, 1798, Lipscomb, X, 49.
33 Jefferson to Kosciuszko, Feb. 26, 1810, Libr. of Congress, Jefferson Papers.
34 Jefferson to Kosciuszko, June 18, 1798, *ibid.*
35 Jefferson to Kosciuszko, March 14, 1801, Lipscomb, XIX, 122.
36 Kosciuszko to Jefferson, 26 Thermidor (Aug. 14, 1800), Mass. Hist. Soc., Jefferson Coll.

tion, "that the first Post of the State which always is beset by flatterers, intrigants, hypocrites and by Men of bad will, should be surrounded by Men of Character of honest talents and of strict probity . . . Do not forget yourself in your station be always virtuous, a Republican of justice and probity without pomp and aspirations, in one word remain a Jefferson and my friend."[37]

Shortly after his inauguration, Jefferson, acknowledging these letters, personally advised the General of "the return of our fellow-citizens to the principles of '76." "It would give me exquisite pleasure," he added, "to have you here a witness to our country and recognize the people whom you knew during the war."[38] This induced Kosciuszko to renew his felicitations and advices: "I congratulate the United States of America on the choice of your person for their President; there will be no more doubt that Republicanism must be inseparable with honesty, probity, and strict justice, and that man should be honored more for his virtues and knowledge, than for his luxury. Your ever memorable message made greatest impression in Europe, even people of opposing opinion admired it, they maintained only that such beautiful promises are not fulfilled in reality.

"Knowing well your way of thinking, Your Genius, your ability, your knowledge, your Character, and your good Heart, I silenced some and allayed others."[39]

In subsequent letters Kosciuszko revealed his views on the problems of strengthening the spirit of democracy in the young American republic and of securing her future peaceful development. This was the subject he invariably returned to in almost every letter till his death. He considered it the supreme purpose of the country and proposed to attain it by "giving the youth proper education" in republican ideas through public schools superintended by the national government and, above all, through special semi-military schools for the education of future officers of militia. At first he was of the opinion that one school of the latter type should be founded in each of the states; later he proposed a single national institution. He reasoned that by their comprehension of the "lofty idea of being virtuous Republicans," pupils of these schools would become a force for democracy and peace in the nation.[40]

Kosciuszko also thought that these semi-military schools should be supervised directly by Congress through a special commission and that their curriculum should be well rounded out, embracing not only

---

[37] Kosciuszko to Jefferson, 18 Vendemiaire (Oct. 10, 1800), *ibid.;* the original in French.
[38] Jefferson to Kosciuszko, March 14, 1801, Lipscomb, XIX, 122.
[39] Kosciuszko to Jefferson, undated, Mass. Hist. Soc., Jefferson Coll.; the original in French.
[40] Kosciuszko to Jefferson, Nov. 15, 1805, *ibid.;* the original in French.

military science, but also civics and all branches of human knowledge, especially those subjects which would be most useful to the development of the country. "Never be behind Europe in science," he advised, "and no discovery should escape your attention." [41] In his opinion, such a national school should have facilities for from six hundred to three thousand pupils from all the states of the Union; pupils should be chosen on the basis of examination, rich and poor in equal numbers, so that the latter would have an equal chance of acquiring an education. The choice of the faculty should also be controlled by Congress.

Kosciuszko's general ideas in this regard were perhaps best explained in his letter of February 1, 1812, in which he wrote:

"What would completely assure me that your Republican Government will exist long, is the education of youth founded on a solid basis of Republican principles, on morality and justice, and under the surveillance of Congress to such an extent that none of the professors could be exempt from it. You know that children are more susceptible to a solid and durable impression than ripe age, which is influenced by profit to such a degree that no other consideration, even the most honorable, can attract it; it is in that tender age that all duties toward society and toward Country become engraved. By such an education you can hope to prepare the greatest defenders of your Country and the Support of Republican Government. You cannot expect much from maritime Cities corrupted by foreign trade and by opulence; they will be, if they are not already, for a Monarchical Government. Your estimable Quakkers will do nothing, they are dead men, but not Citizens. Your real strength are the inhabitants of the interior, whose manners, social virtues are susceptible to greatness of soul, generosity. If you strengthen these qualities by a strictly controlled education then you will have attained your purpose and you will live to see your country bringing forth as many heroes as Greece and wiser men than those of Rome."[42]

Not all of Kosciuszko's ideas would comply with present-day standards. His proposed federal control of schools might seem obnoxious today. Still it was by no means inconsistent with contemporary thought. Constantly, in his messages to Congress and in his private letters, even in his last will, Washington espoused the idea of a national university under the jurisdiction of "the general government" in the Federal City.[43] He was also of the opinion that "a plan of universal education ought to be adopted in the United States."[44] Kosciu-

41 Kosciuszko to Jefferson, undated, but about 1807, *ibid.;* the original in French.
42 Kosciuszko to Jefferson, April 1, 1812, *ibid.;* the original in French.
43 Washington to Jefferson, March 15, 1795, Fitzpatrick, XXXIV, 147.
44 Washington to Gov. Robert Brooke, March 16, 1795, *ibid.,* XXXIV, 150.

szko likewise deserves credit for suggesting that poor and rich students be given equal educational opportunities.

Kosciuszko also thought much about the national defense of the United States. He contributed to it a manual, *Manoeuvres of Horse Artillery,* which he wrote in French in 1800 at the request of General William R. Davie; it was translated into English by Col. Jonathan Williams, and published by the United States Military Philosophical Society in 1808.[45] "This is a branch of the military art which I wish extremely to see understood here, to the height of the European level," wrote Jefferson of the book.[46] The handbook, the first of its kind in American military literature, was used in the American army. It gained for Kosciuszko the title of the Father of the American Artillery,[47] perhaps a too flattering one, but rightly stressing the book's importance in the development of the United States Army.

Justly pointing out to Jefferson, "You are more lucky than Europeans; Thanks . . . to your far neighborhood with Other Powers,"[48] he still advised him to make all males from eighteen to forty-five years old liable to service in the militia. He considered a large regular army dangerous, "as one should always fear the ambition of a President who by the influence of gold, dignities could easily change the State of things by bringing this regular corps over to his side."[49] Echoing the fears of the authors of the American Constitution, he also insisted on diminishing the influence of future Presidents by depriving them of the right to appoint judges and magistrates, transferring this power to Congress.[50]

To promote civic virtues and democratic zeal, Kosciuszko proposed to institute a republican decoration, such as he planned to introduce in Poland during the Insurrection: "A Token of gold, of silver of iron attached to the dress . . . for those who have shown more attachment and devotion to the Republican Government, more Justice, Probity, disinterestedness, Love of their parents; For inventions in the Arts, in the Sciences and especially in Agriculture; and at last, for all those virtues and Social qualities which alone should distinguish us one from another."[51]

---

45 Manoeuvres of Horse Artillery by General Kosciusko. Written at Paris in the Year 1800, at the Request of General Wm. R. Davie, then Envoy from the United States to France. Translated. with Notes and Descriptive Plates, by Jonathan Williams, Col. Comdt. of the Corps of Engineers, and President of the U. S. Military Philosophical Society. Published by Direction of the Society, New York: Sold by Campbell S. Mitchell. 1808. 77 p. and 18 plates.

46 Jefferson to Jonathan Williams, Oct. 28, 1808, Lipscomb, Xii, 185.

47 Griffin, "General Thaddeus Kosciuszko," *Am. Cath. Hist. Researches,* new series, VI (1910), 204-206. See also: Brink, "Kosciuszko—Forefather of the American Artillery," *Field Artillery Journal,* XXII (1932), 303-313; McKee, "The Father of American Artillery," *National Republic,* Sept. 1926, 30-31; Ganoe, *History of the U. S. Army,* 112.

48 Kosciuszko to Jefferson, August 15, 1817, Mass. Hist. Soc., Jefferson Coll.; the original in French.

49 Kosciuszko to Jefferson, March 1, 1811, *ibid.;* the original in French.

50 Kosciuszko to Jefferson, undated, but about 1807, *ibid.*

51 Kosciuszko to Jefferson, March 1, 1811, *ibid.;* the original in French.

Thomas Jefferson
A Philosopher a Patriote and a Friend
Dessiné par son Ami Tadée Kosciuszko.
Et Gravé par Mr. Sokolnicki

THOMAS JEFFERSON
by Kosciuszko

The General did not neglect to spur his friend to action in accord with these principles and to urge him to aim at greatness. "A statesman like you," he wrote, "and, above all, with your disposition and your learning, must strive to give unity of action to his nation and to establish (its) respectable and strong character . . . For God's sake, do not be undecided, act with determined energy befitting a Great Man which you have to be."[52] Jefferson's term of highest office, Kosciuszko reminded the President, was an opportunity "to perform solid and durable good to the whole Nation."[53] But he warned: "Even today your rising power arouses much distrust among your neighbors. You will be destroyed — but if you comprehend the present circumstances which give you all possible advantage over your Enemies . . . I can foretell your success — but one has to decide quickly, act with celerity and great strength . . ."

Kosciuszko closed with a truly classic sentence, full of that profound wisdom and strength which sometimes came from his pen: "Do not deceive yourself, it is pusillanimity and indecision which destroy Nations, but never their valor and ardor."[54]

Kosciuszko also remembered his friend with little gifts. In 1800, he sent Jefferson some books which, however, to the General's sorrow, were lost in transit.[55] Later, he sent the President, several copies of a drawing by his own hand, most probably the well known portrait of Jefferson, which he had made during his stay in Philadelphia. Jefferson presented one copy of it to Madison and divided the rest among his family.[56]

During Jefferson's presidency, correspondence between the two men remained rather one-sided. Jefferson answered Kosciuszko's letters only if they dealt with imperative matters, or with Kosciuszko's financial affairs. Jefferson's letters of this period were short and dry, almost official in tone. But this did not by any means indicate neglect or coolness on his part. The truth was that he was afraid to write, owing to his official position. This behavior of his friend evidently touched Kosciuszko. In his heart he could not overcome his disappointment. When Jefferson again became a common citizen and returned to Monticello, he tried at once to make up for his long semi-silence with a long letter marked by the old sincerity. Apologizing for his rare and brief answers, he explained that he had abstained from writing freely, for fear that his letters might be intercepted by

52 Kosciuszko to Jefferson, Nov. 5, 1805, *ibid;* the original in French.
53 *Ibid.*
54 Kosciuszko to Jefferson, undated, ab. 1807, *ibid;* the original in French.
55 Kosciuszko to Jefferson, 26 Thermidor (Aug. 14, 1800), and undated ab. 1801; *ibid.*
56 Jefferson to Madison, May 5, 1802, Libr. of Congress, Jefferson Papers. This engraving is not in the Jefferson Memorial Home, Charlottesville, Va. One copy is in the Polish R. C. U. Museum.

the British or French, and "be imputed injuriously to our country" or expose Kosciuszko to persecution. He assured the General that all his "anxieties" about the future of America "were worthy of your philanthropy and disinterested attachment to the freedom and happiness of man." He then quite minutely acquainted him with the details of his administration.[57]

Though Jefferson's repentance soothed Kosciuszko's sense of injury, he could not restrain himself from making a friendly rebuke.

"It is true," he wrote, "that I had the rare, the very rare honor of receiving your letters, even if they were dry and brief; I have also neglected myself in writing to you out of fear of being importunate. I felt sorry, I confess, to number you among many people, who change their sentiments according to circumstances. — Excuse me now if my friendship, so warm, is cooling off; but be persuaded that my esteem is always the same as I never ceased to be convinced that nobody more than you unites, with natural qualities and learning, a more perfect disinterestedness and generally more abilities necessary to consolidate the Republic and to render the Country more flourishing—During the whole term of your Presidency I have been completely unacquainted with events in your country and all here were surprised that I did not receive any news from you, but perhaps you might suspect me of being imprudent. Nevertheless the last letter which you were good enough to write me, brought me great pleasure; with greatest interest I have read in it the details of your deeds — A statesman like you, naturally, focusses his attention on great things, on all these objects which can render his government stable and strong enough to act against enemies, interior and exterior . . . and to secure happiness and tranquility to the greatest possible number of inhabitants."[58]

Sometime later Kosciuszko added another word of praise: "You have done much for the safety of your Country and much for science in all its necessary branches."[59]

During America's difficulties with Spain, Kosciuszko advised Jefferson to occupy Florida, assuring him that by this bold act he "would give a high idea of your nation and its character to all powers and this would impress them to make an alliance with you."[60] In 1807, the General came to the conclusion that war between the United States and Spain could only be delayed, but not avoided.[61]

---

57 Jefferson to Kosciuszko, Feb. 26, 1810, Lipscomb, XII, 365.
58 Kosciuszko to Jefferson, March 1, 1811, Mass. Hist. Soc., Jefferson Coll.; the original in French.
59 Kosciuszko to Jefferson, Feb. 1, 1812, ibid.; the original in French.
60 Kosciuszko to Jefferson, Nov. 15, 1805, ibid.; the original in French.
61 Kosciuszko to Jefferson, undated, but ab. 1807, ibid.

The outbreak of the war with Great Britain found Kosciuszko wholeheartedly on the side of America. At the very beginning of the war, he warned British diplomats that soon they would be ignominiously driven out. "I gave them my Word of honor as to that," he boasted before Jefferson. "You do not know, I told them . . . their bravery as well as I do — You will see, my Dear Friend, that I have foretold the defeat of the British, so sure I was of the noble Character and the national bravery of your Countrymen."[62]

The war enlivened the exchange of views between the friends. When Jefferson expressed the opinion that the cession of Canada must be made an imperative condition of the future treaty of peace,[63] Kosciuszko, who during the Revolution persistently advocated its conquest, disagreed.

"The righteous war you have commenced against England," he wrote, "should not frighten you, it will be just the same as against any other power which would refuse to deal with you on the basis of equality between nation and nation. Your country is rich, large and populous; your inhabitants are good, active and courageous. But do not be too ambitious to acquire the whole of Canada, the excess of security would soften you; I should think that your line of demarcation should run from some point of lake Champlain or the St. Lawrence river to the South sea in order that you may not have other powers on your back."[64]

Kosciuszko tried to impress Jefferson with the necessity of a proper selection of army leaders, of "prudent . . . military dispositions," good approvisation and strict discipline of the army; he advised greater use of light artillery, which he considered especially suitable to the topography of the country.

Contrary to the first expectations of both friends, the course of the war dragged on inauspiciously for America. Jefferson considered the first year of the war lost, though he had no doubt as to its ultimate result. At the end of 1813, after a detailed review of events, he affectionately wrote to Kosciuszko:

"I know that no native among us takes a livelier interest in them than you do. The tree which you had so zealously assisted in planting you cannot but delight in seeing watered and flourishing. Happy for us would it have been if a valor, fidelity and skill like yours had directed those early efforts which were so unfortunately confided to unworthy hands . . . However from one man we can have but one life, and you

---

62 Kosciuszko to Jefferson, April 1816, *ibid.*; the original in French.

63 Jefferson to Kosciuszko, June 28, 1812, Lipscomb, XIII, 168.

64 Kosciuszko to Jefferson, May 30, 1813, Polish R. C. U. Museum, Kosciuszko Papers, no. 65; the original in French.

gave us the most valuable and active part of yours, and we are now enjoying and improving its effects. Every sound American, every sincere votary of freedom, loves and honors you, and it was its enemies only and the votaries of England who saw it with cold indifference and even secret displeasure your short-lived return to us . . . God bless you under every circumstance, whether still reserved for the good of your native country or destined to leave us in the fulness of the time with the consciousness of successful efforts for the establishment of freedom in one country and of all which man could have done for its success in another. . . . The lively sense I entertain of all you have done and deserved from both countries, can be extinguished only with the lamp of life, during which I shall ever be, affectionately and devotedly yours."[65]

When victory at last crowned the American war effort, Kosciuszko rejoiced heartily. With evident satisfaction, he reported to Jefferson that, with the exception of himself, "all were surprised and astonished, moreover your reputation considerably rose and the Names of Addison[66] and Jefferson are repeated thousand times by all lips . . . It is you whom England respects most highly and whom she also fears, but not the Allied Powers and Ministers who all are Corrupt."[67]

When Jefferson again kept silent for a longer time than it suited the Polish exile, Kosciuszko remembered himself with a kind reproach: "How tranquilly you repose on your laurels so justly acquired and on your General Reputation and, besides, so beloved by your Co-citizens. But this does not excuse you from forgetting your Friends in Europe who love you as much as your Compatriots. You owe me two or three letters."[68]

But Jefferson was unable to make good that debt. Exactly a month before his death Kosciuszko wrote his last letter to his American "Aristides." As if foreseeing his imminent end, he opened the letter with the gloomy remark: "We all are advancing in Years . . . my dear and respectable Friend." He then wrote of the hopeless situation of Poland, of the duplicity of European cabinets, and his closing thoughts were devoted to America.

"Your Canal from the Lake Erie to the North River amazes everybody in Europe except me, who know so well your Co-citizens — I always saw them Great in everything."

---

65 Jefferson to Kosciuszko, November 30, 1813, Lipscomb, XIX, 205.

66 Evidently a slip of pen; he meant Madison.

67 Kosciuszko to Jefferson, April, 1816; Mass. Hist. Soc., Jefferson Coll.; the original in French.

68 Kosciuszko to Jefferson, June 3, 1817, ibid.; the original in French.

Almost at the edge of his grave, Kosciuszko returned to his old plans. "You are happier than Europeans," he continued, "thanks to your government, better adapted to the nature of man . . . This does not hinder you from establishing a Great Civil-Military School in your Country under the immediate supervision of a commission of Congress. Pay my homage to Mr. Monroe, your President, I do not cease to repeat to him the absolute necessity of such a School."[69] And the General closed the letter: "I embrace you thousand times, not in a French manner, but from the bottom of my Heart."[70]

That was his last message to the man he loved and to the happier New World, which he disinterestingly had helped to found and which he desired to see still happier.

[69] In fact, he wrote to Monroe on the subject, congratulating him also on his election, on Feb. 20, 1817, National Archives, Records of the Dept. of State, Appointment Papers, 1813-1820.

[70] Kosciuszko to Jefferson, Sept. 15, 1817, Mass. Hist. Soc., Jefferson Coll.; the original in French.

X.

"THE ONLY TRUE POLE"

"I want to be ever and inseparably with you, I want to join you to serve our common country . . . Like you I have fought for the country, like you I have suffered, like you I expect to regain it. This hope is the only solace of my life."

These words Kosciuszko addressed to the officers of the Polish Legions in answer to their enthusiastic letters welcoming him to France. Simultaneously with his efforts in behalf of America, the General busied himself with the affairs of Poland. He came to France still believing in her sincerity and in her mission as a moral force destined to burst the chains of slavery in Europe. He was forced to accept the high-sounding homages of officials and citizens. He heard their far-reaching promises, which he believed with the simplicity of his heart, and which sometimes moved him to deep emotion. "To the tears of Kosciuszko!" shouted Bonneville, a French writer, at one of the banquets, when tears appeared in the General's eyes on hearing a toast for a new Poland to be regained with France's aid.[1]

But all these French honors and promises were a tragic farce. The Directory, denounced in the Council of Ancients as a "coalition of thieves worse than the coalition of kings," considered Kosciuszko but a tool in its political machinations. It lied to him brazenly and misused his sincerity.[2] His sudden appearance in France drew on him the attention of the world. "The arrival of Kosciuszko has elicited not a little attention here," wrote John Quincy Adams, the Minister at Berlin, to Rufus King.[3] The very presence of the renowned champion of freedom on France's soil strengthened her political position; it constituted a threat to powers which, having swallowed Poland, now stood united in the Second Coalition against France.

One of Kosciuszko's first acts on landing in France was to write a letter to Tsar Paul renouncing his oath of allegiance and refusing to accept his gift of money. But even this act was abused by the Directory. It induced Kosciuszko to sign a prepared communication[4] unnecessarily couched in strong terms. The first sentence of the letter

---

1 *Gazette Nationale*, XXIX, 338, as quoted in Korzon, *Kosciuszko*, 510.
2 Askenazy, *Napoleon a Polska*, III, 43.
3 Aug. 2, 1798, Polish R. C. U. Museum, Kosciuszko Papers, no. 119.
4 Askenazy, *loc. cit.*, III, 44.

was so formulated as to sting the Americans. Cobbett immediately seized the occasion to attack again the "Spurious Envoy" of Poland "hanging around the heels" of the "French Sultans."[5] The letter sharpened the fears of the partitioning powers. The Tsar issued an ukase ordering Kosciuszko's arrest, whenever the General should appear within the borders of the empire. Russian, Prussian and Austrian agents kept his every move under strict surveillance. There was a period when he did not dare to visit his friends, nor even to write to them for fear an intercepted letter would reveal his plans regarding Poland.[6]

Kosciuszko declined to accept the active command of the Legions, or to take a French pension. He became, however, the Legions' moral leader and unofficial, but recognized, representative before the Directory.[7] He constantly solicited the latter's aid to satisfy their material needs. Alas, that aid came but rarely and in an all too meager measure. Young officers, stealing from Poland through hostile borders rallied around Kosciuszko with filial devotion, and with fatherly affection he cared for them. Above all, he watchfully guarded the ideological direction of the whole movement. He persisted in demanding from the French the preservation of the Polish character of the troops. When a new Polish force, the so-called Danube Legion, began to organize in 1799, Kosciuszko proposed, very significantly for his state of mind in that period, that the officers and men should swear "hatred to kings and aristocrats," but for political reasons he was overruled by the Minister of War, Crance. He ordered Joseph Wybicki, the author of the Polish national hymn, to compose a "republican catechism" for soldiers. According to his view, the Legions were to be a school of patriotism and civic virtues; they were "destined to carry the gift of liberty to the country and the lot of light to their countrymen."[8]

One of the first acts of Napoleon after his return from Egypt was to pay homage to "the hero of the North." He visited Kosciuszko at his modest dwelling at rue de Lille, N. 545, and endeavored to win him for his gigantic plans. But that first meeting at once revealed the deep psychic contrast between the two men: a military and political genius, full of illimitable ambition, and a simple republican, a model of modesty and honesty, whose only ambition was to serve his country and humanity; a Caesar and a Cincinnatus, as a Polish

5 *Porcupine's Works*, X, 88.
6 Lafayette to Johann Wilhelm von Aschenholz, Nov. 24, 1798, "Lafayette Letters," *Bostonian Soc. Publ.*, IV, second ser. (1924), 95.
7 Jefferson to Niemcewicz, Jan. 11, 1801, Libr. of Congress, Jefferson Papers.
8 Kosciuszko to the soldiers of the Legions, Aug. 22, 1798, Kukiel, *Dzieje Oręża*, 59.

historian so aptly characterized the two men.[9] "Beware of that young man," Kosciuszko is said to have warned the Directory. The coup-d'etat of the 18th Brumaire deepened the chasm between the two Generals. In the eyes of Kosciuszko, it was an act of brutal force committed on a republic, and he did not hesitate to condemn it openly. Subsequent rapprochement between Napoleon and Tsar Paul, the peace of Luneville of 1801, which again ignored the Polish question, and the unhappy end of the Polish Legions sent by Napoleon to suppress the insurrection of Toussaint l'Ouverture in San Domingo, still further separated Kosciuszko from the Corsican. "Do you know, General, that the First Consul spoke of you?" Consul Lebrun said at a public reception in the presence of many important personages. "I never speak of him," coldly replied Kosciuszko.

The conduct of the Emperor Napoleon further widened the drift. One of the best Napoleonic historians[10] regretfully stated that this was to the detriment of Poland, France and Europe. Even for the price of some immediate advantage for Poland, Kosciuszko refused to abdicate an inch from his high moral principles, or from those rights of Poland for which he had shed his blood in the Insurrection. It cannot be denied that his personal dislike of Napoleon influenced his stand, at least to some extent.

There were many Poles who disagreed with Kosciuszko, even some who attacked his political attitude. During the Duchy of Warsaw, the majority of the Polish nation enthusiastically followed the star of Napoleon despite Kosciuszko's opposite views.

Under the burden of these disappointments and unpleasant experiences, Kosciuszko quite seriously began to lean to the thought of his return to America. He announced that intention immediately after Jefferson's election[11] and the latter assured him that, notwithstanding Federalism and the threat of war with France, the nation "shall be able to preserve here an asylum where your love of liberty and disinterested patriotism will be forever protected and honoured and where you will find in the heart of the American people a good portion of that esteemed affection which glows in the bosom of the friend who writes this."[12]

A year later Kosciuszko again wrote Jefferson: "I believe that I will be able to admire you this year and then to deposit my ashes in a land of freedom where honesty and justice prevail."[13] Even as

9 Askenazy, *loc. cit.*, III, 167-172.

10 Askenazy, *Thaddeus Kosciuszko*, 20.

11 Kosciuszko to Jefferson, 26 Thermidor (Aug. 14, 1800), Mass. Hist. Soc., Jefferson Coll.

12 Jefferson to Kosciuszko, Feb. 21, 1799, Libr. of Congress, Jefferson Papers.

13 Kosciuszko to Jefferson, undated, but ab. 1801, *ibid.*

late as 1803, he still persisted in that thought. After a visit with Kosciuszko, Monroe assured Jefferson that "he thinks seriously of returning to the United States."[14] But the General procrastinated, as new plans about Poland preoccupied his mind.

Having finally lost his faith in France, Kosciuszko returned for awhile to his insurrectionary idea of regaining Poland's freedom with the nation's own resources. He published anonymously a pamphlet in which he explained that view. One of the maxims proclaimed by it was: "A nation desiring independence necessarily must have faith in its own strength. If it does not have that feeling, if it does not aim to sustain its life by its own effort but by foreign help and favor, one can truly foretell that it will win neither happiness, nor virtue, nor glory." Answering arguments of those who considered the Polish peasantry still unripe for freedom, because of its low social position and lack of education, Kosciuszko demanded its emancipation as the principal condition of raising its mental level and its standard of living. Once freed, the peasants will progress by themselves, he contended.

From the American point of view, the pamphlet was most interesting. The purpose of Kosciuszko was to convince his countrymen that if America, with a much smaller population and more modest resources was able to throw off its foreign yoke, Poland would be successful too, if she only persisted in her attempts. He advised the Poles to finance the war with paper money, as America had done; to conduct it along the lines of American strategy; even to organize a Polish Congress, functioning as the American Continental Congress had done, as the supreme national authority. To assure the quick growth of population, he counselled early marriages which he had seen practiced in America.[15] It was another attempt of his to introduce American ideas into Poland.

The pamphlet was suppressed. It brought still harsher treatment by Napoleon's government upon the author. Again Kosciuszko fell under police surveillance, and this time it was the French police. Disheartened by these experiences, he gradually withdrew from political affairs and closed himself in the quiet of private life. He "literally suffocated in Paris, felt himself out of place there."[16] In 1801 he moved to the home of Peter Joseph Zeltner, the first Minister of the Helvetian Republic, at Berville, near Fontainebleau, where he was to spend the next fourteen years. There Napoleon again tried to reach him during his first Polish War of 1806-7. At that moment the situa-

14 Sept. 20, 1803, Hamilton, ed., *Writings of Monroe*, IV, 77.
15 Sobieski, "Kościuszko i Pułaski," Koneczny, ed., *Polska w Kulturze Powszechnej*, I, 101.
16 Fiszer, "Pamiętnik," 272.

tion seemed propitious for Poland. "Never was there a more promising prospect of that unhappy country regaining its existence," wrote Niemcewicz to Jefferson,[17] and many Poles thought the same. Overcoming his dislike of Napoleon, Kosciuszko did not refuse peremptorily; he demanded only that the Emperor make a public promise to rebuild Poland and to give her a liberal constitution, providing for a legal equality of all inhabitants. When, however, Fouche, Napoleon's Chief of Police, who brought the Emperor's proposition, declared that any demands on the Emperor were out of question, Kosciuszko retorted that "he would not go blindly, nor would he expose thousands of his countrymen." "I know he is always doing what he thinks is right, and he knows my prayers for his success, in whatever he does," wrote Jefferson about that time to Niemcewicz.[18]

When his French and Polish friends pressed him for some concessions for the sake of Poland, Kosciuszko outlined to Fouche new demands much more far-reaching; the restoration of Poland in her historical confines, freedom and land for the peasants and a constitution modeled after the English, which clearly shows that at that time he had lost hope of introducing the American republican system in Europe.

The Emperor could not, even if he had wanted to, fulfill these demands under the circumstances; undoubtedly he considered the point referring to the English constitution a personal affront.[19]

Gradually Kosciuszko's political views began to undergo a new, deep transformation. More and more he leaned to a new solution of the Polish problem; disappointed by France, he now began to look to Russia for Poland's salvation. The new Tsar, Alexander I, was known for his liberalism. While still a Grand Duke, he had declared himself a friend of humanity and of Poland. Together with his close friend, Prince Adam George Czartoryski, son of the protector of Kosciuszko when the General was a youth, he dreamed of making Russia and Poland happy and of restoring the latter to her former greatness. The beginning of his reign was marked by a pro-Polish policy. He entrusted Czartoryski with the management of Russian foreign affairs. He made him curator of the University of Vilno, which enabled Czartoryski to develop the educational system greatly in the whole of Russian Poland. Under Czartoryski's influence, a new era of political concessions seemed to dawn for that part of the dismembered country. The Tsar made efforts to gain Kosciuszko's friendship, and it was to him that Kosciuszko's eyes now turned as the future liberator of Poland.

---

17 April 10, 1807, Libr. of Congress, Jefferson Papers.
18 April 22, 1807, Libr. of Congress, Jefferson Papers.
19 Kukiel, "Legiony," *Polska, Jej Dzieje i Kultura*, III, 40.

For a time, events made this pro-Russian orientation unfeasible. The Duchy of Warsaw, organized by Napoleon from some parts of central Poland retaken from Prussia, never gained Kosciuszko's approval. It did not restore even the name of Poland. With the fall of Napoleon, however, hopes for realization of the new program rose high. Allied troops occupied France. The Tsar entered Paris. Kosciuszko at once turned to Alexander with proposals concerning Poland. The Tsar sent his own carriage for the General, received him with greatest honors, embraced and kissed him before his court. At another public reception Alexander and his brother, the Grand Duke Constantine, taking Kosciuszko under the arm, led him through the throng shouting: "Room, room; behold the great man!" For himself, Kosciuszko declined to accept anything;[20] all he wanted was freedom for Poland. His program submitted to the Tsar was similar to that which he had proposed to Napoleon a decade ago. It provided amnesty for Polish political offenders, freedom for the peasants, the restoration of the old independent Kingdom of Poland with at least the greater part of its territory and a constitution modeled after the English. Firmly believing in the sincerity of Alexander's Polish sympathies, Kosciuszko even proposed that the Tsar should proclaim himself the king of the resurrected state. The Tsar countered with a solemn and written promise, though only a general one, to rebuild "the valiant and admirable nation to which you belong."

The transformation of Kosciuszko's political views toward the end of his life was most surprising. A former enemy of Russia, defeated, imprisoned and persecuted by her, he turned to the very same power for protection and help for Poland. It was not opportunism; above all, it was Kosciuszko's strong faith in the justice of the Polish cause. But he also believed that the chasm which divided the two foremost Slavic nations for centuries, could be bridged. The primary condition of a durable understanding, he rightly thought, was a complete redress for wrongs committed.

But at the Congress of Vienna all of the Tsar's promises went with the winds. Called by Czartoryski to the Austrian capital to attend to the Polish cause, the old General left his Berville home never to return to it again. At first the Tsar tried to remain faithful to his pledges.[21] But opposed by England, threatened with war by the other partitioning powers, he abandoned his stand. Again Kosciuszko's hopes fell. The decisions of the Vienna Congress regarding Poland amounted to a new partition; they constituted an autonomous King-

---

20 Kosciuszko to Jefferson, March 14, 1815, Mass. Hist. Soc., Jefferson Coll.; the original in French.

21 Justus Erick Bollman to James A. Bayard, Dec. 20, 1814, "Papers of James A. Bayard," *Annual Report of the Amer. Hist. Association for the Year 1913*, II, 361.

dom of Poland, but smaller even than the former Napoleonic Duchy of Warsaw, and subject to autocratic Russia. They incorporated the Polish Eastern provinces with Russia. It was much less than even Napoleon had given to Poland. It was a complete abnegation of Kosciuszko's program. His letter to the Tsar reminding him of his promises remained unanswered. "European politics . . . are nothing else," wrote the afflicted Kosciuszko to Jefferson, "than an art of the best seduction."[22] "Their object . . . is plunder," Jefferson condemned the participants of the Congress.[23]

Turning his back on this perfidy, Kosciuszko decided to settle in Switzerland, which seemed to him the only remaining haven of freedom on the European continent, now overwhelmed by the reactionary forces of the Holy Alliance. He understood well that his nation had no other choice than to submit to this new outrage; but he, who had led the nation in its fight for Liberty, Integrity and Independence, could not bow his head before this decision.[24] Though invited by the Tsar to return to Poland, he refused to do so, preferring further exile to any favors of the despot. "I do not want . . . to return to my country until it will be restored in its entirety with a free constitution," he explained to Jefferson.[25] Some time later he wrote to him again:

"Yes, My Dear Friend, I thought of good laws, Tsar Alexander promised me a Constitutional Government, Liberal, Independent, even the emancipation of our unhappy Peasants and to make them Proprietors of the lands which they hold; by this alone he would immortalize himself, but it disappeared as smoke. — I am now in the town of Soleure in Switzerland, looking at the Allied Powers which break their good faith, commit Injustices against small States and treat their own people like wolves treat sheep."[26]

After the Congress of Vienna, Jefferson tried again to induce his desolate friend to leave Europe, the scene of his disappointments, and to move to America.[27] Kosciuszko declined. He now considered it his duty to remain to the last as near as possible to his beloved and unhappy country, to her poor and unfortunate people, the comforting of whom became the necessity of his heart. Amid the political turmoil of Europe, notwithstanding his personal failures, Kosciuszko still considered himself "the only true Pole" in the world. In his last letter to Jefferson before his death he wrote:

---

22 March 14, 1815, Mass. Hist. Soc., Jefferson Coll.; the original in French.
23 To Gallatin, Oct. 16, 1815, Lipscomb, XIV, 358.
24 Askenazy, *Thaddeus Kosciuszko*, 21-22.
25 March 14, 1815, Mass. Hist. Soc., Jefferson Coll.; the original in French.
26 Undated except for April, 1816, Mass. Hist. Soc., Jefferson Coll.; the original in French.
27 This letter of Jefferson seems to be lost in the original, as well as in the press copy, but the contents of a subsequent letter of Kosciuszko clearly point out that such an invitation was sent by Jefferson.

"I greatly and with all my gratefulness appreciate your gracious invitation, but my Country lies heavy upon my heart, and there are also my friends, my acquaintances, and sometimes I like to give them my advice. I am the only true Pole in Europe, all others are by circumstances subject to Different Powers. Perhaps you may say that this is the most unhappy country, yes, no doubt, but just for that reason it is in the greatest need of advice. Everywhere, my dear and Respectable Friend, one can be independent if he thinks right, reasons right, has a good heart, human sentiments, and a Character firm and candid . . ."[28]

---

[28] Sept. 15, 1817, Mass. Hist. Soc., Jefferson Coll.; the original in French.

XI.

KOSCIUSZKO'S DEATH

With all Europe trembling under the constant thunder of guns, with great historical events passing over his head with kaleidoscopic swiftness, the Polish exile, except for brief periods of political activity, lived the comparatively quiet life of a man resigned to passiveness and forced inactivity. Caustically John Ward Fenno called him "the decaying remnant of a life gloriously devoted to danger, in the cause of liberty."[1] Though physically much improved, Kosciuszko never recovered completely, and remained till his death only "in tolerable health."[2] Peter Joseph Zeltner, his host, a light-minded and insincere man, secretly acting against Poland and Kosciuszko's plans during the Legion era, won his friendship by his, true or pretended, republicanism and by his outward pleasant appearance.[3] Far from suspecting this duplicity, Kosciuszko became attached to his household primarily because of Zeltner's wife, Angelica, nee Drouyn de Vaudeuil de Lhuys, young, comely and of a very agreeable disposition. For her and her children's sake he became so intimately connected with the Zeltners that they all lived as one family. At least it satisfied his longing for the warmth of a home of his own. A Polish lady who watched them closely for a long time, assures us that Kosciuszko's influence on Mrs. Zeltner was most elevating. A typical Parisian, "she undoubtedly would have done what many of them did, had not Kosciuszko led her by hand through life. Under his influence she was devoted to her home and children."[4] Always he treated her with evident respect, never with improper familiarity. In turn, she felt for him love and respect mixed with some awe at the greatness of his name. In all their relations there was nothing which might suggest any suspicion of improper conduct; though he lived in an epoch of licentiousness, Kosciuszko passed through life free from any love scandals.

According to the same lady, Kosciuszko made an agreement with the Zeltners "that he would pay them three francs a day for his livelihood, but neither he nor they kept that in mind. The blending of feelings also caused a fusion of finances — and that was the reason why

---

1 *U. S. Gazette,* Nov. 6, 1798.
2 Jefferson to Niemcewicz, Jan. 11, 1801, Libr. of Congress, Jefferson Papers.
3 Askenazy, *Napoleon,* III, 126-8.
4 Fiszer, "Pamiętnik," 256-7.

he felt as in his own home with the Zeltners. Without any embarrassment, he invited us to the family table and the children of the Zeltners seemed to be his own . . . All four accompanied him continually, filled his room with their noises, climbed to his knees and completely took possession of him; he caressed or chided them. The youngest of them all was a six-months daughter who bore his name — Thaddea. I often saw him walking through the streets of Paris with her in his arms. He reproached the mother when she neglected anything in proper care of them; he also rebuked her when he observed any dereliction on her part in the household, or any coquetry or prodigality. Usually he tried to give a jocular turn to his censures.

"His living quarters comprised several unheated and unfurnished rooms, through which one passed to the last room where fire burned and some of the most indispensable pieces of furniture stood. Here he slept and received visitors, often while still in bed or in his dressing gown. Whoever visited him once, could freely visit him at any time without fear of embarrassing him; he did everything in the presence of his guests, as if he were alone, and as he received his friends only, he thought they would not take it amiss."[5]

Severing all relations with those connected with Napoleon's government, Kosciuszko preferred to sentence himself to a life of obscurity rather than compromise his opinions. Nevertheless distinguished foreign visitors sought to meet him.[6] A few disgraced French generals, learned men, litterati, artists, a few ladies, all decided republicans and now oppositionists, made the intimate circle of his friends during the Consulate. He liked music and sometimes arranged concerts for them at the Zeltners' house. Among his most frequent French visitors at that time were: Generals Moreau and Macdonald, Lucien Bonaparte, the mathematician Monge, the historian Segur, the poet Boufflers, the politicians Lesage-Senault and Garat, the tragedian Chenier, former Consul Lebrun and Lafayette. With the rise of Napoleon to power, this circle gradually melted away; Lafayette was perhaps the only one who preserved a steady friendship with him. The Marquis attended Polish celebrations of Kosciuszko's Patron Saint,[7] periodically arranged by the Parisian Polish colony; they were almost the only public festivals, usually celebrated in the most splendid manner, which the aging man did not refuse to participate in, "in order not to deprive the Poles of that only occasion to show the world how much they honor their common country in him."[8] Together with Lafayette,

5 *Ibid.*
6 Among them were the Irish patriot O'Connell (Lafayette, *Memoires,* II, 207) and Charles James Fox (Trotter, *Memoirs,* 229-231).
7 Lafayette to Jefferson, Nov. 6, 1806, Lafayette, *Memoires,* II, 226.
8 Paszkowski, *Dzieje Kościuszki,* 202.

Kosciuszko took part in the Fourth of July dinners arranged by the American colony.[9] Together they intervened in behalf of Kollontay and other Poles still imprisoned by Austria for taking part in the Insurrection.[10] To the end of his life Lafayette kept Kosciuszko's portraits, next to Washington, at Lagrange and in his Paris hotel.[11]

Sketching and turnery remained Kosciuszko's hobbies; the drawings he usually threw away, but the small trinkets turned by himself he gave as presents to his friends. Gardening became his favorite occupation at Berville. Above all he loved roses, and kept thousands of them in his small garden. Monroe, then on a mission to France concerning Louisiana, reported to Jefferson in 1803: "I saw Genl's LaFayette and Kusciusko often. They are the men you always knew them to be . . . Kusciusko lives near the barrier St. Andre not far from St. Antoine, where he cultivates his own garden. Col. Mercer[12] and myself on our visit found him returning from it with his water pots."[13] In his last years, he occupied himself with the making of wooden clogs, which he planned to introduce among the peasants in Poland as a preventive against rheumatism and other diseases. Perhaps the old exile, turning clogs for the benefit of peasants in a far-off country, looked somewhat quixotic, but the action illustrates the goodness of his heart.

The best pen portrait of Kosciuszko at this time has been left by Madame Fiszer. According to her, he was completely unlike all his contemporary portraits; others who knew him confirm this, too. His features were irregular, his face full of wrinkles, his mouth wide and tightly closed, his teeth rare, and his nose turned-up. His thick brown hair, now turning gray, covered his forehead and fell in long locks on his shoulders. The features of this homely and rugged face were, however, mitigated by a subtleness and mildness which attracted and inspired confidence.[14] Most striking were his eyes, shining and lively; when he spoke with animation, they seemed to illuminate his whole face. Paszkowski says that it was impossible to see him thus and not to succumb to his charm.[15]

He was of middle stature, lean, with soldierly bearing; his movements were quick. He was not talkative and spoke quietly, but laconically, sometimes with discreet irony, often in a jocular mood. "Exacting, but tender and jovial, he did not afflict though he commanded obedience."[16] Among friends he was most cordial, among strangers

9 Lafayette to an unknown addressee, 16 Thermidor, 1800, Cloquet, *Recollections,* 251.
10 Janik, *Kołłątaj,* 445.
11 Cloquet, *loc. cit.,* 177 and 248.
12 John Francis Mercer of Virginia.
13 Sept. 20, 1803, Hamilton, ed., *Writings of Monroe,* IV, 77.
14 Fiszer, "Pamiętnik," 255.
15 Paszkowski, *loc. cit.,* 248.
16 Fiszer, "Pamiętnik," 257.

reserved. If he felt hurt by something, he left the company without giving an explanation; nevertheless he was not very touchy; he never took offence at the innocent jokes of others or at their inattention. However, he was very obstinate in his prejudices, and it was most difficult to convince him of error. In his behavior he impressed those with whom he came in contact with his deepseated sincerity and democracy. Notwithstanding his modesty and plain appearance, he had a sense of personal dignity and one glance of his eyes or his ironic silence was enough to subdue those who dared to be too familiar.[17]

He liked to surround himself with young girls and young men and played with them like a boy. To women he was most courteous and ceremonious.

He never spoke of two things: of himself and of the past. The famous Madame de Stael meeting him in a Polish salon, asked him outright: "General, please tell us about your revolution." He answered her: "Madame, I have been a soldier and I have fought," and turning to the lady of the house he said to her in Polish: "Keep this woman away from me, or I will leave," which he did in fact.[18]

He usually dressed in a dark blue coat, black tie, boots with facings, a hat with a wide, round brim; he never wore any decorations. On solemn occasions he put on a black frock coat, in which, however, he felt embarrassed.[19]

According to Xavier Zeltner, the son of Francis Xavier Zeltner, the Landvogt of Soleure, with whom Kosciuszko lived after his removal to Switzerland, the General led a very regular life. He rose early, in the summer at five, in the winter at six o'clock, dressed and prepared his coffee over a spirit-lamp. It seems that he became a habitual coffee drinker during the American Revolution. A diarist remembered that during the Insurrection he drank, at all times of the day, much coffee differently prepared, "hot, cold and iced." Having read his newspaper or a book, he spent two or three hours teaching the Zeltner children, a duty which he voluntarily took upon himself. Finished with the lessons, he took a ride on horseback when the weather was fine; on rainy days he walked in his room. At four or five in the afternoon he dined and usually with a good appetite and in the best of spirits. Strawberries were his favorite fruit. At dusk he liked to sit and chat with his hosts and friends, and when the candles were lighted, he played chess or a game or two of whist, another of his favorite recreations. At about ten the game was stopped and he retired.[20]

17 *Ibid.*, 261 and 265.
18 *Ibid.*, 262.
19 *Ibid.*, 256.
20 Zeltner, "Personal Reminiscences," *U. S. Service Mag.*, IV (1865), 141.

He was careless in his correspondence; he never mastered the English or the French language, and even his Polish letters and his state papers often lacked literary polish. Not infrequently, however, his writings disclose the deepness and beauty of his thought. He never cared much for preserving his papers.

It is difficult to pass a definite judgment on his religious life. He never touched the subject in his correspondence and there are only a few inadequate testimonies of contemporaries. It seems that, though born and reared a Roman Catholic, he did not escape the influence of the Age of Enlightenment. His youthful sojourn in France, his long service in America, the general atmosphere of the epoch, certainly did not contribute to the strengthening of his devotion to the Church. Madame Fiszer says that he "professed the universal religion of good men."[21] In his private letters he generally used the term Providence when speaking of God.[22] But under these appearances of religious liberalism, the core of his heart was full of Christian faith so manifest in his deeds. Zeltner assures that every morning upon rising he said his prayers. In a letter to Boudinot, Kosciuszko disclosed that he prayed for the health of Boudinot's daughter, Mrs. Susan Vergerau Bradford.[23] He started the Insurrection with God's name on his lips and publicly showed all respect to the Church. He was never a Freemason.[24] Even if he did not approve of the monastic life, as Madame Fiszer relates, yet out of his funds he endowed a poor girl who wished to become a nun.[25] To a blind priest he volunteered as a reader. When a petitioner inadvertently stepped upon his beloved tame bullfinch and killed it, Kosciuszko, forgetting his own grief, consoled the much distressed man and, giving him a gold piece, said: "Here, my poor man, for your pain."[26] He became a servant of the poor. "To see a poor man and not to give him something was impossible for him."[27] Famous is the anecdote of his horse which halted before every beggar. Kosciuszko's heart was responsive to all human sorrow. The weak, the down-trodden, the neglected, were always on his mind. He continually pleaded their causes and devoted to them almost the whole of his income.[28] According to Jefferson, the single purpose of Kosciuszko's life was "the freedom and happiness of man."[29] Kosciuszko stressed the need of education as necessary to attain these ideals, whether he

---

21 Fiszer, "Pamiętnik," 275.
22 Korzon, *Kosciuszko*, p. 609, note 393.
23 Kosciuszko to Boudinot, no date, but ab. Sept. 1797, Polish R. C. U. Museum, Kosciuszko Papers, no. 46.
24 Załęski, *O Masonii*, 128.
25 Fiszer, "Pamiętnik," 275.
26 Zeltner, *loc. cit.*, 142.
27 Michelet, *Kościuszko*, 35.
28 Zeltner, *loc. cit.*, 139-140.
29 Jefferson to Kosciuszko, June 1, 1798, Lipscomb, X, 49.

spoke to his own countrymen, or to Americans or others. When he made his will shortly before his death, giving freedom to the peasants on his small paternal estate, Siechnowicze, he admonished them to establish suitable schools. In his testament for America, he advocated not only freedom, but also education for Negroes. He loved Poland above all, but he also loved and much admired America, always upholding it to all as a model state. Francis Xavier Zeltner truly said of him that his heart "throbbed for the whole world."[30] During his forced inactivity in France, the General complained to Jefferson: "As for myself, far from my homeland, I do nothing, you undoubtedly know the reason, I am resting in inactivity and am of no service to humanity."[31] Years before, he formulated his simple philosophy on this point in words written to Gen. Greene:

"Are we ought to like only our Compatriots, not allowance to be made for one sort of Strangers; from your Philosophical turn of mind I would expect of enlarging the limits of our affection contracted by prejudice and superstition towards the rest of mankind, and more so for whom we have a Sincier Esteem, let him be Turck or Polander, American or Japon."[32]

With his virtues, his attainments, and his fame, he retained a noble modesty. Mary Williams, an English writer, beautifully said of him that "he seems to regret that great deeds do sentence great men to fame."[33]

The following advices written for a boy reflect the beauty of Kosciuszko's soul and disclose the principles of his moral code:

"Rising at 4 o'clock in summer and at six o'clock in winter, Your first thought must be directed towards the Supreme Being, worshipping him for a few minutes; Put yourself at once to work with reflexion and intelligence, either to your prescribed duty, with the most scrupulous exactitude, or to perfect yourself in some science of which you should have a true mastery. Be always frank and loyal . . . ; and always speak the truth; never be idle, be sober and frugal and even hard for your own self but indulgent towards others; shun selfishness and egotism; before speaking something or answering, reflect well and reason . . . Never fail to make obvious your gratitude in all circumstances to a Person who takes charge of Your happiness . . . Look forward to his desires, his wishes, be attentive . . . , always look for an occasion to render yourself useful. Because you are a Stranger in the country you must double your cares and efforts to earn legitimately the confidence and the preference over the natives by your merit and

30 "Last Years of Kosciuszko," *Harper's Mag.*, XXXVII, 483.
31 May 30, 1813, Polish R. C. U. Museum, Kosciuszko Papers, no. 65; the original in French.
32 Jan. 20, 1786, Huntington Libr., Greene Papers, HM 8056.
33 Paszkowski, *Dzieje Kościuszki*, 202.

your superior knowledge. If a secret is entrusted to you, keep it religiously; in all your actions you must be upright, sincere and open, no dissimulation in any of your talk, never argue, but seek truth serenely and modestly; be polite and considerate to everyone, agreable and obliging in society, always humane and succour the poor according to your means; read instructive books to embellish your Mind or better your heart, never degrade yourself by making bad acquaintances, but be always with persons full of morals and of good reputation; at last, your conduct must be such that everyone approves of it."[34]

During the last months of his life Kosciuszko felt the weight of his loneliness and his many past disappointments so heavily that he tried to escape the painful recollections by long excursions on horseback into the surrounding country. The atmosphere of the home of the Swiss Zeltner was not too sympathetic. Francis Xavier Zeltner was of a rash character; his wife, in contrast to the lady of Berville, was a woman of little education; they quarreled often.[35] Somehow Kosciuszko could not find a responsive soul among the small circle of his Swiss acquaintances. The town physician, a priest, a few local officials and businessmen, were all who made up the list of his usual visitors. Sometime an old friend, or a countryman stumbled upon his modest dwelling. They were welcome, but still could not quench his longing for Poland. "I beg you," he wrote to one of his Polish friends, "often to send me news about yourself, but above all about our dear Fatherland; it returns to my thoughts every night. From all my soul I wished to serve my Country — I have been unsuccessful and it gives me much pain."[36]

Before his death Kosciuszko disposed of his European estate. He had never touched a penny of the money given him by Paul I, leaving it all these years in a London bank; now he divided the sum between Gen. Francis Paszkowski, a former Polish officer of the Insurrection, who had attended him in his exile, and Emily Zeltner, daughter of the Swiss Zeltner, whom he had so tenderly served as a teacher. He divided the rest of his funds and effects among other members of both Zeltner families. He ordered his sword to be laid in his coffin, and the sword of John Sobieski presented to him by the Polish Legions, to be returned to the nation. He stipulated also that his funeral should be modest and its cost should not exceed one thousand francs; his body should be carried to its grave by beggars, to whom he also left cash gifts.

---

34 Written for Conrad Zeltner, 17 year old son of Francis Xavier Zeltner, in August, 1817; the original in French, in private possession of Dr. Boleslaw Mastai of New York; cf. "Rady Tadeusza Kościuszki," *Dziennik Chicagoski,* April 23, 1894.

35 Fiszer, "Pamiętnik," 274.

36 Korzon, *Przedśmiertna Męczarnia,* 9.

Surrounded by the Zeltner family, Kosciuszko died peacefully on October 15, 1817, after a brief illness brought on by an exerting horseback ride. His funeral took place on October 19, with Catholic church rites, in the presence of a large number of clergy, members of religious orders, representatives of civil authorities, school children "and crowds of the poor who remembered his kindness."[37] His body was temporarily interred in a vault of the local Jesuit church.

"It is with the deepest regret I have to announce the Death of our dearly beloved friend and much revered Correspondent the Worthy — the Great — the good & Virtuous Genl Kosciuszko," Barnes hastened to inform Jefferson one day in December of 1817, when he unexpectedly read the sad news in a local newspaper.[38]

Soon particulars of his death reached Jefferson by Francis Xavier Zeltner. "It is with the greatest pain," wrote Kosciuszko's host, "that I have to announce a terrible loss which we have suffered in the person of the Great and Immortal General Kosciuszko, he died in my arms on the fifteenth of this month in consequence of a violent fever against which all the efforts of art and exertions of friendship were fruitless. This great man who has honored me with his friendship and his confidence for over twenty years retired two years ago to the bosom of my family where he hoped to pass his life unless circumstances more favorable than he ventured to hope would allow the rebirth of his unhappy Country, and in that event, he would be summoned into the midst of his compatriots. A few weeks before his sickness he communicated to me the last letter he wrote to you, and a few days before his death he still told me of you, of your interesting Country, of its progress in sciences, of its population, of the power of that only Republic of the World, a worthy subject of our wishes . . ."[39]

Answering Barnes, Jefferson dwelt only briefly on his feelings upon the reception of the mournful news. "I will not trouble you with vain condolences," he wrote, "& expressions of regret on the death of a mutual friend . . . & which we both lament."[40] But to Zeltner, a stranger, he wrote more extensively:

"To no country could that event be more afflicting nor to any individual more than to myself. I had enjoyed his intimate friendship and confidence for the last 20 years, & during the portion of that time which he past in this country, I had daily opportunities of observing personally the purity of his virtue, the benevolence of his heart, and his sincere devotion to the cause of liberty, his anterior services during our revolutionary war had been well known & ac-

---

37 From the funeral records of the Church of SS. Ursus and Victor at Soleure, Oct. 27, 1817, Korzon, *Kosciuszko,* 690.

38 Dec. 30, 1817, "Edgehill" Randolph Papers in the Alderman Library; this source referred to hereafter as "Edgehill" Randolph Papers.

39 Oct. 29, 1817, Mass. Hist. Soc., Jefferson Coll.; the original in French.

40 Jan. 5, 1818, *Mag. of History,* no. 36, p. 294.

knowledged by all. when he left the U. S. in 1798. he left in my hands an instrument, giving, after his death, all his property in our funds, the price of his military labors here, to the charitable purposes of educating and emancipating as many of the children of bondage in this country as it should be adequate to . . . I am therefore taking measures to have it placed in such hands as will ensure a faithful discharge of his philanthropic views. . . ."[41]

On October 31, the American colony in Paris assembled at St. Roche Church to take part in a Mass for the repose of the soul of the "great and good man — the friend of freedom."[42] In the crowd there were many Frenchmen who had fought with him in America, and many Poles whom he had led in the Polish Insurrection.[43] Lafayette was also present to pay tribute to him whom he considered "a perfect type of courage, honor and Polish patriotism."[44] Many recognized in Kosciuszko "one of the greatest men of the epoch."[45]

The Congress of the United States also honored the deceased General during the session of January 20, 1818, when William Henry Harrison of Ohio, the ninth President of the United States, announced in the House that "Kosciuszko, the martyr of liberty, is no more!" In a long address he sketched his life and concluded:

"His fame will last as long as liberty remains upon the earth; as long as votary offers incense upon her altar, the name of Kosciusko will be invoked. And if, by the common consent of the world, a temple shall be erected to those who have rendered most service to mankind, if the statue of our great countryman shall occupy the place of the 'Most Worthy,' that of Kosciusko will be found by his side, and the wreath of laurel will be entwined with the palm of virtue to adorn his brow."[46]

Harrison proposed that, "not . . . to perpetuate his fame — but our gratitude," all members of the House should wear black crepe on the left arm for one month. "In the short debate on this question, the merits of Kosciuszko, the advocate of freedom, and the friend of man, were fully admitted; but it was shown, that no such respect . . . had been paid to any of the departed worthies, native or foreign, who had aided in the achievement of our independence, except in the single case of General Washington."[47] Whereupon Harrison withdrew his resolution; at least he had "acquitted his conscience," he said.

---

41 July 23, 1818, Mass. Hist. Soc., Jefferson Coll.
42 Isaac C. Barnet to Jefferson, Nov. 30, 1817, Libr. of Congress, Jefferson Papers.
43 The description of the services is in the *Detroit Gazette,* Feb. 26, 1818.
44 Lafayette to an unknown addressee, Feb. 12, 1830, *Memoires,* II, 441.
45 Arnault, *Souvenirs,* IV, 272.
46 *Annals of Congress,* XXXI, 795-798.
47 *Ibid.,* XXXI, 800.

In 1818 the body of Kosciuszko was sent to Poland and buried in the cathedral of Cracow, there to rest among the kings and national heroes of that country. His heart, enclosed in an ornamental urn, became one of the most precious relics in Polish museums. The town of Soleure wanted at least a part of his earthly remains and it kept his intestines which were interred in the Zuchwil cemetery.[48] In 1820, the Senate of the Free City of Cracow, the last remaining vestige of Poland's independence, decided to pay him honor in a unique way, by building on the outskirts of the city a high mound made up of soil from Kosciuszko's battlefields and of that Polish earth which he so generously loved. For three years men, women and children carried earth in hands, baskets, and wheelbarrows, and collected funds for the necessary expenses. The Cracow Senate asked Jefferson to take charge of contributions in America. Jefferson, however, felt unequal to the task, because of his age and turned the matter over to President Monroe, "the friend of his (Kosciuszko's) fame."[49] Notwithstanding his "profound respect for the character of General Kosciusko" and "his important services" to the cause of liberty of this country, Monroe had doubts as to the success of the proposal; citizens were overburdened with financial demands of the country and even a subscription for a monument to Washington had failed recently.[50] The matter had to be dropped. A few years later, cadets of the United States Military Academy erected the first American monument of Kosciuszko on American soil.

For the same reason Jefferson also declined to collaborate with two men who intended to write a biography of Kosciuszko soon after his death. For the first one, Antoine Jullien, a Frenchman and personal friend of Kosciuszko, he enlisted the aid of Gen. Armstrong.[51] The second would-be biographer of Kosciuszko, John H. James of Cincinnati, was openly discouraged by Jefferson for various reasons: to avoid competition with Jullien, because of the scarcity in American archives of documents pertaining to Kosciuszko's activity in Europe, and because of Jefferson's doubts as to James' literary abilities.[52]

Truly, what pen can rival the rhymes of great poets, who immortalized Kosciuszko even during his life? Their lyres have transformed

---

48 Bronarski, *Tadeusz Kościuszko,* 39.

49 Jefferson to Monroe, Aug. 13, 1821, Libr. of Congress, Jefferson Papers.

50 Monroe to Jefferson, Sept. 6, 1821, *ibid.*

51 Correspondence on the subject in the Libr. of Congress, Jefferson Papers, except for one letter of Jefferson to Armstrong, March 20, 1818, in the Kahanowicz Coll., p. 42, no. 97 and another, from the same to the same, May 20, 1818, in the Alderman Libr., Jefferson Coll. On July 1, 1818, Armstrong wrote to Jefferson: "I have a number of the General's letters, but they are written in bad English and have besides very little connexion with political events or public men." Most probably these letters were destroyed in the fire which occurred at Armstrong's house.

52 James to Jefferson, June 13, 1820, and Jefferson to James, July 7, 1820, Libr. of Congress, Jefferson Papers.

his name into "an everlasting tone,"[53] enchanting all noble souls. Jefferson paid him the highest tribute he paid anyone: "He is as pure a son of liberty as I have ever known, and of that liberty which is to go to all, and not to the few and rich alone."[54] To America and Poland he forever remains a model of the most sublime patriotism and the loftiest idealism. In him the world recognizes one of the foremost champions of human rights. His noble figure towers above the road of humanity like a signpost marking not only the past, but also pointing to a better and more ideal future. It will enrapture generation after generation to great deeds, at least as long as nobility remains alive in the breasts of men.

Through the dark days that are before Poland, the ideals of Kosciuszko will continue to encourage the Poles to work and to suffer for that Poland which he so nobly and so untiringly served, and for which he sacrificed his entire being.

---

53 Keats, "To Kosciuszko."
54 Jefferson to Gates, Feb. 21, 1798, Lipscomb, IX, 441.

XII.

KOSCIUSZKO'S AMERICAN ESTATE

Some attention should be devoted to the American estate of Kosciuszko, the administration of which he left in the hands of Jefferson, who in turn entrusted its immediate control to John Barnes of Georgetown. This matter occupies much space in their correspondence.[1]

Originally amounting to about twelve thousand dollars Kosciuszko's funds were invested in thirty shares of the Bank of Pennsylvania, at four hundred dollars each and bearing eight per cent interest. In 1801 Barnes, with Jefferson's permission, converted one third of these shares into a government loan.[2] The financial crisis of 1814 resulted in the failure of many banks and in a depreciation of bank papers.[3] Happily Jefferson foresaw the coming catastrophe. Blaming the legislators for bringing the country "to the precipice" by unnecessary multiplication of banks, and fearing "universal bankruptcy," he took steps in time to save the investment of his friend. "We should be unfaithful stewards to leave the worthy Kosciusko in danger of wanting bread," he wrote to Barnes.[4] "Duty . . . requires that we should save him while we can."[5] He ordered Barnes to get rid of all the remaining shares of the Bank of Pennsylvania and to look for some safer investment. Just at that time the government was opening a subscription for a loan of twenty five million dollars, which though bearing six per cent interest, allowed an increase of the nominal value of the capital. Selling the twenty shares of the Bank of Pennsylvania at one hundred thirty six dollars each (a total of eleven thousand forty dollars), Barnes bought certificates of the United States Loan for twelve thousand five hundred dollars.[6] Now, thought Jefferson, "it will be

---

[1] Most of the Barnes correspondence with Jefferson, as well as the Kosciuszko accounts for the later years are in the "Edgehill" Randolph Papers, Alderman Library. Accounts for the earlier years, together with some pertinent letters and documents, are in the Mass. Hist. Soc., Jefferson Collection. Jefferson's letters to Barnes are mostly in the Library of Congress, Jefferson Papers. William Abbatt reprinted those pertaining to Kosciuszko's funds, in *The Magazine of History*, vol. IX (1915), no. 36.

[2] Jefferson to Kosciuszko, March 14, 1801, Lipscomb, XIX, 122; in fact, there were 45 shares of the Bank of the United States, at the nominal value of $100 each and bearing 8 per cent interest.

[3] Shultz and Caine, *Financial Development of the U. S.*, 152.

[4] Feb. 23, 1814, *Mag. of History*, no. 36, p. 285.

[5] Jefferson to Barnes, Jan. 29, 1814, *ibid.*, p. 284.

[6] Jefferson to Kosciuszko, June 28, 1814, Mass. Hist. Soc., Jefferson Papers; Barnes to Jefferson, May 2, and May 24, 1814; Barnes' accounts of June 25, 1814, and April 8, 1815, "Edgehill" Randolph Papers.

safer than in any deposit on earth, and it will place him beyond those risks which might close his days in want."[7]

When the transaction came through in the middle of the financial chaos, Jefferson sighed with evident relief. Returning to the subject in a letter to Barnes, he rejoiced:

"How fortunate is it, my dear Sir, that we have saved our friend Kosciusko, by withdrawing his funds from the bank in the moment we did, for him to have lost his capital, the price of his blood spilt for us, & now his only resource for life, would have overwhelmed me with affliction while I should have lived."[8]

In 1816 the funds were again relocated. The Treasury notes of 1801 were converted into forty-six shares of the Bank of Columbia, at one hundred dollars each and bearing eight per cent interest.[9] At the time of Kosciuszko's death, according to Jefferson's accounts, his property consisted of the latter shares, valued at four thousand six hundred dollars, and two certificates of the United States loan of 1814, one worth $11,363.63, and the other $1,136.36. Thus Kosciuszko's American estate, at the time of his death, represented a total of $17,099, besides interest.[10]

It may be said to the credit of Jefferson and Barnes that all these transactions were made very judiciously and advantageously to Kosciuszko. The investments produced about one thousand dollars of interest yearly,[11] and constituted Kosciuszko's main support. The regular transmission of funds was, therefore, of utmost importance to him. The usual procedure was to buy bills of reliable export merchants, who needed money in the United States, in exchange for their money in France, but Barnes found it often "extremely difficult to do this in good bills and without loss."[12] The "risque & anxiety of finding bills of exchange" also worried Jefferson much,[13] and Kosciuszko suffered, too, by the irregularity of remittances and from high discounts. An arrangement made by Jefferson with John A. Morton, "a substantial and friendly house" of Baltimore, proved for a time very satisfactory to all three friends. Morton agreed to transmit funds to Kosciuszko without charge, to "give the General a proof that I feel the

---

7 Jefferson to Barnes, June 28, 1814, *Mag. of History,* no. 36, p. 287.

8 Sept. 30, 1814, *ibid.,* p. 288.

9 Barnes' accounts of March 21, and April 21, 1816, "Edgehill" Randolph Papers.

10 Jefferson to Barnes, Feb. 17, 1817, *Mag. of History,* no. 36, p. 293; to William Wirt, Feb. 5, 1820; to Benjamin L. Lear, Sept. 25, 1821; note of Lear of Oct. 4, 1821, Library of Congress, Jefferson Papers.

11 So for instance Kosciuszko received $1,000 in 1800, $1,025 in 1803, but only $950 in 1805, and $850 in 1809. The largest annual interest he received was $1,110 in 1812.

12 Jefferson to John A. Morton, April 9, 1812, Mo. Hist. Soc., Jefferson Papers.

13 Jefferson to Barnes, Jan. 27, and April 30, 1812, and June 28, 1813, *Mag. of History,* no. 36, pp. 279-280, 282.

interest of his welfare which he has a right to expect from every American."[14] The outbreak of the war with Great Britain in 1812 thwarted that arrangement very shortly. "Embargo & blockade and consequent cessation of nearly all intercourse with Europe"[15] made all Barnes' endeavors to deliver money to his friend fruitless. Still in 1812 Jefferson succeeded in transmitting the usual dividend to Kosciuszko through the American diplomatic mail, appealing in this connection directly to President Madison and invoking his aid to help "one of our most genuine foreign friends."[16] Further progress of the war closed this avenue, too. In 1814 Kosciuszko found himself in an unhappy state. Jefferson rightly considered him "not a man of business"[17] and he was not prepared for such an emergency. At one time his funds became completely exhausted and he was obliged to contract debts. With uneasiness he alarmed Jefferson:

"The time passes in expectation and my anxiety grows in proportion to my small revenue . . . I am already in debts, which angers me much and for ought in the world I would like to break my word."[18]

A little later he complained again: "I have nothing to live on," and in his despair he asked Jefferson to transfer all his funds to Europe.[19]

Unable to find the usual means of relieving Kosciuszko's distress, Jefferson again appealed to the federal government for aid. "I know that your esteem for our mutual friend Kosciuszko will interest you in relieving the suffering under which he now is in Paris," he wrote to Monroe, the Secretary of State, asking him for "any means . . . of remitting to the General his annual funds."[20] Simultaneously he turned to George W. Campbell, the Secretary of the Treasury, with an identical request, reminding him that Kosciuszko's "revolutionary services and general devotion to the cause of liberty have rendered him dear to this country."[21] Entrusted with the letters, Barnes found both Secretaries anxious to help "the good Genl. K. — but at present nothing could be done."[22] He succeeded in supplying Kosciuszko with needed cash not earlier than the fall of 1815.

It happened once that Kosciuszko's money helped Jefferson in a moment of need. Upon retiring from the presidency, he found him-

---

14 Morton to Jefferson, April 24, 1812, Mo. Hist. Soc., Jefferson Papers.

15 Jefferson to Kosciuszko, June 28, 1814, Mass. Hist. Soc., Jefferson Coll.

16 Jefferson to Madison, Aug. 5, 1812, Libr. of Congress, Jefferson Papers.

17 Jefferson to Barnes, April 17, 1812, *Mag. of History*, no. 36, p. 280.

18 July 14, 1814, Mass. Hist. Soc., Jefferson Coll., the original in French.

19 Kosciuszko to Jefferson, March 14, 1815, *ibid.;* the original in French. For the purpose of transferring the funds, Kosciuszko enclosed a new power of attorney for Jefferson, executed by Isaac Cox Barnet, the American Consul in Paris (Mass. Hist. Soc., Jefferson Coll.). As Barnes succeeded, at last, in sending considerable cash to Kosciuszko, Jefferson decided to wait with fulfilling the request till the General's further instructions.

20 May 8, 1814, Libr. of Congress, Jefferson Papers.

21 May 8, 1814, *ibid.*

22 Barnes to Jefferson, May 24, 1814, "Edgehill" Randolph Papers.

self in a difficult financial position and heavily in debt. "Accounts came in a mass so overwhelming as to exceed all" his "resources by ten or twelve thousand Dollars." He was undergoing "a thraldom of mind never before known to" him, ever so scrupulous in his obligations. The debts were pressing and a friend could accommodate him with only a part of the sum needed. To Jefferson "sunk in affliction," Barnes suggested the use of Kosciuszko's funds in the emergency. Jefferson eagerly accepted the proposal. He felt most sure that Kosciuszko "would be delighted with the opportunity of accommodating him."[23]

"The proposition was like a beam of light," he advised Kosciuszko; "& I was satisfied that were you on the spot to be consulted the kindness of your heart would be gratified . . .to lift a friend out of distress."[24]

Of course, Kosciuszko was entirely satisfied. "I approve of everything you have done with my fund," he replied. "I have all confidence in you."

He had only one request, that he might receive his interest regularly as he was "not rich."[25]

Jefferson borrowed forty-five hundred dollars in United States notes of Kosciuszko's funds and charged the debt to his whole estate which, according to himself, was fifty times that amount, "in the event of any accident to" himself. He promised Barnes that "the punctual paiment of the interest shall be sacredly attended to."[26] He kept his word most faithfully. He even paid interest for two months caused by his inability to find Kosciuszko's certificates in the "mass of" his "papers."[27] In 1814 he ordered the sale of his flour with a loss in order to pay the interest on time.[28] He repaid the loan in full in 1815,[29] and it was this money which Barnes used to buy the shares of the Bank of Columbia. This little known episode throws significant light on the honesty of the "Aristides" of Virginia and on his relations with Kosciuszko.

Barnes' Kosciuszko accounts, kept with exemplary conscientiousness, still remain a testimonial to his probity. In his correspondence with Jefferson, Barnes usually referred to his distinguished client as "the good General Kosciuszko." Till his death he preserved a deep love and admiration for the General. Before his death in 1826, he left

23 Jefferson to Barnes, June 15, 1809, *Mag. of History*, no. 36, p. 276.

24 Feb. 26, 1810, Libr. of Congress, Jefferson Papers, and Jefferson to Barnes, June 15, 1809, *Mag. of History*, no. 36, p. 276.

25 Kosciuszko to Jefferson, March 1, 1811, Mass. Hist. Soc., Jefferson Coll.; the original in French.

26 June 15, 1809, *Mag. of History*, no. 36, p. 276.

27 Jefferson to Barnes, Jan. 29, 1810, *ibid.*, p. 277.

28 Jefferson to Barnes, June 28 and August 20, 1814, *ibid.*, pp. 287-288.

29 Jefferson to Barnes, April 15, 1815, *ibid.*, p. 289.

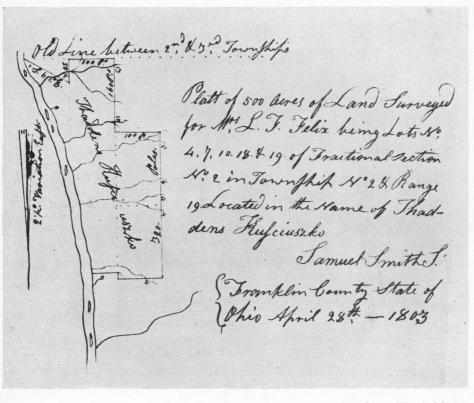

MAP OF KOSCIUSZKO'S LAND
by Samuel Smith

many legacies for humanitarian purposes and to Jefferson he willed, besides his own portrait, a printed portrait of Kosciuszko, a gift from the General himself,[30] "as a token of grateful remembrance . . . of his deceased and distinguished and much lamented friend whose memory will be ever dear to this country."[31] Such was the man on whom Kosciuszko depended in financial matters and never to his regret.

Almost immediately after Kosciuszko's death, three parties applied to Jefferson with claims to the General's American estate. John Armstrong demanded $3,704 and interest in behalf of his minor son, Kosciuszko Armstrong, on the basis of the will of 1806. Francis Xavier Zeltner of Soleure claimed the whole estate on the basis of another will of 1817. Lastly, children of Kosciuszko's two sisters, living in Russian Poland, started action, as his nearest relatives, to take possession of the whole estate, through the Russian Minister in Washington, Peter Poletica.

Convinced that the matter "is likely to become litigious,"[32] and to "take a longer course of time than I have left of life," the aged Jefferson felt obliged to confide to someone younger than himself the "sacred & delicate trust . . . of my deceased friend."[33] On May 12, 1819, he appeared before the Circuit Court of Albemarle County, Virginia, and proved Kosciuszko's will of 1798, but refused to accept the executorship.[34] In this regard he turned to General John Hartwell Cocke of Fluvianna County, his neighbor, and "the most diligent, correct and worthy man in the world."[35] Cocke, however, declined to undertake the task because he foresaw difficulties in carrying out Kosciuszko's desire of freeing and educating the Negroes: "in the first place from the scarcity of Schools about me & 2-ly from the prejudices to be encountered in obtaining admission for negroes — to say nothing of the effect which might be produced on the minds of my own people."[36] With the help of William Wirt, the Attorney General of the United States, Jefferson succeeded, however, in transferring the matter to the Orphan's Court of the District of Columbia, which, being a federal court, both considered the only authority competent to handle the matter.[37] In 1821 this court granted the administration of Kosciuszko's estate to Benjamin L. Lear of Washington, D. C., to whom Jefferson

---

30 This portrait was sent to Barnes by Kosciuszko in response to his request (Barnes to Kosciuszko, April 28, 1815, "Edgehill" Randolph Papers). "I should Esteem (it) and place among the Several, of my most Valued friends," acknowledged Barnes. The picture, in a black frame, is not among the Jefferson relics at the Jefferson Memorial at Monticello.

31 Jackson, "John Barnes," Records of the Columbia Hist. Soc., VII (1904), 41.

32 Jefferson to Poletica, May 27, 1819, Howard, Reports, XIV, 414, Ennis et al. v. Smith.

33 Jefferson to William Wirt, Nov. 10, 1818, Libr. of Congress, Jefferson Papers.

34 Scribner's Monthly, XVII (1879), 615.

35 Jefferson to John Armstrong, March 12, 1819, Libr. of Congress, Jefferson Papers.

36 Cocke to Jefferson, May 3, 1819, Alderman Libr., Jefferson Coll.

37 Jefferson to Lear, Sept. 25, and Lear to Jefferson, Oct, 4. 1821, Libr. of Congress, Jefferson Papers.

transmitted all the Kosciuszko properties. Till his death in 1834, Wirt, at the request of Jefferson, acted as counsel of the trust.[38]

Thus Jefferson justifiably disposed of the matter, which was too burdensome for his dwindling strength. Like Cocke, Lear also had doubts "how far the will can be executed compatibly with the Laws of Virginia & Maryland, — wh: regard with jealousy the education of that description of persons,"[39] but Jefferson was convinced that "the foreign claims" would ultimately be rejected and that "there will be no difficulty of carrying the trust into execution."[40] At first, Jefferson thought that Kosciuszko's noble wish could be eventually fulfilled in Virginia. Before his death, however, he nevertheless approved[41] Lear's project of using the Kosciuszko fund for the endowment of "The Kusciusko School," which the African Education Society of New Jersey planned to organize for the vocational and academic training of Negroes.

This society, controlled by the Presbyterian Church, aimed to encourage the emigration of free Negroes to Africa for the purpose of civilizing it and thus cutting off the slavery trade at its source. On becoming one of the trustees of the Society, Lear promised to put the Kosciuszko fund at its disposal on condition that the Society would collect an equal amount of money; the manumitted pupils of the school would go to Africa to carry the light of the Christian faith and of civilization into the dark continent, thus spreading the fame of the philanthropy of their benefactor already known for "his valor, his patriotism, and his devotion to liberty." The school, however, never came into existence, because of the prolonged litigation over the fund and the final decision of the judiciary.[42] Lear himself did not live long enough — he died in 1832 of cholera — to see the end of the contest, which became more and more entangled by appeals of the claimants from the decrees of the lower courts, the appearance of Col. B. Henry Lubicz Klimkiewicz, a false pretender to the estate, and even political interference and pressure. Death caused other changes in the administration of the fund and among the claimants. The fund ultimately doubled in its value, before it could be distributed. For over three decades the case dragged before legal tribunals. It occupied the attention of Presidents.[43] Several times it came before the United States Court under various aspects. It stirred up sharp debates in two

---

38 Jefferson-Wirt correspondence in the Libr. of Congress, Jefferson Papers.

39 Lear to Jefferson, Oct. 4, 1821, *ibid.*

40 Jefferson to Lear, Sept. 25, 1821, *ibid.*

41 "Kosciusko," *Niles' Register*, Aug. 26, 1826.

42 Cf. Wright, *The Education of Negroes*, subchapter "The Kusciusko School," pp. 92-97. Some details also given in Mazyck, *George Washington and the Negro*, 143-149; T., "Kosciusko School," *Mag. of Am. History*, VIII (1882), 437, etc.

43 John Tyler to Andrew Jackson, Sept. 20, 1842, *Tyler's Quarterly Mag.*, VI (1925), 221 and Tochman's pamphlets, *passim.*

Congresses and for several years caused much ado in the press of the country.

The main cause of the notoriety gained by the case was the engagement of Major Gaspard Tochman, a Polish political exile, by some descendants of Kosciuszko as their attorney. Tochman fought against Russia in the Polish Revolution of 1830-31; after its suppression, he was compelled to flee the country, while his property in Poland was confiscated. In 1837, he arrived in America, became a naturalized citizen of the United States, and in 1845 was admitted to practice law in state and federal courts. His part in the Polish Revolution, and, even more, his public lectures describing the sufferings of Poland at the hands of Russia, delivered in this country in 1842-4,[44] made him *persona non grata* in the eyes of the Russian Legation in Washington, still officially representing the interests of Kosciuszko's descendants. The Russian Minister, Alexander Bodisco, found it most difficult to reconcile Tochman's rights as a naturalized American citizen with the autocratic laws of Russia, according to which the Major was a criminal and a rebel. There seems to be no doubt that Bodisco transgressed some laws of this country and of the international code in trying to browbeat Tochman. The Minister questioned Tochman's right to represent subjects of Russia, though they happened to be descendants of Kosciuszko, and though their case was in the hands of American courts. Ignoring the usual method of communicating through the Department of State, Bodisco interfered with the orderly process of the law by addressing a letter directly to one of the judges of the Orphan's Court in Washington, which had jurisdiction over the case.[45] The Minister also attacked Capt. Ladislaus Wankowicz of the Russian army, sent to America as plenipotentiary by one group of Kosciuszko's descendants, and had his property in Poland confiscated when the Captain associated with Tochman.[46] Tochman twice appealed to the Department of State and directly to the White House for protection, but both Secretaries, Buchanan and his successor, Clayton, preferred not to interfere.[47] Congressman Lewis C. Levin of Pennsylvania, who smelled foreign intrigue everywhere, was the first to attack openly Bodisco in the forum of the House. He accused him of "preposterous exercise of authority," of an attempt to deprive an American citizen of his constitutional rights, of "rushing into an American court like a true Cossack" and "at the point of his spear, hurling Justice from her throne."[48]

---

44 Tochman, *Strike But Hear.*

45 Memorial of Tochman to Pres. Polk, March 19, 1847, Tochman, *Petition* of Dec. 1847, 28; *idem, Expose,* 30.

46 Memorial of Wankowicz to the U. S. Senate, Jan. 3, 1849, *30 Congress, 2d Sess., Senate Documents, Misc. No. 8,* pp. 1-3.

47 Buchanan to Tochman, Nov. 21, 1846, *31 Congress, 1 Sess., Executive Documents, No. 50,* p. 5; and Clayton to Philip R. Fendall, May 11, 1850, *ibid.,* p. 7.

48 *Congressional Globe,* 30 Congress, 1 Sess., House, June 5, 1848.

Other members of Congress seconded his attack, among them Senators Isaac P. Walker of Wisconsin and Henry S. Foote of Mississippi, both severely censoring Bodisco's behavior.[49] Tochman's most powerful ally was, however, Senator Reverdy Johnson of Maryland, a recognized authority on constitutional law, who not only stood in his defense, but also volunteered as a professional aid in carrying on the case of Kosciuszko's estate against Bodisco's highhandedness.[50] The dispute became so sharp that it led to a brawl between Bodisco and Wankowicz on the streets of New York[51] and to a violent exchange of insults and even to a challenge to a duel between the contesting lawyers.

The case ultimately came to an end in 1852, when the United States Supreme Court decided that as far as his property in this country was concerned, Kosciuszko died intestate, having revoked his will of 1798 by a clause in the will of 1816.[52] This will had been written by a professional lawyer employed by Kosciuszko and the invalidation of the American will was obviously against Kosciuszko's intent, — a fact which the Court itself admitted. "After my death, you know the fixed destination" of the money, he wrote to Jefferson a month before his death. In the opinion of the court, however, Kosciuszko's bequest for the freeing and educating of Negroes could not take effect, "because of the uncertainty of its dispositions and objects of the bounty." The court ordered the estate distributed among the grandchildren and great-grandchildren of two of Kosciuszko's sisters, Anna Estko and Catherine Zolkowska. It amounted to $37,924.40 plus interest since June, 1847, the date of the last account of the administrator, altogether about $50,000.[53]

The Armstrongs were not successful in vindicating their legacy. At one moment of the long legal struggle they succeeded in obtaining a decree, allowing them the bequeathed sum with interest, all in all about $10,000.[54] The Supreme Court, however, after first rejecting their appeal because of lack of probate,[55] ultimately voided Kosciuszko's will of 1806 as also revoked by the will of 1816.

The claims of the Zeltners to the whole American estate of Kosciuszko were also set aside as unfounded. The suit of the false pretender, Klimkiewicz, abated by his death. This, in brief, is the story of Kosciuszko's legacy for the benefit of colored people in America.

49 *Ibid.*, 31 Congress, 1 Sess., vol. XXI, part 1, pp. 964 and fol.

50 Johnson, *Remarks.*

51 Tochman, *Expose, passim,* and his *Supplemental Petition,* 1; cf. Kozłowski, *Spadki,* 34.

52 Howard, *Reports,* XIV, 400-434, Ennis et al. v. Smith et al.

53 "The Heirs of Kosciuszko," *Niles' Register,* Aug. 7, 1847, p. 368.

54 Tochman, *Petition* of Dec. 1847, 6—7; idem, *Supplemental Petition,* 36; idem, *Expose,* 25.

55 Peters, *Reports,* VIII, 52-74, Armstrong v. Lear; see also Wheaton, *Reports,* XII, 167, Armstrong v. Lear. A large collection of legal documents pertaining to the long litigation over Kosciuszko's estate is in the National Archives, Division of Justice Department Archives.

Though his intentions were not carried out, he nevertheless justly deserves the title of a pioneer of their emancipation.

Another financial matter mentioned in Jefferson's correspondence with Kosciuszko was the land grant for his services in the Revolution. Soon after his landing in Philadelphia in 1797, Kosciuszko was presented with a land warrant by a government official. According to the evidently incorrect reports of the press, the General in turn presented this warrant as a gift to a Welsh farmer, Thomas by name, who was a passenger on the Adriana, and "of whom he had received a high opinion."[56] The fact is that Kosciuszko showed little interest in the grant, at least while in America. The military lands distributed among the veterans of the Revolution were in sparsely settled western territories; had he chosen to remain in America, he would have preferred to live in one of the eastern States, near his friends, as he, in fact, indicated.

Evidently, however, Kosciuszko had left with Jefferson some oral dispositions concerning the grant. Sometime in 1800, or perhaps in 1799, Col. John Armstrong, one of Kosciuszko's former companions-in-arms,[57] located the land for him on the east side of the Scioto River, in what is now Perry Township, Franklin County, Ohio.[58] As a Colonel in the Continental Army, Kosciuszko was entitled to five hundred acres and accordingly Armstrong selected five one hundred acre lots.[59] President Adams signed the warrant for Kosciuszko on May 7, 1800.

"I have got your land warrant located and have received for you the patent for 500 acres of land on the Scioto river," wrote Jefferson to Kosciuszko. "I am informed they are fine lands, and I believe it the rather because they were located by Col. Armstrong who is well acquainted there and has done a great deal of business for others in consequence of his knowledge of the country. he refused to recieve anything for you for this service, saying he had done a great deal of duty with you & under you during our war, and was sufficiently rewarded by the pleasure of doing anything to serve you."[60]

---

56 *U. S. Gazette,* Sept. 6, 1797; also *Kentucky Gazette,* Sept. 27, 1797. Cobbett immediately made the most of the news and attacked Kosciuszko as a mercenary. "If a man fights for the sheer love of liberty," he wrote, "let him have the honour of it; but let him not enjoy this honour with the wages of a *mercenary* in his pocket . . . These fellows are all *Cincinnatuses,* if you believe their canting professions; but, when you come to the trial, you soon find that a coach and pair suits them better than a *plough.* The *tract of land,* you see, which you have furnished our liberty hero with a charming opportunity of becoming a *Cincinnatus,* he gave away as unworthy of his attention." (*Porcupine's Works,* VII, 114).

57 Not to be identified with Gen. John Armstrong, aide to Gates, author of the Newburgh Addresses and diplomat. According to Heitman, *Hist. Register,* 75, this John Armstrong came from North Carolina.

58 It extended from the Delaware County line well below the village of Dublin, on the opposite side of the Scioto (Galbraith, "Kosciusko Lands," *Ohio Mag.,* Nov. 19, 1907, pp. 325-329). See also: Wittke, *We Who Built America,* 419, note.

59 They were lots numbered 4, 7, 10, 18 and 19 of the second quarter of the second township in the nineteenth range of the military tract (Military Land Warrant No. 1219, Patent Records of the Gen. Land Office, vol. I, p. 188).

60 May 7, 1800, Libr. of Congress, Jefferson Papers.

At first Kosciuszko intended to rent the land to some deserving settlers on profitable terms. He answered Jefferson:

"I beg of you to send Thousands thanks from me to Colonel Armstrong for his goodnese, This land require som setlement. Can you procure one or more farmers of good reputation each for a Hundred acres. I should give them Land for nothing for five years on condition that after that terme will pay me the rente one procent Lesse than authers in that part of the Country, or upon any condition you thing proper."[61]

However, two years later he sold the land to Madame Louise Francoise Felix, a French emigrant, for nine thousand livres, and the act of sale was executed before the American Minister, Livingston, on July 29, 1802.[62] Immediately thereafter she sailed with her family for America and with the help of Jefferson and Armstrong reached the place.[63] In 1803 the land was surveyed for her by Samuel H. Smith, the cost of the survey being charged to Kosciuszko.[64] Soon, however, Madame Felix became dissatisfied. She complained of the poor soil, lack of water and of similar grievances, but Jefferson dismissed all of them as groundless.[65] This ends the story of "the Kosciuszko lands," the name of which has been preserved locally even to this day.

---

61 26 Thermidor (August 14), 1800, Mass. Hist. Soc., Jefferson Coll.

62 Polish R. C. U. Museum, Kosciuszko Papers, no. 59.

63 Jefferson to Armstrong, Dec. 21, 1802, Mass. Hist. Soc., Jefferson Coll.

64 S. H. Smith to Col. Thomas Worthington, Feb. 26, 1804, and Worthington to Jefferson, March 24, 1804, ibid.

65 Jefferson to Armstrong, July 12, 1803, ibid.

APPENDICES

A.

KOSCIUSZKO'S ACT OF INSURRECTION

(From *Dunlap and Claypoole's American Daily Advertiser,* August 22, 1794.)

The wretched state in which Poland is involved is known to the universe; the indignities offered by two neighboring powers, and the crimes of traitors to their country, have sunk this country into this abyss of misery. Catherine II, who in concert with the perjured William has sworn to extirpate even the name of Poland, has accomplished her iniquitous designs; there is no species of falsehood, or perjury, or of treason, which those governments have hesitated to commit, to satisfy their vengeance and their ambition. The Czarina, while she impudently promised to guarantee the entire possessions and the independence of Poland, has afflicted it with every species of injury; and when Poland, weary of bearing the shameful yoke, had recovered the rights of her sovereignty, she employed against her, traitors to their country. She supported their sacrilegious plots with all her military force, and having artfully diverted, from the defence of his country, the king to whom the diet had confided the National forces, she shamefully betrayed the very traitors themselves. By such arts, having made herself mistress of the state of Poland, she invited Frederick William to take part of the plunder, to recompense him for having broken a most solemn treaty with the Republic, under imaginary pretexts, whose falsity and impiety accord only with tyrants; but in fact to satisfy the boundless ambition of extending his tyranny, by an invasion of the adjacent nations.

These two powers, confederated against Poland, have violently seized the immemorial and incontestable possessions of the Republic; and for this purpose, have obtained, in a diet, convoked with this view, a forced approbation of their usurpations. They have compelled the subjects to take an oath, and to a state of slavery, by imposing on them the most grievous burthen, and acknowledging no law but their arbitrary wills, by a new language and unknown in the law of nations, have audaciously assigned to the existence of the Republick a rank inferior to all other powers, in making it appear every where, that the laws, as well as the limits of sovereigns depend absolutely on their caprices; and that they regard the North of Europe, as a prey doomed to the rapacity of their despotism.

But the remainder of Poland has not been able to purchase any amelioration of its fate, at the price of such cruel misfortunes. The Czarina, in concealing her ultimate designs, which must be prejudicial to the powers of Europe, in the mean time sacrifices Poland to her barbarous and implacable vengeance. She tramples under her feet the most sacred rights of the liberty, the safety, and property of citizens. Opinions and Freedom of thought in Poland find no shelter from her persecuting suspicions, and she attempts even to enchain the very speech of the citizens. None but traitors find any indulgence with her, and these are encouraged that they may commit every species of crimes. The property of the revenues of the public are becoming the prey of her rapacity. The property of our citizens has been seized; because the country was subdued, these plunderers have divided among them the charges of the Republic, that they might seize the spoil; and in usurping impiously the name of National Government, tho' the slaves of a foreign tyranny, they have done whatever their wills dictated.

The Permanent Council, whose establishment was imposed upon us by a foreign power, suppressed legally by the national will, and recently re-established by traitors, has by order of the Russian minister, overleaped the bounds of its power, which it has received with meanness from the same minister, in re-establishing, reforming, suppressing arbitrarily the constitutions which had just been framed and those which had been abolished. In a word, the pretended government of the nation, the liberty, the safety and property of the citizens are in the hands of the slaves of a servant of Czarina, whose troops deluge the country, and serve as a rampart to support these detestable men.

Borne down by an immense pressure of evils, vanquished by treachery, rather than by force of foreign enemies, destitute of all protection from the national government; having lost our country, and with her the enjoyment of the most sacred rights of liberty, of personal safety and of property; having been deceived, and becoming the derision of some nations, while we are abandoned by others; we citizens, inhabitants of the Palatinate of Cracow, by sacrificing to our country our lives, the only good which tyranny has not condescended to wrest from us, will avail ourselves of all the extreme and violent measures, that civic dispair suggests to us. Having formed a determined resolution to perish and entomb ourselves in the ruins of our country, or to deliver the land of our fathers from a ferocious oppression, and the galling yoke of the ignominious bondage, we declare in the face of Heaven and before all the human race, and especially before all the nations, that know how to value liberty above all the blessings of the universe, that to make use of the incontestable right of defending ourselves against tyranny and armed oppression, we do unite, in the spirit of Patriotism, of civism and of fraternity, all our forces; and persuaded that a fortunate issue of our arduous enterprize depends principally on our strict union, we renounce all the prejudices of opinion, which have divided or may still divide the citizens, inhabitants of the same territory, and children of one common country; and we pledge ourselves to each other to spare no sacrifices whatever, but on the other hand to use all the means which the sacred love of Freedom can inspire in the breast of man; all that despair can suggest for his defence.

The deliverance of Poland from foreign troops, the recovery of the entire possessions of the state, the extirpation of all oppression and usurpation, as well external as internal, the re-establishment of the national liberties and the independence of the Republic are the sacred objects of our insurrection. But to insure success to our undertaking, it is necessary that an active power should direct the national force. Considering attentively the actual situation of our country, and of its inhabitants, it appears necessary to resort to extreme and decisive measures; to wit, those of naming a commander in chief of the armed force of the nation, to establish a temporary Supreme National Council, a Commission of Good Order, a Supreme Criminal Court of Appeals, and a subordinate Criminal Court in our Palatinate. For this purpose, with the consent of the assembly, we ordain as follows:

1. We elect and declare by this act, Thaddee Kosciuszko sole commander in chief of all our armed forces.

2. The said commander in chief, shall immediately convene a Supreme National Council. We confide to his civic zeal the choice of the members, who shall compose it; and also to care of organizing the Council. The chief himself shall have a seat in the Council as an active member.

3. The organization of the armed force of the nation shall be entrusted solely to the chief; as also the nomination of military officers of every grade; he shall also employ his force against the enemies of his country, and of this actual insurrection. The Supreme National Council shall, without any delay, fulfill the orders and dispositions of the commander in chief, elected by the free will of the nation.

4. In case the chief Kosciuszko, by reason of sickness or otherwise, shall not discharge the duties of his important office, he shall name his lieutenant after having communicated for this purpose, with the Supreme Council; chief interim, and the Council shall appoint in the place of T. Kosciuszko, another commander in chief. In both cases, the supreme chief of the forces, not being immediately appointed by the nation, but by the Supreme Council, shall be subject to the orders of the said Council.

5. The Supreme Council shall have the care of the public treasury, for maintaining the forces and providing for the expences of the war; as also for supporting this insurrection. Therefore the Council is authorized to ordain temporary imposts, to dispose of all national property and funds, and to negociate loans in this or foreign countries. The same Council shall ordain the levy of recruits, shall furnish the national troops with every thing necessary for the war; arms, ammunition and clothing. They shall endeavor to procure a sufficiency of provisions for the nation and the army; maintain order; watch over the safety of the country; and removing all obstacles and disconcerting all plans prejudicial to our great object, they shall take care that public justice be administered with promptitude and energy. They shall endeavor to negociate with foreign powers for support and assistance. In short they shall endeavor to rectify public opinion, and rouse a national spirit, that Liberty and their country may become the most powerful incentives with all the Poles, to make the greatest sacrifices for the public good. These are the principal duties imposed on the Supreme National Council.

6. We create in our Palatinate a Commission of Good Order, by organizing it for the present in a particular manner. This Commission shall be among us, a single organ, a chief executive magistrate of the armed forces and Supreme Council. It shall be bound to execute all their orders and all their regulations, conformable to their powers. The Supreme Council shall prescribe immediately the organization and particular duties of this commission. We on our parts engage strictly to execute their decrees.

7. The Supreme Council shall prescribe the arrangement, the proceedings and the fixed principles of the supreme criminal jurisdiction, which shall sit near the Council.

8. As in the present circumstances, we cannot conveniently choose suitable persons to form the Supreme Criminal Tribunal except those of the Palatinate, therefore we charge the Council to make choice of judges from among the persons, who, by the last free territorial dietines and elections of the cities, were designated for those judicatures.

9. The Tribunal shall have cognizance of all crimes against the nation, and all proceedings contrary to the object of this sacred association, as also of all crimes against the safety of the country. All these crimes shall be punished with death.

10. We commit to the commander in chief of our armies, the power of establishing a Council of War, according to military rules and customs.

11. We reserve to ourselves most solemnly, by the act prescribed, that none of the temporary powers, we have now established, shall hereafter either separately or collectively form any of the acts which shall compose a national constitution. Every act of that nature shall be regarded by us, as a usurpation of national sovereignty, like that against which we are now struggling, at the hazard of our lives.

12. All the temporary powers created by the present act, shall exist in full force, until we have obtained the object of our present association, that is, until Poland shall be delivered from foreign troops, and of all armed forces, opposed to this our association; and until the entire possession of our territorial rights shall be secured. Of this the commander in chief and the Council shall be bound to notify the citizens, under the most rigid responsibility of their persons and property. Then the nation, assembled by its representatives, shall cause to be rendered an account of its labors and of the proceedings of the temporary authorities, and shall publish to the world their gratitude towards the virtuous children of their country, by recompensing their labor and sacrifices in proportion to their real services. Then they will decide on their future prosperity and that of the most distant generations.

13. We require the commander in chief of the forces and Supreme Council, to inform the nation, by frequent proclamations, of the true state of public affairs, without concealing or disguising the most disastrous events. Our despair is at its height; and the love of our country knows no bounds. The most cruel misfortunes, and the most insurmountable difficulties shall neither enfeeble nor discourage our virtue and civic valor.

14. We pledge ourselves to each other and to the whole nation, for our firmness in enterprize, for our fidelity to the principles, and our obedience to the national authorities, expressed and decreed in this act of association. We conjure the commander of our forces and the Supreme Council, by the love of their country, to employ all the means capable of delivering the nation and saving the Polish territories. By depositing in their hands the power of commanding our persons and our estates, during the combat of Liberty with despotism, of justice with oppression and tyranny, we desire that they may keep constantly in view this great truth, that THE SAFETY OF A NATION IS THE SUPREME LAW.

Done at Cracow, March 24, 1794, in an assembly of Citizens, inhabitants of the Palatinate.

(Here follows some thousands of signatures.)

Conformable to the original — GASPAR MECISZEWSKI,
Commissary of Good Order of the Palatinate.

DIAGNOSIS OF KOSCIUSZKO'S PHYSICAL CONDITION
BY BRITISH PHYSICIANS

(Library Company of Philadelphia, Ridgway Library, Rush Papers, 7246 F.39)

General Koscuoski received a wound at the lower part of the hind head, with a blunt Sabre, which both bruised, and most probably divided the Nerve, upon the right side that supplies the posterior portion of the Scalp with sensibility — Since that time the Scalp at the upper and the posterior part has been without feeling — The stroke of the Sabre, it is also probable produced some degree of concussion of the Brain, by which the General was rendered insensible for a short time after the accident, and has since been often subject to considerable pains in the head.

The effects of the Injury done by the wound on the head are gradually wearing off, and the Scalp will probably in time recover it's sensibility, tho, that we do not think a matter of much importance — It is of more consequence that while any pain is felt in the head, he should continue to live with great temperance, not drinking any wine that is not mixed with water and not eating of any thing that is heating or high-savoured.

He should further be attentive to the state of his Body, to procure daily the proper Evacuation; and for that purpose we recommend the continuance of the present opening Medicine of Sulphur and Cream of Tartar, which he has found to have the desired effect —

The Paralytic state of the Thigh and Leg is owing to another wound he received at the same time in the Hip, with a Cossack pike — This instrument had penetrated deep so as to divide, or injure extremely, the Sciatic Nerve, near the place where it passes out of the great Sciatic Notch.

The paralytic state of the Thigh and Leg, as well as the irregular action of the Bladder, are the consequence of this wound —

Nerves, which have been rendered useless in consequence of any external injury are capable of being restored more perfectly to their Functions, than Nerves which have become paralytic from internal causes —

It is a good while however, before Nerves which have received a great external injury begin to show signs of recovery at all —

The reason of it is this; that if Nerves have been lacerated or cut through by external violence, it is a considerable time before the injured parts are regenerated —

When they are fully regenerated the Nerves, recover their functions but by degrees, and more or less perfectly according to the magnitude of the original injury —

Their restoration to their Functions is greatly promoted by the following means, which we would recommend to General Koscioski,

1st The Limb should be exercised in every possible way, and that the General may more readily understand what we mean by this, we will shortly state what should be the management of it for one day — It should be rubbed well three times a day for twenty minutes or half an hour at a time — The rubbings will be more easy & perhaps more effectual from the use of a Liniment, and we have accordingly annexed a prescription for one — Besides rubbings with the hand for the time mentioned, the Flesh of the Thigh and Leg should be gently pressed between the hands, and all the Joints (the hip knee and Toes) should be bent, to give them their natural motion, and to preserve the pliability of the Limb — After each rubbing the General should try to move his Toes, his foot, his Leg and Thigh as much as possible, be it ever so little and should continue some time to repeat his efforts in this way.

These efforts and trials frequently repeated, contribute much to the gradual restoration of motion and strength in the Limb —

2d The recovery of Sense and motion of the Limb will probably be promoted by the use of tepid Bathing; nor do we apprehend at present any inconvenience similar to what the General experienced when he formerly made trial of it. But the Bath should be properly tempered, with the heat not exceeding ninety two degrees of Farenheit's Thermometer—

The General should not at first stay long in the Bath, but the time may afterwards be gradually encreased. He may begin with five minutes and by degrees go as far as half an hour—

It will be enough to bathe every other day and it is not material at what hour of the day the Bath is used — it may be either in the morning or Evening —

He should try to move and exercise the limb while in the Bath —

The Douche or pumping warm Water on the limb may likewise be tried, if a favorable opportunity offers—

3d Besides exercising the Limb in the manner directed, and using the tepid Bath, we would further recommend the use of Electricity to promote the restoration of the action of the Muscles.

The Electricity should be made to pass in gentle sparks, through the Muscles of the Legs and Thigh, so as moderately to excite their contraction — And this may be done everyday at any time that is convenient—

In exercising the Limb in bathing and in applying Electricity, we have one general caution to give, which is that none of these means be used so as to excite pain—

There is still considerable pain felt upon pressing on the part where the wound was received in the Hip, and there is also an acute pain that frequently shoots through the whole Limb to the Toes — these Symptoms probably indicate an imperfect restoration of the Nerve, and therefore the Friction and other means recommended, should be used with that moderation, that would not excite pain —

By following the plan we have laid down for the General, we are of opinion that he will probably recover in a considerable degree, the use of the Limb, but the progress will be slow, particularly at first, and this he must not be discouraged by —

We feel peculiar interest in the success of the plan above used — It gives us the most heartfelt satisfaction to think, that we may possibly contribute to the comfort of a man, whose Character and Exertions in behalf of his country, have called for the admiration of the whole civilized world.

Lond, 3d 6/97

G. Baker
J. Hunter
Wm Farquhar
M. Baillie
Gil Blane
Dav. Pitcairn
W— Saunders
T. Cline
T. Heate
Chilver

C.

THE JEFFERSON AND KOSCIUSZKO CORRESPONDENCE

(This correspondence covers the period from Kosciuszko's departure from America in 1798 till his death. Jefferson's letters have been published for the most part and only such of his letters, or parts of them, are being given in full here as have been omitted in various editions of his writings; all other letters are briefly summarized to give the reader proper understanding. References pertain to the full text, or printed parts of the text, of the letters in the editions of Jefferson's *Writings* by Henry A. Washington (9 vols., New York, 1853-1854), by Paul Leicester Ford (10 vols., New York, 1892-1899), and Andrew A. Lipscomb (20 vols., Washington, 1903-5). In 1879, Franciszek Paszkowski published a collection of Jefferson's letters to Kosciuszko, then in his possession, in a pamphlet: *Listy Jeffersona, Prezydenta Stanów Zjednoczonych Ameryki Północnej, do Kościuszki,* Kraków, 1879, 28 pp.; it contained several letters never before published in this country. With very few exceptions, Kosciuszko's letters to Jefferson are being printed here for the first time).

1. *Jefferson to Kosciuszko*

Philadelphia, June 1, 1798.

(Kosciuszko's departure not yet known. Niemcewicz much affected. Jefferson takes care of some of Kosciuszko's effects left on departure. Alien bill struggles for passage.)

(Washington, IV, 248; Lipscomb, X, 47)

2. *Jefferson to Kosciuszko*

Philadelphia, June 18, 1798.

I wrote to you my dear and respectable friend on the 30th of May (by Volney) putting it under cover, as I do this to our friend Jacob Van Staphorst, at Paris. Capt. Lee of the ship Adriana has brought for you as a present from the Whig Club of England an elegant Sabre, mounted in gold and inscribed "The Whig Club of England to General Kosciuszko" said to have cost two hundred guineas. Capt. Lee understanding according to the general opinion that you were gone to the medicinal springs in Virginia deposited it with me for you were I sure it would find you at Paris I would have sent it by this opportunity but it is a thing which ought not to be put to hazard. I will therefore wait your orders. it would be easiest for us to send it to Amsterdam to N. & J. Van Staphorst & Hubbard but this you will decide on. in the meantime I send you a letter which accompanies it. not a doubt is entertained here but that you are gone to the springs. our affairs continue to go on from bad to worse. if we can remain at peace this year, our citizens will see through the delusion of the present moment, and republicanism will be saved in this country. if we are invaded, an union comes on of necessity, with a power under whose auspices everything fatal to republicanism is to be apprehended. meaning to leave this place day after tomorrow, I had packed away my cypher with my papers which puts it out of my power to avail myself of that. I am anxious

137

to hear of you and from you never having heard a little since you left us. my sincere prayers for your health and life attend you & the most affectionate Adieux.

(Library of Congress, Jefferson Papers)

3. *Kosciuszko to Jefferson*

(Two letters written by Kosciuszko about July, 1798, and delivered to Jefferson by Gerry, are acknowledged in Jefferson's letter of Feb. 21, 1799 [no. 5]. Both are evidently lost.)

4. *Kosciuszko to Jefferson*

(Undated, but written about the beginning of October, 1798)

My dear Friend

The Amicable disposition of the Gouvernement of France are realy favorable to the interest of the United States, by the recent prouves they give, you ought not to doubt that they choose to be in pease and in perfect harmonie with America. before it was misrepresented by Some the facts relative to your Country, but now they are perfectly acquiented wyth yours and their interest and Mr. Logan eyewitnes of the Sentyment they have towards the Nation Of the United States. At present it is a duty of every true American as you, to publishe and propagate their friendship, and to Compele your Gouvernement by the Opinion of the Nation to the pacifique Mesures with Republique of France, otherwise you cannot but to loose every thing even your Liberty by a conexion so intimet wyth England which increasing son influence can easily subdue and exercise son despotique pouvoir as before. write me soon as possible of the effects which the news by Logans arrival will produce in America, as well of by the Election of the members for Congress, you may rely upon my indevours here but you most work in America wyth your friends and Republicans and (one word illegible) their reall interest. I will not hasard my Opinion concerning the affaires of different Nations of Europe. Mr. Logan, can give Some Scachess[1] as to my pecuniary affaires. I beg you would pay a friendly attention that I may receive punctualy my money here at Paris. inclosed I send a letters received from Amsterdam by which it apear that the money was returned to the Treasury long ago, but they had not inclination to pay me. now I beg you would receive from Mr. Wolcott and to send me immidiatly by Amsterdam to Paris. if you will find a difficulty to receive the money please to publishe thos letters that the public should know their Characters. if the sword which was ofered to me by Patriots in England arived in America be so good to Send me to Paris.

> Your for ever
> Sincier Friend
> T. Kosciuszko

The Compliments to all
my friends Matt
and fernell

(Mass. Hist. Soc., Jefferson Coll.)

---

1 He meant perhaps "sketches."

5. Jefferson to Kosciuszko

Philadelphia, February 21, 1799

My dear Friend

Your two letters by Mr. Gerry came to my hands not till Dec. 25. Mr. Gerry who arrived in September, delivered them to a person to bring to this place and here they were kept till I should arrive here which was expected to be the 1st of December at the meeting of Congress; but I did not come till the 25th of December, about 10 days after I recieved a third letter from you, without a date. Not knowing by what conveyance it came. we were then within a month of having your 2d dividend drawn. 6 int February. since that time river being frozen up, no vessel has sailed. this must account for the very long interval between your first letter & this answer, and even now we do not know of any vessel bound for Amsterdam; but as I leave this place in a few days, I write this letter and leave it with Mr. Barnes to be forwarded by the first conveyance.

Mr. Barnes into whose hands all the details of your affairs are confided, has drawn your two dividends of 480 Dollars each. he will therefore with this letter remit to Mr. Van Staphorst & Hubbard 1000 Dollars, including the proceeds of sales. we attempted to sell at auction some of the articles you left, such as kitchen furniture etc. and they sold for next to nothing. I therefore directed that such other articles as were of greater value should be estimated by some person of skill and sold at private sale. in this way your fur was valued by an honest furrier here at 25. Doll. according to the price of Martins here it would not have fetched 10 D. at vendue some silver spoons were sold at their weight. the table linen & some other articles will be attempted to be sold on valuation. but as your clothes could not be sold in any way, worth attention, and may be useful to yourself, I have directed them to be sent to Amsterdam. the freight will be trifling. as I had never seen Mr. Niemcewicz from the time I left this, last summer, I know nothing respecting your box of plate. I supposed he had accepted it answering to your desire. but the night before last he arrived here, and in conversation mentioned that he had left it in the care of Dr. Rush for you. I pressed him to take it, but he declined and yesterday delivered it to Mr. Barnes. I immediately examined it. it consisted of 4 candlesticks and a pr. of snuffers. 4 bottle slides, 2 goblets, 3 waiters and a bread basket with inscriptions on every article which could suit only yourself, and consequently that they could be sold only for the value of the metal, sacrificing the workmanship. I had them weighed and found they weighed 216 ounces which are worth here exactly so many French crowns of 6 livres as therefore it was nearly as convenient to remit them in this form as in that of money I determined they should go with the clothes to Amsterdam. there you can take them either as they are or sell to as great if not greater advantage. at the same time shall go the sword sent for you by the Whig Club of England. the whole will be shipped as your baggage to Van Staphorst & Hubbard. I have obtained from the Secretary of the Treasury a positive authority to Williams, Van Staphorst & Hubbard as bankers of the U. S. to pay you that part of your demand which has from misunderstandings been so long unreceived. it is for 7162 florins banco. I did very much wish to have recieved the money here and invested it in bank shares as it would have added near a fourth to your annual income from hence. but this could not be obtained. you will therefore consider this sum as an additional remittance now made, over & above the thousand dollars before mentioned. if you chuse to have it invested here Mrss. J. Staphorst & Hubbard can easily transmit it here, where it can be placed so as to bring in 8 per cent interest. I desire them to send you a copy of Mr Wolcott's letter. I am now, I think, through the whole of your affairs to this time, and Mr. Barnes will write you more in detail. he will also hereafter remit your dividend half yearly as it is received, to wit, in August & February.

(The rest of the letter pertains to the XYZ affair and to Jefferson's hopes for peace; it is reproduced in Lipscomb, X, 115, and Washington, IV, 294. The original is in the Library of Congress, Jefferson Papers).

6. *Kosciuszko to Jefferson*

15th of September (1799)

Dear Sir

I had the honor of receiving a letter from you dated the 25th of March,[2] with a bill from the Treasury of the United States for which I send you my best thanks. By your order came to my hands the first divident of the Pennsylvania Bank. Mr. Barnes has send me likwise two Cases loaded with my things, which are now upon the road to Paris. before I came from America Mr. Clay[3] has been appointed by me to acte as my proxy at the meeting of Stok Holders upon Pensylvania Bank. the desir of Mr. Barnes to be apointed in his place I refere to you you may do as you please because you have suficient Power from me. The Theatre of the World is of such kind that I cannot sai nothing in favor. Be so good howev to belive that my affection Friendship and Esteem for you will be everlasting.

T. Kosciuszko

(Archives and Museum of the Polish R. C. Union, Kosciuszko Papers, no. 10A).

7. *Jefferson to Kosciuszko*

May 7, 1800

My dear General

I have duly received your letter of Sept. 15 and with that pleasure with which I always hear of your health. Mr. Barnes remits by this conveyance to Mrss. Van Staphorst & Hubbard for you 1082 Dollars, being the last dividends. I have got your land warrant located and have recieved for you the patent for 500 acres of land on the Scioto river. I am informed they are fine lands, and I believe it the rather because they were located by Col. Armstrong who is well acquainted there and has done a great deal of business for others in consequence of his knowledge of the country. he refused to recieve anything for you for this service, saying he had done a great deal of duty with you & under you during our war, and was sufficiently rewarded by the pleasure of doing anything to serve you. I send you a plot of the land. — you know the fever in which you left us. All that is subsiding. the public opinion is running fast back into it's ancient and natural channel; within one twelvemonth from this time it will exactly what you & I would wish. Our great quadrennial election comes on in about 6 months even now there would be no question of it's result but that, from peculiar circumstances, there is danger that Pennsylvania will not

---

2 Evidently this endorsement pertains to the foregoing letter which Barnes had no chance to send earlier.

3 Perhaps Matthew Clay of Virginia, at that time a Republican member of Congress.

be able to give any vote. however, independent of that, a victory just obtained
by the republican party in the elections of New York is considered by both
parties as going far toward deciding the great election, even should Pennsylvania not obtain it's vote. An accomodation with France will entirely tran-
quilize our affairs.

(Library of Congress, Jefferson Papers)

8. *Kosciuszko to Jefferson*

(August 14, 1800)

My dear Sir

I have the honor to receive your letter of 7th of May in which you gave
me a notice of 1082. Dollars being the last dividents for me and that you send
over by Mr. Barnes likwise a skitch of my land. I beg of you to send Thousands
thanks from me to Colonel Armstrong for his goodnes, This land require som
setlement. Can you procure one or more farmers of good reputation each for a
Hundred acres. I should give them land for nothing for five years on condition
that after that terme will pay me the rente one procent lesse than authers in that
part of the Country, or upon any condition you thing proper. You have so
many friends her that I most beforehand pay you the first my respects as to
the President of the United States. I hope you will be the same in that new
station always good, true Americane a Philosopher and my Friend, it may hapen
under your helme I shall returne to America, but not otherwise. I do not see
a great difficulty for your self to make accomodation with France what I know.
I send you by this conveyance a new book to remember me by. accept my
thanks for the troubles I gave you and be assured of my friendship Esteem,
Consideration, respect and Constant love for ever Adieu

T. Kosciuszko

Paris 26 Thermidor
rue de Lille N 545
the peace kwite made with Austria
I have received a letter of exchange from Mr. Barnes for 1082 Dollars

(Mass. Hist. Soc., Jefferson Coll.)

9. *Kosciuszko to Jefferson*

(October 10, 1800)

Cher Ami

Enfin la Vertu triomphe si ce n'est pas encore dans le vieux du moins dans
le nouveau Monde. Le peuple de moeurs et d'un jugement solide appercoit
qu'il faut vous nominer pour être heureux et independant et il ne se trompe
pas. je joins mes voeux à la voix Generale. Souvenez vous apendant que le
premier Poste de l'état qui est toujours entouré des flateurs, des intrigants, des
hipocrites et des Gens mal pensants, soit environé par les Gens a Caracter a
talents honetes et d'une probite stricte, il faut que les places dans l'interieur
comme l'exterieur soyent occupées par les Gens a principe et d'une conduite ir-
reprochable jointe avec les connoissances et l'activité. et je vous recommande
pour Paris au lieu de Mr Muray[4] Mr. Barlow qui a tant des qualités que s'il

---

[4] William Vans Murray, Minister of the United States to the Batavian Republic and
Envoy extraordinary to the French Republic.

étoit votre Ennemi personel (qu'il en faut beacoup) je l'aurai tout de même recommandé a cette Place il à tout ceque vous souhaiteriez dans une personne pour cette poste importante pour vous. Les Gens de l'elle trempe vous aideront dans votre grand travaille pour le bonheur de votre Pays; ne Vous vous oubliez pas a votre poste soyez toujours vertueux Republicain avec justice et probité san faste et ambition en un mot soyez Jefferson et mon ami

T. Kosciuszko

Paris 18. Vendemiaire An. 9
rue de Lille N 545

(Mass. Hist. Soc., Jefferson Coll.)

10. *Jefferson to Kosciuszko*

Washington, March 14, 1801

(Barnes converts part of Kosciuszko's funds into a government loan. Jefferson hails the return of citizens to the principles of '76, but complains that Kosciuszko's letters are too barren of details concerning himself. Jefferson expects Kosciuszko will empower him to buy land for the General in his neighborhood).

(Lipscomb, XIX, 122; Paszkowski, 11).

11. *Kosciuszko to Jefferson*

Sir

J'ai eu l'honneur de recevoir votre lettre par Mr Dauwson, y trouvant les expressions de votre bonté pour moi et les peines que vous vous donnez sans cesse pour mes affaires; je les grave au fond de mon Coeur à jamais vous promettant ma sincere reconoissance. Je felicite les Etats Unis de l'amerique sur le Chois qui ont fait dans votre personne pour leur President; Il n-y aura plus de doute, que Republicanisme doit être inseperable avec l'honneteté, probité et la justice stricte, et que l'homme doit être plus honoré par ses vertues et ses Connoissances que par son luxe. Votre discours à jamais memorable a fait la plus grande impression en Europe, les hommes mêmes de l'opinion contraire ont admire, ils pretendent seulement que des si belles promesses ne serot pas effectuees en realité.

Sachant bien votre facon de penser, Votre Genie, votre habilité, vos connoissances, votre Caracter, et votre bon Coeur; j'ai fait taire les uns et j'ai tranquilisé les autres. Je suis faché que plusieures livres trés curieux que je vous ai envoyes ne vous sot pas parvenus. A l'egard de mois je crois que cette anneé j'yrais vous admirer et deposer apres mes cendres sur une terre de liberté, ou il y a des meures l'honettes et la justice.

Agreez Les assurances d'admiration de mon estime et de mon respect.

(Undated, but evidently written in 1801, and endorsed by Jefferson as received on April 24. Mass. Hist. Soc., Jefferson Coll.)

12. *Kosciuszko to Jefferson.*

(This letter of 25 Frimaire [December 15, 1801], in which Kosciuszko asks Jefferson to secure places for officers of the Polish Legions in the U. S. Army, is evidently lost).

13. *Jefferson to Kosciuszko*

Washington, April 2, 1802

(Jefferson informs Kosciuszko that the United States is reducing its army and there is no possibility of employing Polish officers. The session of Congress is drawing to a close. Besides reducing the army, Congress reduced also the number of civil offices. These economies permitted the suppression of all internal taxes. The internal political situation is becoming calm).

(Lipscomb, X, 309; Washington, IV, 430)

14. *Kosciuszko to Jefferson*

Inclosed I have the honor to send to you from Mr. Pougens. Permit me Sir to recomend to you his desires, you know his merit and his talents. Accept my best wishes and be convinced of my sincier friendship and respect

T. Kosciuszko

rue de Province N 43

(Undated, but endorsed by Jefferson: October 5, 1802. Boston Public Library. The letter of Pougens which evidently was enclosed, is now in the Library of Congress, Jefferson Papers. It is an offer of books for sale).

15. *Kosciuszko to Jefferson*

Je sai que vous avez tres grande influence dans votre pays par votre Caracter, vos talents, vos lumieres, et par votre Poste mais c'est une juisance pour vous seulement, votre Pays ne tire pas aucun avantage. Si vous ne vous exercéz pas à faire un solide et durable bien pour la Nation entiére, durant votre Pouvoir; Vous voulez avoir toujours votre Gouvernement Républicain mais ou sont les materiaux pour soutenir la même opinion surtout apris votre mort. si vous ne donnez pas a votre jeunesse une éducation propre, si vous ne veuillez pas sur tous les écoles civiles, si vous ne prescrivez les principes uniforme et conforme au Gouvernement d'aujourdhui si vous establissez encore dans chaque Province une Ecole Militaire d'ou les sujets sortant pour etre Officiers de la milice ajouteront encore plus de paix par leur conaissance et leur lumieres a cette haut idée d'etre Republicain vertueux autrement je ne vous responds de rien. Un homme d'Etat comme vous et surtout avec ses disposition et ses lumieres doit chercher a donner a sa nation unité d'action et d'etablir un Caracter respectable et puissant que jusq'a presant on ne le voi pas, et vous etes en état de la faire, si vous agissez avec fermeté dans les circonstances d'aujourdhui ou tout vous favorisent. mais il faut se decider vite et si vous envoyez des troupes pour prendre la posession de la floride, vous donerez à toutes les puissances une haute idée de votre nation et de son Caracter, et on s'impressera de faire une Alliance avec vous. Si vous manguez cet unique moment, vous perdrez tous les fruits pour toujours, et soyez persuadé qu'on vous reprocherat n'avoir pas profiter, de n'avoir rien fait pour votre pays, de negliger les moyens que votre influence vous donnait, de grace ne soyes pas indecie, agissez avec une energie et fermeté analogue a un Grand Homme que vous devez l'être. pardonnez moi si j'ecris avec trop de liberté mais mes sentimens sont sinceres pour

vous je vous aime vous êtes un seule espoir pour l'umanité entiere et je voudrai
que vous soyez l'Exemple a l'age future mes respects et mes homages

T. Kosciuszko

(Undated; endorsed by Jefferson as received Nov. 15, 1805; Mass. Hist.
Soc., Jefferson Coll.)

16. *Kosciuszko to Jefferson*

Sir

Permetez moi de vous recommander Mr Neef Professeur; il va à Phila-
delphie pour tenir une école d'après le Sisteme de Pestalozi ayez le bonté de
la protéger. La marche de Pestalozi dans son éducation Elémentaire de la jeunesse est; de suivre exactement la Nature c.v.d. de parler aux yeux de l'enfant,
ce que le frape de nomer l'objet, en suite de faire observer sa forme, sa pro-
prieté, son usage etc. etc. par la il forme son jugement et augmente sa memoire;
vous voyez par la que l'enfant de Pestalozi suivant par la proportion a ces
forces intellectuelles peut devenir habile dans toutes les sciences et dans peu de
tems vous me devez plusieurs letters en réponse des miennes, ce pendant soyez
persuade de mon attachment le plus sincere et de mon amitié la plus constante.
faites moi l'honneur d'agreer mes Sentimens de la haute Consideration.

T. Kosciuszko

Paris 10 Mars.

(Evidently written in 1806. Mass. Hist. Soc., Jefferson Coll.)

17. *Kosciuszko to Jefferson*

Citoyen President

Par Mr Foulton allant en Amerique vous recevrez la presante dans la
quelle je vous exprime du fond de mon Coueur l'estime le respect et l'amitie
Sincere, ces Sentiments de Conviction dureront autant que vous fairez bien
pour l'humanitê et que vous agirez comme a present avec l'admiration univer-
selle recevez en meme tems les Assurances de ma haute Consideration de mon
respect et de mon attachement invariable   T Kosciuszko

24 Avril. Paris

(Evidently written in 1806. Mass. Hist. Soc., Jefferson Coll.)

18. *Kosciuszko to Jefferson*

Je profite d'un moment avant le depart de Mr Monroe pour exprimer
mes Sentimens d'une Amitié Sincere pour Vous — et donner mon opinion
dans peu des mots sur une Contestation de votre Pays avec l'Espagne — Par
une attention bien refléchée tout homme conviendrat que vous ne pouvez éviter
mais éloigner seulement l'Epoque de la guerre avec elle — que soit peut être
une autre puissance dans un tems propre a elle séconderat ses vue avec les
siennes dans une pai profonde, avec des Alliances uniantées, contre vous interets; et que deja votre grandeur naissante donne beaucoup d'ombrage a vos
voisins. vous serez ruiné — mais si vous saississez les circonstances presentes qui
vous donnent tout l'avantage possible sur vos Ennemies; regardez devant vous

toutes les puissances de l'Europe qui sont occupes de garder leur Existances je peu prononcé de votre reusite—mais il faut se decider promptement, agir avec celerité, et un grand vigeur, et quand on vous verrat agir avec un ferme Caracter, on chercherat votre alliance par preference je vous repond — ne vous trompez pas cela pusilanimitè et indécision qui abime les États, mais non pas leur valeur et leur ferventé Vous etes seule a qui on peut dire la verité — de grace ayez donc soin de votre pays de son bonheur et de votre reputation, jè n'entre pas dans les details elles sont dans la bouche de notre comun Ami — Je vous conseillerai aussi d'etablir les Censeurs pour les Ecoles Civiles prés dans les membres du Congrés, pour donner plus des principes republicaines dans votre jeunesses. — je serai aussi d'avis de former une Ecole militaire pour sixcent persones riches et pauvre par moitié ce serat un pepiniére pour toutes les Connoissances necessaires pour votre pays. Car ne soyez jamais en arrière dans les Connoissances de l'Europe et qu'aucun decouverte ne vous échape pas — faitez encore élevé vos juges et vos Magistres par les Membres du Congres, pour diminuer l'influence dun president apres vous car vous devez penser que le President ne doit être plus que le premier Oficier exécutif rien autre chose et alors vous serez Imortel. Agreez mes Homages et mon Amitié

T Kosciuszko

(Undated, but evidently written in 1807. Mass. Hist. Soc., Jefferson Coll.)

19. *Jefferson to Kosciuszko*

Washington, May 2, 1808

("During the present paroxysm of the insanity in Europe, we have thought it wisest to break off all intercourse with her." Seaports are put into a state of defense, but a bill providing an enlargement of militia has been put off to the next session of Congress. The regular army is being augmented).

(Lipscomb, XII, 44; Washington, V, 281).

20. *Jefferson to Kosciuszko*

Washington Feb. 25, 09

My dear friend

This will be handed you by Mr. Coles[5] the bearer of public despatches by an Aviso, who has lived with me as my Secretary being one of my wealthy neighbors. I will say nothing to you on the Situation of our country because his intimate knoledge of our affairs, and the unreserved confidence you may repose in him will enable you to learn from him whatever you desire. he is worthy your friendly attentions & I ask them for him. he will particularly state to you the difficulties to which we are reduced by the very trying measure of the embargo, rendered necessary by the edicts of the belligerents against our Commerce. the loss of fifty millions of exports annually is become more intolerable than war, which would not cost us the third of that & we should take something from our enemies. if therefore these edicts are not repealed before the meeting of congress in may, war must probably be declared. Can you by consultation with bankers or Merchants tell us how in that event we

---

5 Edward Coles, "a most worthy, intelligent and well-informed young man" (Jefferson to Dupont de Nemours, March 2, 1809—Lipscomb, XII, 259).

are to remit your quarterly dividends from hence. perhaps it may be more easy for you to sell bills on Mr Barnes than for him to get Bills in Europe. he is at present in a bad state from a fall which has entirely, tho I hope only temporarily disabled his right arm, so that he will not be able to write you by this Occasion. his life is precious to us both, as another agent so faithful & so punctual could not be found.

I am within a few days of retiring to the shades of Monticello for which I have been long panting. there at length I hope I shall find rest and happiness among my family, my friends, my farm and books. you talked once of becoming a neighbor. it would add more to my happiness than I believe to yours. persons long accustomed to the Society and excitements of large Cities languish under the monotony of a country life. God bless you my dear General & give you happiness as long as you have life & life as long as you wish it.

Th. Jefferson

(Mass. Hist. Soc., Jefferson Coll.; Paszkowski, 12).

21. *Jefferson to Kosciuszko*

Monticello, February 26, 1810.

(In the first part of the letter Jefferson rejoices that, as a private citizen again, he can write freely. He gives a very detailed description of the preparedness of the country for an eventual war during the last years of his administration. He then describes his private life).

From this portion of my personal condition, I must turn to another of unpleasant hue, and apologize to you for what has given me much mortification. for some time before I retired from the government I anxiously endeavored to have all outstanding accounts called in, & no new ones contracted, that I might retire, at least without any embarrasment of debt. Wholly occupied with the care of the public affairs, I was obliged to trust to others for that of my own: and in the last moments of my stay in Washington, notwithstanding my precautions, accounts came in in a mass so overwhelming as to exceed all my resources by ten or twelve thousand Dollars. a friend accomodated me readily with a considerable part of the deficiency, to be reimbursed out of the first proceeds of my estate. while sunk in affliction as to the residue, mr Barnes suggested that the public were paying off the whole of the 8. percent stock, that he had not yet recieved yours of that description, or reinvested it in any other form: that he had thought of placing it in bank stock, but, he supposed, if I should pay you an interest equal to the dividends on bank stock, it would be indifferent to you from what hand your profits came: & that the 4500. D. of yours then disengaged, would entirely relieve my remaining deficiency. the proposition was like a beam of light; & I was satisfied that were you on the spot to be consulted the kindness of your heart would be gratified, while recieving punctually the interest for your own subsistence, to let the principal be so disposed of for a time, as to lift a friend out of distress. I therefore gave mr Barnes a proper written acknolegement of the debt, & he applied your 8 percent principal to the closing of my affairs. I was the more encouraged to do this, because I knew it was not your intention to call your capital from this country during your life, & that should any accident happen to you, it's charitable destination, as directed by the paper you left with me, would not be at all delayed. I have set apart an estate of 3000 D. a year which I have at

146

some distance from Monticello, & which is now engaged in reimbursing what was furnished by the friend I alluded to. it will be nearly accomplished by the close of this year. two more years will suffice for the residue of that, & yours; when this part of your funds can again be invested in some of the monied institutions. the diversion of it from them for 4. or 5. years, will in the mean time have saved me. but the affliction is a sore one, & needs the solace of your approbation.

(Libr. of Congress, Jefferson Papers; the beginning and the end of the letter in Lipscomb, XII, 365; Washington, V, 506; the whole letter in Paszkowski, 14).

22. *Kosciuszko to Jefferson*

Mon digne Ami

Il est vrai que jai eu rarement tres rarement l'honneur de recevoir de vos lettres, qui même etaient sèches et courtes, aussi ai je negligé de vous écrire craignant d'etre importun. il me repugnait, je l'avoue, de vous ranger au nombre des hommes, qui changent de sentiment en raison des circonstances — Pardonez moi maintenant si mon amitie aussi assembleé se refroidire; mais soyez persuadé que mon estime à toujours été la même, car je n'ai jamais cesse d'être convaincu que personne plus que vous, ne reunit aux qualites naturelles et acquises, un desinteressment plus parfait et generalement plus de dispositions propres, a consolider la République et rendre l'Etat plus florissant — Pendant tout le tems de votre Presidence jai complettement ignoré ce qui se faisait chez vous et tout le monde ici était surpris, que je ne recusse aucune de vous nouvelles; mais peut être me supposiez vous imprudent. nonobstant tout, la derniere lettre que vous avez eu la bonté de m'écrire m'afait grand plaisir; j'y ai lu avec le plus vif intérêt le détail de vos faits — Un homme d'État tel que vous fixe naturallement son attention en grand, sur tous les objets qui peuvent rendre son gouvernement stable et assez fort pour agir contre les ennemis, interieurs et exterieurs, juste envers tous, et procurant le bonheur et la tranquillité au plus grand nombre possible de ses habitants — Votre idee est très juste d'Enregimenter la jeunesse partout; j'ajouterai seulement depuis l'age 18. jusqa 45 ans, Pourquoi aussi ne pas former une force de Milice assez suffisante pour tous les accidents et qui pourvoit faire même le service dans les forts, plutot que de soufrire un corps régulier tel petit quel soit; Car il faut toujours craindre l'embition d'un President, qui avec l'influence de l'argent, des dignites, peut aisement changer l'Etat des choses en sattachant ces corps réguliers. Les examples ne sont pas rares, et disons franchement une triste et dure vérité, c'est qu'on peut corrompre presque tous les hommes; nous aimons si passionement d'être distingues des autres que nous saissons les moindres faveur de la fortune pour nous elever au-dessus deux. Pour parer a cet inconvenient il me semble que vous n'auriez besoin que de l'Ecole militaire mais augmanteé jusqu'au nombre de *3000* composé de jeunes gens de toutes vos provinces, sous l'inspection immediatte du Congrés, et dont on choisirait d'apres examen les individus propre a être Officiers dans la Milice et dans le Corps d'artillerie qui seule doit être toujours sur pié a raison de l'exercice continuel qui'l exige — Je serais d'avis qu'on fit chez vous ce que je voulais faire dans mon Pays cest-a-dire une marque de distinction Republicaine. Un Bonet en or, en argent en fer appliqué sur l'habit comme il se pratique en Europe pour les Crachats, mais pour d'autres choses par exemple pour ceux qui auroient prouvés plus d'attachement et dé-

147

vouement au Gouvernement Republicain, plus d'Equité, de Probité, de desin-
terressement, d'Amour pour ses parents; Pour la découverte dans les Arts, dans
les Sciences et surtout dans l'Agriculture; Enfin pour toutes les vertus et qualites
Sociales qui seules doivent nous distinguer les un des autres.

J'approuve tout ce que vous avez fait avec mon fond j'ai toute ma confiance en vous; je demande seulement que l'interêt soit payé regulierement, et
desirerais beaucoup qui'il fut possible de l'envoyer par d'autre voie que par
Angletere, car de cette maniere je perds beaucoup et je ne sui pas riche.

Je vous embrasse de tout mon coeur.

Agreez mes sentiments d'Amitié d'Estime et de la Consideration la plus
distinguee   T. Kosciuszko

1 Mars 1811
(Mass. Hist. Soc., Jefferson Coll.)

23. *Jefferson to Kosciuszko*

Monticello, April 13, 1811.

(Notwithstanding the difficulty of preserving neutrality, the country remains in peace and continues to prosper. Its financial situation is good. Spanish
America is all in revolt).

(Lipscomb, XIII, 40; Washington, V, 585; Paszkowski, 18).

24. *Jefferson to Kosciuszko*

Monticello, May 17. 11
Dear General:
I have written you a long letter by mr Barlow & in that inclosed you one
from mr Barnes covering a bill of exchange for £200. sterling. referring to that
for all other things, the object of the present is merely to inclose the second
of the same bill of exchange, and to get it put under the cover of the Secretary
of State's dispatches. I shall seek a third opportunity of sending the third, or
get mr Barnes to do it, in order to multiply the chances of one of them getting
safely to you. ever affectionately yours

Th. Jefferson
Gen'l Kosciuszko

(Mass. Hist. Soc., Jefferson Coll., in Polish translation: Paszkowski, 21).

25. *Jefferson to Kosciuszko*

Monticello July 8. 11
My dear General and friend
I recieved your letter of Mar. 1. by our yesterday's post and by it's return
of to-day I hasten a word of answer in the hope it may reach Mr Barlow &
Mr Warden[6] before they actually sail, which they are to do in the course of
the week. it is principally to answer on a single point. you have thought my
letters, while in office, rare, short & dry. they certainly were so. but it was

---

6 D. B. Warden, a businessman who lived in Paris and met with little financial success; "Perfectly good-humored, inoffensive man, a man of science" (Jefferson to Madison,
Dec. 8, 1810, Lipscomb, XIX, 177).

purely from the fear that my correspondence might bring on you the suspicions or censure of the government under which you were living. it would have delighted me to have detailed to you from time to time, our measures and our views; because I know that no one felt a livelier interest in our welfare: but I know that my letters might fall into the hands of the English & be published, or into those of the French government who might make you responsible for what I wrote. I reserved therefore a free communication until I should be a mere private citizen, and made it fully in my letter of Feb. 26 of the last year, which I am rejoiced to hear you have received. from a fear that you had not, I enclosed a duplicate of it in mine of Apr. 16 of the present year, which has been ever since that date in the hands of mr Barlow & mr Warden, & I suppose will get to your hands at the same time with this.

I will write to mr Barnes to attend specially hereafter to your wish of recieving your remittances otherwise than thro' London. I am sorry that of the present year had been previously invested in a London bill & inclosed to you. I have recommended specially to mr Barlow to consider whether an exchange of funds here & there might not be an accomodation to him as well as you.

I thank you most particularly for the last paragraph of your letter. it has relieved me from a load of uneasiness which rested on my mind till I could recieve your approbation of what I had done. nothing shall be so sacred to me as a regular paiment of the interest: and should your situation require at any time an anticipation of it, and the means occur of turning a draught on me to account, it shall always be punctually honored, accept the assurances of my unchanged affections & respect

Th. Jefferson

(Mass. Hist. Soc., Jefferson Coll., in Polish translation in Paszkowski, 21).

26. *Kosciuszko to Jefferson*

Mon cher Aristide

J'ai eu l'honneur et le sensible plaisir de recevoir vos deux lettres et celle de Mr Barnes avec une lettre d'exchange. En les relisant dans ma solitude: (car je suis à la campagne a 16 lieux de Paris prés Fontainbleau:) J'ai vu que vous avez fait beacoup pour la sureté de votre Pays et beaucoup pour les connoissances dans tous les genres nécessaires. Mais qui me dira positivement que votre Gouvernement Républicain durerat long tems; Si l'education de la jeunesse n'est pas établie sur la base fixe des principes Republicaines sur la morale et la justice, et Surveillé par le Congrés même afin qu'aucun Professeur ne puisse s'en ecarter. Vous savez que les enfants sont plus susceptibles d'une impression solide et durable, que l'âge mure ou l'intérêt parle avec tant de force qu'aucune autre considération le plus honorable ne l'emporte pas; C'est dans cet âge tendre que se grave mieux tous les devoires de la société et envers sa Patrie, C'est de cette Education que vous devez espérer d'avoir les plus grands défensseurs de votre Pays et les Soutiens du Gouvernement Républicain. Vous ne devez pas attendre autant des Villes maritimes corrompues par le commerce étranger et par l'opulence, ils seront s'ils ne sont déjá pour le Gouvernement Monarchique. Vos estimables Quakkers ne feront rien ils sont les hommes Moreaux mais non pas Citoyens. Votre véritable force consiste dans les habitants de l'intérieurs ou il-ya des moeurs des vertus sociales susceptibles de grandeur d'Ame et de générosité si vous renforciez ces qualites par une education strictement surveillér alors votre but sera rempli, et vous verez sortir de votre Pays autant de Héros que de la Grece et plus sages que de Rome.

Je vous embrasse tendrement et agreez l'assurance des Sentiments d'Estime, d'attachement et de haute Consideration que je vous ai voues pour la vie

T. Kosciuszko

1 Fevrier 1812 a Berville
Adressez vos lettres pour moi
a Mr Hottinger a Paris

(Mass. Hist. Soc., Jefferson Coll.)

27. *Jefferson to Kosciuszko*

Monticello, June 28, 1812.

(War with England broke out. In the last thirty years the country grew prosperous and gained much strength and now enters the war under very favorable auspices. From the economical point of view it is self-sufficient, and to prove it, Jefferson describes his own estate. The addition of Canada "must be a *sine qua non* at a treaty of peace.")

(Ford, IX, 361; Lipscomb, XIII, 168; Washington, VI, 67; Paszkowski, 23).

28. *Jefferson to Kosciuszko*

Monticello Aug. 5. 12.

Dear General

I wrote you a long letter of June 28. in which I inclosed you a bill of exchange for 5500. francs by duplicate, the 1st of which had been inclosed to you by mr Barnes. the object of the present letter is merely to forward the triplicate of the same bill, to guard against accidents, as the dangers of the sea are somewhat increased by the war in mine of June 28. I omitted to mention that I had received yours of Feb. 1.

(Americans entered Canada. Privateers are busy on the sea and cutting up "more of the commerce of England than all the navies of Europe.")

(Library of Congress, Jefferson Papers. The second part of the letter reprinted in Lipscomb, XIII, 182; Washington, VI, 77; Paszkowski gives the whole letter, p. 26).

29. *Kosciuszko to Jefferson*

(This letter of Dec. 1, 1812, is evidently lost; Jefferson acknowledges its receipt in his letter of Nov. 30, 1813 [no. 31]; the following is its duplicate).

30. *Kosciuszko to Jefferson*

Paris, mai 30, 1813.

Mon Cher Ami,

Je vous remercie pour les détails que vous me donnez sur votre patrie. Je vois que votre génie, votre prudence et votre attachement pour elle a tout préparé d'avance pour sa sureté. Les operations militaires sont faciles maintenant.

La guerre juste que vous avez commencée contre l'Angleterre ne pout pas effrayer, il en serait de même contre toute autre puissance qui ne voudrait point agir avec sur le pied d'égalité de nation à nation. Votre pays est riche, grand et peuplé; vos habitants sont bons, actives, et courageux. Mais ne soyez point trop ambitieux d'acquérir tout le Canada, trop de sécurité vous amollira; je serais d'opinion que votre ligne de démarcation fut de quelque point du lac Champlain ou de la rivière St. Laurent jusqu'à la mer du Sud afin que vous n'ayez rien aux autres puissances derrière vous. Je ne doute pas ques vos dispositions militaires ne soyent sagement combinées et prêtes à secourir les divers corps d'armée, d'après la connaisance générale du pays, de vos nationaux et par celle de la direction des forces de vos ennemis. Je pense aussi qu'il soit utile de se servir de beaucoup d'artillerie légère à pied et à cheval, car vos bois ne sont pas serrés et la promptitude de l'artillerie pour se porter ou il est nécessaire, décide souvent du gain de la bataille.

L'approvisionnement suffisant de l'armée est le premier besoin, vient ensuite la sévérité de la discipline, points sur lesquels personne ne disputerait pas. A l'égard de vos généraux il importe d'en faire un bon choix. L'activité, la prudence et un attachement non douteux pour leur patrie doivent être préferés à d'autres qualités et surtout exclure de cet emploi tout homme intéressé. Que vos généraux attaquent toujours les premiers vos ennemis et sur deux points, s'il est possible. Punissez sévèrement la surprise, par là vous inspirerez la confiance aux habitants et une grande circonspection aux militaires. Je suis jaloux des améliorations que vous faites dans votre propriété et par là de l'exemple que vous donnez à vos compatriotes, tant qu'à moi je ne fais rien loin de ma patrie, vous en savez sans doute la raison, je reste dans l'inaction et ne suis d'aucun service pour l'humanité. Je vous embrasse de toute mon âme T. Kosciuszko.

Vous me rendez un grand service en s'aarangeat avec Mr. Morton à qui je dois des remerciements pour la manière la plus obligeante que j'ai été traite à Paris, et par l'exactitude de son correspondant.

(Archives and Museum of the Polish R. C. Union, Kosciuszko Papers, no. 65).

31. *Jefferson to Kosciuszko*

Monticello, Nov. 30, 1813

(A long letter on the disappointing course of the war ending with a warm tribute to Kosciuszko).

(Lipscomb, XIX, 200).

32. *Kosciuszko to Jefferson*

(This letter of Jan. 24, 1814, has been lost; it is mentioned in Jefferson's letter to Kosciuszko of June 28, 1814 [no. 34], and in Barnes' letter to Kosciuszko, dated April 28, 1815, the original of which is in the Alderman Libr., "Edgehill" Randolph Papers).

33. *Kosciuszko to Jefferson*

Mon Cher Ami

Je Crois que nous souffrons tout deux cette Année Vous par l'Angleterre et moi par vous, Car je nai pas touché les interets de ma petite somme placée chez vous, pour l'année passée de 1813. et dont cependant jaurais un grand besoin. Je connois que la Guerre a pu empecher les communications avec la France, Mais tâchez de m'envoyer par l'Angleterre ou par la Hollande.

Je vous embrasse mille fois avec toute mon Amitié et mon Estime

Sincere   T Kosciuszko

Paris 15. Mai 1814.

(Mass. Hist. Soc., Jefferson Coll.)

34. *Jefferson to Kosciuszko*

Monticello June 28. 14

My dear friend & General.

Your letter of Jan. 24. has been recieved and has realised the fears we had for some time entertained that you would be suffering from the failure of the annual remittance from hence. mr. Barnes had been constant in his endeavors to find some channel of remittance: but from the embargo & blockade and consequent cessation of nearly all intercourse with Europe, it had been absolutely impracticable. the medium of mr Morton, with which you had been so well contented, was particularly pressed on his correspondent here, and had failed, as well as other public and private channels which he tried. he has availed himself of the first moment we heard of the peace between France & England to procure a remittance thro' the latter country; and now forwards a bill of exchange for £400. sterl=1644.D.44.c. drawn by Boice & Kurtz on Wm Murdoch of London at 60. Days sight. this bill he has endorsed to Messrs Barrings brothers & co. of London; to whom I have written urgently to remit the proceeds to you as speedily as may be.

The abuse of the institution of banks in this country by their infinite multiplication, and the immense mass of paper they have thrown into circulation beyond the competent amount, has brought on a great depreciation of their paper, and imminent danger that all will blow up and end in universal bankruptcy. and as the particular moment, like that of the day of judgment, cannot be foreseen, but, when it comes, involves incuverable loss, I thought I owed it to your friendship & confidence, to attend to the danger in time, and secure you against a total loss of your capital. it happened fortunately too, that the US. opened a loan at the same time, the permanent security of which is beyond that of any other deposit, I believe, in the world; and altho' the annual interest they give is less than the bank profits, yet as we found we could get an advance of 38 per cent on the original amount of your bank stock, so as to increase your capital of 8000. D. in the Pennsylvania bank to upwards of 11,000 D. in the funds of the US. the smaller rate of interest on a capital so much enlarged, will be something more than equivalent to the larger profit on a smaller capital, in bank stock. I accordingly directed mr Barnes to subscribe 10,000 D. for you in the loan of the US. and to sell out your bank stock. this he had effected, and after the operation should be completed, and the balance remaining on hand, after paying the subscription of 10,000 D. shall be known, the surplus also shall be invested in the same loan by a purchase of it's stock. you will experience no difference in your present income; but should you chuse to recieve the capital at the epoch of paiment, it will be of about 11,000 D. instead of 8000. and on the whole I am in hope you will approve the transfer, as well for it's ultimate profit as it's permanent security.

Great events, my dear friend, have happened at Paris. I hope and believe they will be for the benefit of the world in general, and I especially wish they may be so to your country, & to yourself personally. how they will operate on us is doubtful, but we have minds prepared to meet anything rather than dishonor. but the transactions in Europe generally are too little known here to justify any further observations or conjectures. under all circumstances I am faithfully your affectionate friend

Th. Jefferson

(Mass. Hist. Soc., Jefferson Coll.; Paszkowski, 27).

35. *Kosciuszko to Jefferson*

Mon Cher Ami

Le tems se passe en attente et la nécessité augmente en proportion de mon petit revenu, de Grace cherchez moi un autre moyen de m'envoyer de l'argent; Je suis deja aux emprunts ce qui me fache beacoup, et je ne voudrais pas manquer à ma parole donnée pour le monde entier. Que fait Mr Barnes de qui je n'ai rien aucune nouvelle ni l'Année passée ni celle-ci. Obligez le je vous prie à m'envoyer plusieures lettres d'echanges par differents voys, afin qu'avec une parvenue je puisse tacher l'argent ou la négocier. Je nai pas le tems de repondre à Votre datée d'octobre 1813.[7] mais agreez je vous prie l'assurance de mon Amitié et de ma Consideration la plus distinguee

T Kosciuszko

Paris 14. Juliet 1814.

(Mass. Hist. Soc., Jefferson Coll.)

36. *Kosciuszko to Jefferson*

Mon Cher Ami

Les grands et les petits, les riches et les pauvres de notre Hemisphere, admirent le devouement qui vous aporté a accepter le place de Secretaire d'État, afin d'être utile a votre Patrie par vos connoissances parfaites du Pays, du courage du peuple, de vos grands resources, et de la Politique Europeene qui n'est que l'art de mieux tromper. Comme je suis dans la classe des pauvres, et que je ne veux rien accepter, ni aller dans mon Pays jusq'a qu'il ne soit pas rêtablit en entier avec une Constitution liberale, je vous prierai bien et avec empressement de m'envoyer incessament mes interets, et même (:apres la ratification de la paix avec Angleterre:) le fond de mon Capital pourvou que je ne perde pas beaucoup. A pour cela je joins ici ma procuration d'agire comme vous voudrez. Car je ne rien pour mon entretien.

Agreez l'assurance de mon Estime de mon admiration et de ma Sincere Amitié

T Kosciuszko

---

[7] Evidently he meant November, 1813 (no. 31).

14 Mars
1815

Souvenez Vous d'établir une grande Ecole civile et Militaire en même tems, pour vos jeunes Gens de chaque provinces sans en omettre aucune, et sous la garde et l'inspection imédiate du Congres, Car il faut toujours entretenir l'Esprit Republican avec les moeurs et les connoissances necessaires, seule base solide d'un État libre comme le votre.

(Mass. Hist. Soc., Jefferson Coll.)

37. *Jefferson to Kosciuszko*

(In the letter which follows Kosciuszko acknowledges the receipt of a letter from Jefferson dated July 3, 1815. This letter is missing. Evidently this was the correspondence which George Ticknor delivered to Kosciuszko [see *Coll. of the Mass. Hist. Soc.,* 7th series, vol. I, p. 254]. Kosciuszko's letter dated Soleure, April 15, 1816, and reprinted with addressee unknown, by Skałkowski, "Listy," p. 106, no. 40, evidently was addressed to Ticknor).

38. *Kosciuszko to Jefferson*

Mon cher et tres Respectable Ami

Votre lettre datée le 3 Juliet 1815 m'a fait un tres grand plaisir. J'etois à Paris lorsque l'Angleterre envoya ses trouppes en Amerique et j'ai dis aux Diplomates Anglais qu'au Commencement leurs Armées seront victorieuses à cause du manque d'Officiers en Amerique mais que bientot elles seront chassées ignominieusement et je leur ne donnois ma Parole d'honneur. Vous ne connoissez dis je leur bravoure si bien comme moi — Vous voyez bien mon Cher Ami que j'ai prevu davance la défaite des Anglais, tellement j'ai eté sur d'un Character noble, et d'une bravoure Nationale de vos Concitoyens. Mais en Europe tout le monde a été surpri et éttoné aussi votre réputation s'est accrue considerablement et les Noms d'Addison et Jefferson sont répétés Mille foi par toutes les bouches. — C'est sans doute quelque chose que le Nom la Pologne et nous avons une reconnaissance eternele a l'Empereur Alexandre — mais il ne fait pas une Nation, Comme la Grandeur du Pays avec un nombre considerable d'habitants. l'Empereur Alexandre m'a promit d'agrandir le Duché de Varsovie jusqu' a la Dzwina et Dnieper à nos enciens limites; mais à ses intentions généreuses et Magnanimes, son Gabinet d'execution n'a pas répondu, et il se trouve malheureusement, que le Royaume de Pologne a present est moindre d'un bon tiers que le Duché de Varsovie; J'ai fais un Voyage exprés à Vienne pour savoir au juste et je ne voulois pas retourner en Pologne à l'invitation de l'Empereur lui même, que lorsque je serais persuadé de l'intention réele, et n'ayant pas l'assurance satisfaisante de son Ministre; J'ai ecris à l'Empereur le supliant de m'assurer par un ecrit ce qu'il ma promit verbalement et que je tiendrai cela un secret jusqu'a l'execution; Mais je n'ai pas eu le bonheur de recevoir la réponse, alors je suis revenu en Suisse pour ne pas abuser de la Confiance de mes Concytoyens. — Oui Mon Cher Ami jai pensé aux bonnes lois, l'Empereur Alexandre mà promit un Gouvernement Constitutionel, Libéral, Indépendant, même l'affranchissement de nos Paysans malheureux et les rendre Proprietaires des terres qu'ils possedent. par cela seul il s'mmortaliseroit; mais mais l'est evanui en fumée. — Je sui maitenant dans la Ville de Soleure

154

en Suisse regardant les Puissances Alliées manquant de bonne fois, faisant des Injustices aux autres petits États et agissant avec leur Peuple, Comme les Loups avec les Moutons — Vous voiez mon Cher Ami dans qu'elle position je ma trouve à present; Si Vous croyez qu'il serat plus avantageux pour moi de tirrer les intérets anuelle de mon fond, que de me l'envoyer en Éurope faites le, mais je Vous prie de grace que mes interets soyent reguliérement envoyés car j'en ai grand besoin, et que mon fond soit dans la Banque Sous mon Nom mai non pas sous let votre. Si au contraire il y a une petite perte à essuyer en transportant mon fond en Europe j'aurois preferé sans doute, j'ai ma Confiance toute entiere en Vous faites comme Vous jugez le mieux pour Moi. — C'est Vous que l'Angleterre considére le plus et Vous craint aussi, mais non pas les Puissances Allies les Ministres de quelles sont tous Corompus; Les nouvelles possessions d'Angleterre en Europe Mettent les grands entraves au Comerce partout, et la France bientot perdra toutes ses manufactures par sa protection particulière.

Agreez Mon Cher Ami l'assurance de ma Consideration La plus Distinguee et la plus Affectionée

T Kosciuszko

Soleure Avril 1816

(Mass. Hist. Soc., Jefferson Coll.)

39. *Kosciuszko to Jefferson*

Mon Cher Ami

Comme vous vous réposéz tranquilement sur vos l'Auriers si justement acquis et sur la Réputation Générale et tant chérie encore par vos Concytoyens. Il ne faut pas pour cela oublier vos Amis en Europe, qui vous aiment tout autant que vos Conpatriotes. Vous me devez deux ou trois lettres. Apresat il s'agit de rendre un service éssentiel a une personne de mes Connoissances Mr Poinsot démeurant en Amerique a acheté à Richmond 1200 Acres de terre dans le Comté de Monongalia et que Mr Patrick Henry Gouverneur alors de l'Etat de Virginie lui a delivre le 23 Mai 1785 avec le Contrat, elles sont situees prés de vos terres appéllées le Puk of Otter il payoit déja land taxes et il a aussi le Plan et le titre dont il vous envoit une Copie. Mais revenu en Europe la révolution Fraincaise et les autres evénements l'ont empeché de réclamer sa Propriete. Ayez la bonté de charger quelq'un de votre part, afin qu'il puisse revandiquer cette terre et Vous témoigner avec moi sa parfaite reconnoissance.

Agréez l'assurance de ma haute Consideration

T Kosciuszko

Soleure le 3 Juin 1817

(Mass. Hist. Soc., Jefferson Coll.)

40. *Jefferson to Kosciuszko*

(The contents of the following letter of Kosciuszko, the last he wrote to Jefferson, clearly prove that in the meantime Jefferson had written to Kosciuszko, inviting him to America. Nothing is known of the whereabouts of this letter).

41. *Kosciuszko to Jefferson*

Mon cher Réspectable Ami

Nous avancons tous en Age, c'est pour cela, mon cher et respectable Ami, que je vous prie de vouloir bien (:et comme vous avez tout le pouvoir:) arranger q'apres la morte de notre digne Ami Mr Barnes,[8] quelqu'un d'aussi probe que lui prenne sa place, pour que je recoive les intérêts ponctuellement de mon fond; du quel après ma mort vous savez la destination invariable. Quant a present faites pour le mieux comme vous pensez. J'apprécie baucoup avec tout ma réconnoissance votre Amiable invitation; mais mon Pays me tient beaucoup a Coeur, et puis mes Amis, mes connoissances et quelque fois il m'est doux de leurs donner un conseill. Je suis seul véritable Polonais en Europe, tous les autres par les circonstances sont assujétés a Differentes Puissances. Vous me direz peut-être voila l'état le plus misérable, oui sans doute, mais c'est justement pour cela le plus on a besoin de conseil. Partout mon cher et Réspectable Ami, on peut être independant, quand on penu bien, raisonne bien, qu'on a bon Coeur, les sentiments humains, et un Caractere ferme droit, et ouvert, qui confond toujours le plus Astucieux Diplomate et un être le plus fourbe, fin et bas. Vous n'ignorez pas les Proclamations des Puissances qui promettent les Constitutions liberales à lours Peuples, ses promesses continuent et s'evanouiront comme les poussiéres emportés par les Vents. Votre Canal du Lac Erie jusqu'a la riviére du Nord, surprand tout le monde en Europe, mais pas moi, qui connois si bien Vos Concitoyens je les ai vu toujours Grands en tout. Vous êtes plus heureux que les Europeens; Grace à votre Gouvernement raproché plus de la nature de l'homme, Grace aussi au voisinage tres eloigné des Autres Puissances. Cela n'empeche pas d'établir une Grande Ecole Civilo-Militaire dans votre Pays sous l'imediate inspection de la comission du Congrés. Faites mes hommages à Mr Monroe votre Président, je ne cesse de lui réppéter la nécessitee absolue de cette Ecole.

Je Nous embrasse mille fois, non pas à la maniere francaise, mai du fond de mon Coeur et Agréez l'assurance de ma haute Considération.

T Kosciuszko

Soleure le 15. 7bre 1817.

(Mass. Hist. Soc., Jefferson Coll.)

---

8 Barnes died Feb. 11, 1826.

BIBLIOGRAPHY

PRIMARY SOURCES

a) Manuscript

PUBLIC INSTITUTIONS

Albemarle County Circuit Court, Charlottesville, Va., Will Book no. 1.

Alderman Library, University of Virginia, Charlottesville, Va.: "Edgehill" Randolph Papers; Jefferson Collection.

Archives and Museum of the Polish Roman Catholic Union of America, Chicago, Ill.: Kosciuszko Papers (now including the Kahanowicz-Wachowski Collection of Kosciuszko's papers and relics, recently acquired by the institution).

Archives du Ministère des Affaires étrangères: Correspondance Politique, États-Unis (photostats in the Library of Congress).

Department of the Interior, General Land Office, Washington, D. C.: Military Land Warrant—No. 1219.

Historical Society of Pennsylvania, Philadelphia, Pa.: Gratz Collection; Etting Papers.

The Houghton Library, Library of Harvard University, Cambridge, Mass.: Barlow Papers.

Henry E. Huntington Library and Art Gallery, San Marino, Cal.: Greene Papers.

Ridgway Library, Library Company of Philadelphia, Pa.: Rush Papers.

Library of Congress, Washington, D. C.: Papers of the Continental Congress; Thomas Jefferson Papers; Washington Papers.

Maine Historical Society, Portland, Me.: Fogg Collection.

Massachusetts Historical Society, Boston, Mass.: Pickering Papers; Jefferson Collection; Norcross Collection.

Missouri Historical Society, St. Louis, Mo.: Jefferson Papers.

The National Archives, Washington, D. C.: Division of State Department Archives, Miscellaneous Letters and Appointment Papers, 1813-1820; Division of Legislative Archives; Division of Justice Department Archives.

New York Historical Society, New York, N. Y.: Gates Papers.

New York Public Library, New York, N. Y.: Miscellaneous Manuscripts; Emmett Collection.

Polish Academy of Sciences, Cracow: Kosciuszko Papers, (one letter of David Humphreys to Kosciuszko).

Princes Czartoryski Museum, Cracow: one letter of John Adams to Kosciuszko.

Public Library of the City of Boston, Boston, Mass.: one letter of Kosciuszko.

South Carolina Historical Society, Charleston, S. C., one letter of Kosciuszko.

The University of Chicago Libraries, Lafayette Papers and one letter of Kosciuszko.

PRIVATE COLLECTIONS

Collection of Dr. Boleslaw Mastai of New York, one letter of Kosciuszko.
Correspondence pertaining to Major Elnathan Haskell in the possession of Mrs.
  Richard G. White of Charleston, S. C.

b) Published

DOCUMENTS, COLLECTED WORKS, DIARIES ETC.

Adams, John. Warren-Adams Letters, Being Chiefly a Correspondence among
  John Adams, Samuel Adams, and James Warren. The Massachusetts
  Historical Society, 1917-1925, vol. II.

Adams, John Quincy. Memoirs of John Quincy Adams, ed. by Charles Francis
  Adams. Philadelphia, 1874-77, vol. I.

Adams, Samuel. The Writings of Samuel Adams, ed. by H. A. Cushing. New
  York, 1904-1908, vol. II.

American State Papers. Documents, Legislative and Executive of the Congress
  of the United States . . . Selected and Edited by Walter Lowrie and
  Matthew St. Clair Clarke . . . Washington, 1832. Foreign Relations,
  Class I.

Arnault, A. V. Souvenirs d'un Sexagénaire, Paris, n. d., vol. IV.

Barthélemy, Francois. Inventaire Analytique des Archives du Ministere des
  Affaires étrangéres. Papiers de Bathélemy, Ambassadeur de France
  en Suisse, 1792-1797, (Suisse). Paris, 1889, vol. IV.

Bayard, James. A. Papers of James A. Bayard, 1796-1815, ed. by Elizabeth
  Donnan. Annual Report of the American Historical Association for
  the Year 1913. Washington, 1915, vol. II.

Burd, Edward. The Burd Papers, Selections from Letters Written by Edward
  Burd, 1763-1828, ed. by Lewis Burd Walker. (Pottsville, Pa.), 1899.

Cloquet, Jules. Recollections of the Private Life of General Lafayette. London,
  1835.

Cobbett, William. Porcupine's Works, Containing Various Writings and Selections, Exhibiting a Faithful Picture of the United States of America.
  London, 1801, vols. V—X.

Dickinson, John. The Political Writings of John Dickinson, Esquire, Late
  President of the State of Delaware, and of the Commonwealth of
  Pennsylvania. Wilmington, 1801, 2 vols.

Dunlap, William. Diary of William Dunlap, 1766-1839. The Memoir of a
  Dramatist, Theatrical Manager, Painter, Critic, Novelist and Historian.
  New York Historical Society Collections. New York, 1929-1931, vol. I.

Engestrom, Lawrence, Count. Pamiętniki Wawrzyńca hr. Engestroma, Posła
  Nadzwyczajnego i Ministra Pełnomocnego Króla J. Mci Szwedzkiego
  w Polsce Czasu Sejmu Czteroletniego, później Kanclerza Państwa i
  Ministra Spraw Zagranicznych. Translated by J. I. Kraszewski. Poznań,
  1875.

Gordon, William. Letters of the Rev. William Gordon, Historian of the American Revolution, 1770-1799. Massachusetts Historical Society Proceedings, vol. LXIII (1931).

Haiman, Miecislaus, comp. The Fall of Poland in Contemporary American
  Opinion. Chicago, 1935.

Hiltzheimer, Jacob. Extracts from the Diary of Jacob Hiltzheimer of Philadelphia, 1765-1798, ed. by his grandson, Jacob Cox Parsons. Philadelphia, 1893.

Ingersoll, Charles Jared. Recollections, Philadelphia, 1861, vol. I.

Jay, John. The Correspondence and Public Papers of John Jay, 1763-1826, ed. by Henry P. Johnston. New York and London, 1893, vol. IV.
Life of John Jay with Selections from his Correspondence and Miscellaneous Papers, ed. by William Jay. New York, 1833, vol. I.

Jefferson, Thomas. The Writings of Thomas Jefferson, ed. by Paul Leicester Ford. New York, 1892-99, vol. IX.
The Writings of Thomas Jefferson, ed. by Andrew A. Lipscomb. Washington, 1903-05, vols. I, VII, IX-X, XII-XIV, XIX.
The Writings of Thomas Jefferson ed. by Henry A. Washington. Washington, 1853-4, vols. IV-VI.
The Jefferson Papers, Collections of the Massachusetts Historical Society. Boston, 1900, Seventh Series, vol. I.

King, Rufus. Life and Correspondence of Rufus King, ed. by Charles R. King. New York, 1894-1900, vol. II.

Kosciuszko, Thaddeus. Kościuszko, Listy, Odezwy, Wspomnienia, comp. by Henryk Mościcki, Warszawa, 1917.
Manoeuvres of Horse Artillery . . . Written at Paris in the Year 1800 . . . transl. with Notes and Descriptive Plates, by Jonathan Williams, Col., Comdt. of the Corps of Engineers, and President of the U. S. Military Philosophical Society, Publ. by Direction of the Society. New York, 1808.
Memorial Exhibition, Thaddeus Kosciuszko, the Revered Polish and American Hero, His Patriotism, Vision and Zeal Revealed in a Collection of Autograph Letters . . . the Collection formed by Dr. and Mrs. Alexander Kahanowicz. New York, n. d.
Tadeusz Kościuszko, Jego Odezwy i Raporta, Uzupełnione Celniejszemi Aktami Odnoszącemi się do Powstania Narodowego 1794. Wstęp i Objaśnienia Dołączył Ludwik Nabielak. Z Wydania Paryskiego w Stuletnią Rocznicę Zgonu Naczelnika Wydało Centralne Biuro Wydawnictw N. K. N. Kraków, 1918.

Lafayette, Marquis de. The Lafayette Letters in the Bostonian Society, The Bostonian Society Publications, vol. IV, second series. Boston, 1924.
Mémoires, Correspondance et Manuscrits du Général Lafayette publiés par sa Famille. Bruxelles, 1839, vol. II.

La Rochefoucauld-Liancort, Francois Alexandre Frederic, Duc de. Travels through the United States of North America. London, 1799, vol. II.

Logan, George. Memoir of Dr. George Logan of Stenton, by his Widow Deborah Norris Logan, with Selections from his Correspondence, ed. by their Great-granddaughter Frances A. Logan, with an Introduction by Charles J. Stillé. Philadelphia, 1899.

McHenry, James. The Life and Correspondence of James McHenry, Secretary of War under Washington and Adams, ed. by Bernard C. Steiner. Cleveland, 1907.

Mazzei, Philip. Memoirs of the Life and Peregrinations of the Florentine Philip Mazzei, 1730-1816, transl. by Howard R. Marraro. New York, 1942.

Monroe, James. The Writings of James Monroe, ed. by Stanislaus Murray Hamilton. New York and London, 1898-1903, vols. II, IV and VI.

Moreau de Saint Méry, (Médéric Louis élie). Voyage aux états-Unis de l'Amérique, 1793-1798, by Moreau de Saint-Mery. Ed. with an Introduction and Notes by Stewart L. Mims. New Haven and London, 1913.

Morris, Gouverneur. A Diary of the French Revolution, by Gouverneur Morris, 1752-1816, Minister to France during the Terror, ed. by Beatrix Cary Davenport. Boston, 1939, 2 vols.

The Diary and Letters of Gouverneur Morris, ed. by Anne Cary Morris. New York, 1888, vol. II.

Niemcewicz, Julian Ursyn. "Kosciusco." (Niemcewicz's eulogy on Kosciuszko of Nov. 14, 1817) in H. Niles' Principles and Acts of the Revolution in America, Baltimore, 1822.

Pamiętniki Czasów Moich, Dzieło Pośmiertne Juliana Ursina Niemcewicza. Paryż, 1848.

Niles, H. Principles and Acts of the Revolution in America. Baltimore, 1822.

Otis, Harrison Gray. The Life and Letters of Harrison Gray Otis, Federalist, 1765-1848, by Samuel Eliot Morison, Ph. D. Boston and New York, 1913, vol. I.

Paszkowski, Franciszek. Dzieje Tadeusza Kościuszki, Pierwszego Naczelnika Polaków, przez Generała Paszkowskiego. Kraków, 1872.

Sievers, Jan Jakób. Drugi Rozbiór Polski. Warszawa, 1906, vol. I.

Tarleton, (Banastre), Lt. Col. A History of the Campaign of 1780 and 1781 in the Southern Provinces of North America. London, 1787.

Trotter, John Bernard, Late Private Secretary to Mr. Fox. Memoirs of the Latter Years of the Right Honorable Charles James Fox. London, 1811.

Turner, Frederick J., ed. Correspondence of the French Ministers to the United States, 1791-1797. Annual Report of the American Historical Association for the Year 1903. Washington, vol. II.

Turner, Jacob. Jacob Turner's Book, 1777-1778. The State Records of North Carolina, North Carolina Historical Commission. Goldsboro, 1896, vol. X.

United States Congress. Laws of the United States of America, from the 4th of March, 1789, to the 4th of March, 1815, Philadelphia and Washington, 1815, vol. III.

Abridgement of the Debates of Congress from 1789 to 1856. From Gales and Seaton's Annals of Congress; from their Register of Debates; and from the Official Reported Debates, by John C. Rives. New York and London, 1857, vol. II.

The Debates and Proceedings in the Congress of the U. S.; with an Appendix, containing Important State Papers and Public Documents, and all the Laws of a Public Nature, with a Copious Index. Fifteenth Congress — First Session, Comprising the Period from December 1, 1817, to April 20, 1818, inclusive. (Overall title: Annals of the Congress of the U. S.) Washington, 1854, vol. XXXI.

Congressional Globe: New Series: Containing Sketches of the Debates and Proceedings of the First Session of the Thirtieth Congress, by John C. Rives. City of Washington, 1849.

Miscellaneous Documents Printed by Order of the Senate of the United States during the Second Session of the Thirtieth Congress Begun and Held at the City of Washington, Dec. 2, 1848, Washington, 1849, vol. I. Misc. Doc. no. 8.

Congressional Globe: New Series: Containing Sketches of the Debates and Proceedings of the First Session of the Thirty-First Congress, by

John C. Rives. City of Washington, 1850, vol. XXI, two parts.
Executive Documents Printed by Order of the Senate of the United
States during the First Session of the Thirty-First Congress, 1849-50,
Washington, 1850. Senate Documents, vol. XIII, Ex. Doc. No. 50.
Miscellaneous Documents Printed by Order of the Senate of the
United States during the First Session of the Thirty-First Congress,
1849-50, Washington, 1850. Vol. I, Misc. Doc. No. 11.

United States Supreme Court. Reports of Cases Argued and Adjudged in the
Supreme Court of the United States. January term 1834. By Richard
Peters. Philadelphia, 1834, vol. VIII.
Reports of Cases Argued and Adjudged by the Supreme Court of the
United States. By Benjamin C. Howard. December Term, 1852. Boston, 1853. Vol. XIV.

Warner, Richard, Rev. Literary Recollections. London, 1830, vol. II.

Washington, George. The Writings of George Washington, from the Original
Manuscript Sources, 1745-1799, ed. by John C. Fitzpatrick. Washington, 1931-40, vols. XXX, XXXIV—XXXVI.

Wolcott, Oliver. Memoirs of the Administration of Washington and John
Adams, Edited from the Papers of Oliver Wolcott, by George Gibbs.
New York, 1846, vol. I.

PAMPHLETS

Jay, John. Letters Being the Whole of the Correspondence between the Hon.
John Jay and Mr. Lewis Littlepage, a Young Man whom Mr. Jay
when in Spain Patronized and Took into his Family. New York, 1786.

Jefferson, Thomas. Listy Jeffersona, Prezydenta Stanów Zjednoczonych Ameryki Północnej, do Kościuszki, ed. by Franciszek Paszkowski. Kraków, 1879.

Johnson, Reverdy. Remarks of the Hon. Reverdy Johnson, on the Power of
Congress to Pass the Law of Venue for the District of Columbia, Presented to the Committee of the Judiciary of the House of Representatives in the Case of the Heirs of Gen. Thadeus Kosciusko and Maj.
G. Tochman, April 1848. Washington, 1848.

Kościuszko, Tadeusz. Manuskrypt Tadeusza Kościuszki Opisujący Kampanię
Odprawioną Przeciw Moskalom w Roku 1792. Poznań, 1842.

Littlepage, Louis. Answer to a Pamphlet Containing Correspondence between
the Hon. John Jay, Secretary for Foreign Affairs; and Lewis Littlepage,
Esquire of Virginia, at present Chamberlain and Secretary of the
Cabinet of His Majesty the King of Poland. Philadelphia, 1786.

Morse, Jedidiah. The Present Situation of other Nations of the World, Contrasted with our own. A Sermon: Delivered at Charlestown, in the
Commonwealth of Massachusetts, February 19, 1795. Boston, 1795.

Richards, George. An Oration on the Independence of the United States of
Federate America; Pronounced at Portsmouth, New Hampshire, July
14, 1795. Portsmouth, 1795.

Smith, William Loughton. An Oration, Delivered in St. Philip's Church, before
the Inhabitants of Charleston, South Carolina, on the Fourth of July,
1796, in Commemoration of American Independence. Charleston, 1796.

Tochman, Gaspard, Major. An Exposé of the conduct of Joseph H. Bradley of
Washington, D. C., Counsellor "Employed by the Imperial Russian

Legation," towards Major G. Tochman, of New York, Counsellor Retained by the Next of Kin and Heirs at Law of Gen. Thadeus Kosciusko. December, 1847.

To the Honorable, the Senate and House of Representatives of the United States, in Congress Assembled. Petition of Major G. Tochman, Attorney and Counsel to the Next of Kin and Heirs at Law of Gen. Thaddeus Kosciuszko. Dec. 1847.

To the Honorable, the Senate and House of Representatives of the United States, in Congress Assembled. Supplemental Petition of Major G. Tochman, Attorney and Counsel of The Next of Kin and Heirs at Law of General Thadeus Kosciusko, Containing a Rejoinder to the Answer of Joseph H. Bradley, Esq., "Counsellor Employed by the Imperial Russian Legation." January, 1848.

Wolcott, Oliver. Report of the Secretary of the Treasury, Made in Pursuance of a Resolution of the House, of the 22d Instant, Relative to the Claim of General Kosciusko, against the United States. House of Representatives, Dec. 28, 1797. Philadelphia, (1797).

PERIODICALS

Fiszerowa, Wirydjana z Kwileckich Radolińska. "Pamiętnik Damy Polskiej o Kościuszce," ed. by Adam M. Skałkowski, *Przegląd Historyczny*, Warszawa, Second series, vol. XII, (1934), pp. 245-277.

"The Heirs of Kosciuszko," *Niles' National Register*, Baltimore, Aug. 7, 1847, vol. LXXII, p. 368.

Jefferson, Thomas. "Jefferson's Letters to Kosciuszko." (From the Library of Congress). *The Magazine of History with Notes and Queries*, Tarrytown and New York, vol. IX (1915), extra no. 36, pp. 273-295.

"Kosciusko," *Niles' Weekly Register*, Baltimore, vol. XXX, Aug. 26, 1826.

Kosciuszko, Thaddeus. "Kosciuszko to Maj. Alexander Garden," *The South Carolina Historical and Genealogical Magazine*, Charleston, vol. II (1901), pp. 126-7.

"Listy Kościuszki do Przyjaciół Amerykańskich i Inn.," ed. by Adam M. Skałkowski, *Przegląd Historyczny*, Warszawa, vol. VI, (1926-27), pp. 86-106.

"Rady Tadeusza Kościuszki dla Swego Wychowańca," *Dziennik Chicagoski*, Chicago, April 23, 1894, p. 4.

Niemcewicz, Julian Ursyn. "Niemcewicz en Amérique et sa Correspondance Inédite avec Jefferson (1797-1810)," ed. by Władysław M. Kozłowski, *Revue de Littérature Comparée*, Paris, vol. VIII (1928) pp. 29-45.

"Pobyt Kościuszki i Niemcewicza w Ameryce," ed. by Władysław M. Kozłowski, *Biblioteka Warszawska*, Warszawa, vol. CCLXI (1906), pp. 241-284.

"Rozstanie się Kościuszki z Niemcewiczem w Filadelfji," ed. by Władysław M. Kozłowski, *Kwartalnik Historyczny*, Lwów, vol. XX (1906), pp. 225-252.

"A Visit to Mount Vernon a Century Ago," ed. by Władysław M. Kozłowski, Introduction by Worthington C. Ford, *Century Magazine*, New York, vol. XLI (1902), pp. 510-522.

Ryer, Elizabeth. "The Fur Coat (A Reminiscence)," *The Token and Atlantic Souvenir . . .*, ed. by S. G. Goodrich, Boston, 1833, pp. 342-350.

Tuleja, M., comp. "Z Pobytu Tadeusza Kościuszki w Londynie," *Prawda,* London, Oct. 15, 1917, p. 2.

Tyler, John. "Some Letters of Tyler, Calhoun, Polk, Murphy, Houston and Donelson," *Tyler's Quarterly Historical and Genealogical Magazine,* Richmond, vol. VI (1925), pp. 221-249.

Willett, Susanna. "Mrs. Willett to Gen. Kosciuszko," *Pennsylvania Magazine of History and Biography,* Philadelphia, vol. XXIII (1899), p. 122.

Zeltner, Xavier. "Personal Reminiscences of Kosciusko," *United States Service Magazine,* New York, vol. IV (1865), pp. 136-146.

NEWSPAPERS

The Argus, New York, 1797.

The Aurora and General Advertiser, Philadelphia, 1797-1798.

Carey's Daily Advertiser, Philadelphia, 1797.

Claypoole's American Daily Advertiser, Philadelphia, 1797.

Columbian Centinel, Boston, 1796-1798.

Detroit Gazette, Feb. 6, 1818.

Dunlap's American Daily Advertiser, Philadelphia, 1792-1793.

Dunlap and Claypoole's American Daily Advertiser, Philadelphia, 1794-1795.

Gazette Nationale ou Le Moniteur Universel, Réimpression de l'Ancient Moniteur Seule Historie Authentique et Ináltérée de la Révolution Francaise Depuis la Réunion des États-Généraux Jusqu'au Consulat (Mai 1789—Novembre 1799). Paris, vol. XXIX.

The Herald, New York, 1797.

Independent Chronicle and Universal Advertiser, Boston, 1797.

Kentucky Gazette, Lexington, 1797.

Massachusetts Mercury, Boston, 1797.

The Mirror, Washington, Ky., 1797.

The Time Piece and his Literary Companion, New York, 1797.

United States Gazette, Philadelphia, 1797-1798.

SECONDARY SOURCES

BOOKS

Alden, Rev. Timothy, A. M. A Collection of American Epitaphs and Inscriptions with Occasional Notes. New York, 1814, vol. I.

Allen, Julian. Autocrasy in Poland and Russia or, a Description of Russian Misrule in Poland, and an Account of the Surveillance of Russian Spies at Home and Abroad. Including The Experience of an Exile. New York, 1854.

Askenazy, Szymon, Napoleon a Polska, Warszawa, Kraków, 1918-1919, vol. III.

Benedict, William H. New Brunswick in History. New Brunswick, 1925.

Bonner, William Thompson. New York; The World's Metropolis, 1623-1923. New York, 1924.

Bowers, Claude G. Jefferson and Hamilton. Boston and New York, 1925.

Carpenter, Stephen C. Memoirs of the Hon. Thomas Jefferson, Secretary of State, Vice-President, and President of the United States of America, Containing a Concise History of Those States, From the Acknowledgement of Their Independence, with a View of the Rise and Progress of French Influence and French Principles in that Country. Philadelphia, 1809, vol. II.

Clark, William Bell. Gallant John Barry, 1745-1803, The Story of a Naval Hero of Two Wars. New York, 1938.

De Koven, Mrs. Reginald. The Life and Letters of John Paul Jones. New York, 1913, vol. II.

Dunlap, William. A History of the American Theatre. New York, 1832.

Evans, A. W. W. Memoir of Thaddeus Kosciuszko, Poland's Hero and Patriot. An Officer in the American Army of the Revolution, and Member of the Society of the Cincinnati. New York, 1883.

Eversley, Lord. The Partitions of Poland. New York, 1915.

Fay, Bernard. The Revolutionary Spirit in France and America, A Study of Moral and Intellectual Relations between France and the United States at the End of the Eighteenth Century, transl. by Ramon Guthrie. New York, 1927.

Ganoe, William Addleman. The History of the United States Army. New York and London, 1932.

Gardner, Monica M. Kosciuszko, A Biography. London and New York, 1920.

Gumowski, Marjan, Dr. Portrety Kościuszki, Studja Ikonograficzne do Dziejów Polskich, vol. I. Lwów, 1917.

Haiman, Miecislaus. Poland and the American Revolutionary War. Chicago, 1932.

Halecki, O. A History of Poland. New York (1943).

Hayden, Horace E. Virginia Genealogies. Wilkes-Barre, 1891.

Hazen, Charles Downer. Contemporary American Opinion of the French Revolution, Johns Hopkins University Studies in Historical and Political Science. Baltimore, 1897. Extra vol. XVI.

Heitman, Francis Bernard. Historical Register of Officers of the Continental Army during the War of the Revolution, April, 1775, to December, 1783. Washington, 1914.

Hubotten, Dr. Franz, Prof. W. Haberlin and Prof. H. Vierordt, Biographisches Lexikon der Hervorragenden Arzte aller Zeiten und Volker. Berlin und Wien, 1929-1935, 6 vols.

Humphreys, Frank Landon. Life and Times of David Humphreys, Soldier— Statesman—Poet, "Belov'd of Washington." New York and London, 1917, 2 vols.

Janik, Michał. Hugo Kołłątaj, Monografia. Lwów, 1913.

Johnson, Allen, and Dumas Malone, Dictionary of American Biography. New York, 1928-37, 20 vols.

Keats, John. Poems, ed. by G. Thorn Drury. London and New York, 1896, vol. I.

Konopczyński, Władysław. Dzieje Polski Nowożytnej. Warszawa, 1936, vol. II. Od Sobieskiego do Kościuszki, Szkice, Drobiazgi, Fraszki Historyczne. Warszawa i Kraków, 1921.

Korzon, Tadeusz. Kościuszko, Biografia z Dokumentów Wysnuta. Kraków, 1894. Wewnętrzne Dzieje Polski za Stanisława Augusta (1764-1794). Badania Historyczne ze Stanowiska Ekonomicznego i Administracyjnego. Kraków i Warszawa, 1897-8, vol. III.

Krzemiński, Stanisław. Stanisław Poniatowski i Maurycy Glayre. Warszawa, n. d.

Kukiel, Dr. Maryan. Dzieje Oręża Polskiego w Epoce Napoleońskiej, 1795-1815. Poznań, n. d.
"Kościuszko and the Third Partition." The Cambridge History of Poland, from Augustus II to Piłsudski, (1697-1935). Cambridge, 1941.
"Legiony i Hasła Powstańcze," Polska, Jej Dzieje i Kultura. Warszawa, n. d., vol. III.

Lamb, Martha J. History of the City of New York, its Origin, Rise and Progress. New York and Chicago. 1877, vol. II.

Lord, Robert Howard. The Second Partition of Poland, A Study in Diplomatic History. Cambridge, 1915.

Lossing, Benson J. History of New York City, Embracing an Outline Sketch of Events from 1609 to 1830. New York, 1884, vol. I.

McCrady, Edward Jr., and Samuel A. Ashe. Cyclopedia of Eminent and Representative Men of the Carolinas in the Nineteenth Century. Madison, Wis., 1892, 2 vols.

McMaster, John Bach. A History of the People of the United States, from the Revolution to the Civil War. New York and London, 1924, vol. II.

Mazyck, Walter H. George Washington and the Negro. Washington, (1932).

Mills, W. J. Historic Houses of New Jersey. Philadelphia and London, 1902.

Mitskievitch, Adam. Conrad Wallenrod, transl. by Michael H. Dziewicki. London, 1883.

Patton, John S., and Sallie J. Doswell. Monticello and its Master. Charlottesville, Va., 1925.

Porter, Jane. Thaddeus of Warsaw, A New and Revised Edition with the Addition of New Notes, Etc., by the Author. New York, n. d.

Randall, Henry S. The Life of Thomas Jefferson. Philadelphia, 1863, vol. III.

Randolph, Sarah M. The Domestic Life of Thomas Jefferson, Compiled from Family Letters and Reminiscences, by his Great-granddaughter. New York, 1871.

Russell, Phillips. John Paul Jones, Man of Action. New York, 1930.

Scharf, J. Thomas, and Thompson Westcott. History of Philadelphia, 1609-1884. Philadelphia, 1884, vol. I.

The Sesquicentennial Committee. Revolutionary History of Elizabeth, New Jersey. 1926.

Shultz, William J. and M. R. Caine. Financial Development of the United States. New York, 1937.

Skałkowski, Adam M. "Finis Poloniae," Polska, Jej Dzieje i Kultura. Warszawa, n. d. vol. III.
O Kokardę Legionów. Lwów, 1912.

Sobieski, Wacław. Dzieje Polski. Warszawa, 1938, vol. II.
"Kościuszko i Pułaski w Ameryce," Polska w Kulturze Powszechnej, ed. by Feliks Koneczny. Kraków, 1918, vol. I.

Todd, Charles Burr. Life and Letters of Joel Barlow, LL.D., Poet, Statesman, Philosopher. New York and London, 1886.

Tokarz, Wacław. Warszawa przed Wybuchem Powstania 17 kwietnia 1794 Roku. Kraków, 1911.

Washbourne, Henry. Memoirs of Paul Jones, late Rear-Admiral in the Russian Service. London, 1843, vol. II.

Watson, John F. Annals of Philadelphia and Pennsylvania in the Olden Time. Philadelphia, 1870, vol. II.

Wilstach, Paul. Jefferson and Monticello. New York, 1925.

Wittke, Carl. We Who Built America, The Saga of the Immigrant. New York, 1940.

Wittlin, Joseph. "Tadeusz Kosciuszko," The Torch of Freedom, ed. by Emil Ludwig and Henry B. Kranz. New York and Toronto, 1943.

Wolański, Adam (Tadeusz Soplica). Wojna Polsko-Rosyjska 1792 R., Kampanja Koronna. Kraków i Poznań, 1920.

Wright, Marion M. Thompson. The Education of Negroes in New Jersey. Teachers College, Columbia University, Contributions to Education, No. 815. New York, 1941.

Załęski, Ks. Stanisław. O Masonii w Polsce od roku 1738 do 1822, na Źródłach Wyłącznie Masońskich. Kraków, 1908.

PAMPHLETS

Askenazy, Szymon. Thaddeus Kosciuszko, The Polish Review. London, 1917.

Bristol Development Board. Birthplace of America, Bristol—England, n. p., n. d.

Bronarski, Dr. Alfons. Tadeusz Kosciuszko, Eine biographische Skizze zur Grundung des Kosciuszko—Museum in Solothurn. Solothurn, 1936.

Jullien, Antoine. Rys Życia Wodza Polskiego Tadeusza Kościuszki. Z Francuskiego Pana Jullien. Z dodaniem Opisu Sprowadzenia Zwłok Bohatyra do Krakowa i Złożenia Onych w Grobach Królów Polskich. . . . n. p., 1819.

Korzon, Tadeusz. Przedśmiertna Męczarnia Kościuszki i Żal Pozgonny Narodu. Warszawa, 1917.

Kozłowski, W. M. Spadki Po Kościuszce i Jego Testamenty. (Na Podstawie Dokumentów Nie-Wydanych z Archiwów Amerykańskich). Poznań, n. d.

Michelet, J. Kościuszko, Legenda Demokratyczna. Paryż, 1851.

Tochman, Gaspard, Major. Strike But Hear. Poland, Russia, and the Policy of the Latter Towards the United States. Baltimore, 1844.

PERIODICALS

A. C. G. "Kosciuszko's Will," Scribner's Monthly, New York, vol. XVII (1879), pp. 614-616.

Brink, Elizabeth Camille. "Kosciuszko — Forefather of American Artillery," The Field Artillery Journal. Baltimore, vol. XXII (1932), pp. 303-313.

Dubiecki, Prof. Tadeusz. "Tytuł Amerykanina Jest Święty," Dziennik Chicagoski, August 13, 1926, p. 5.

Gaffney, M. Cecilia. "Kosciuszko's Gift to Jefferson," Poland-America, New York, vol. XIII (1932), pp. 176-178.

Galbraith, John Howard. "The Kosciusko Lands," The Ohio Magazine, Columbus, O., vol. III (1907), pp. 325-329.

Green, Samuel A. "Kosciusko as an Artist," The Magazine of American History with Notes and Queries, New York, vol. IX (1883), p. 73.

Griffin, Martin I. J. "General Thaddeus Kosciuszko," The American Catholic Historical Researches, Philadelphia, new series, vol. VI (1910), pp. 129-216.
"Thomas Lloyd," The American Catholic Historical Researches, Philadelphia, vols. VII (1890), p. 19, and XX (1903), pp. 19-26.

Harvey, Oscar J. "Wilkes-Barre's Earliest Newspapers," Part I, *Proceedings and Collections of the Wyoming Historical and Geological Society* for the year 1922, Wilkesbarre, 1923, vol. XVIII, pp. 58-98.

Hayden, Horace Edwin. "Kosciuszko as an Artist," *The Magazine of American History with Notes and Queries,* New York, vol. IX (1883), p. 73.

Jackson, Cordelia. "John Barnes, a Forgotten Philanthropist of Georgetown," *Records of the Columbia Historical Society,* Washington, vol. VII (1904), pp. 39-48.

Korzon, Tadeusz. "Kwestja Wyjazdu Kościuszki z Ameryki w 1798 r." *Biblioteka Warszawska,* Warszawa, vol. CCLXV (1907), pp. 399-402.

"Kosciusko School," *The Magazine of American History with Notes and Queries,* New York and Chicago, vol. VIII, (1882), p. 437.

Kosznicki, Leon. "Sonet Keats'a do Kościuszki," *Tygodnik Polski,* New York, August 8, 1943, pp. 1-2.

"The Last Years of Kosciuszko," *Harper's New Monthly Magazine,* New York, vol. XXXVII (1868), pp. 478-483.

Liguori, Sister M., Ph. D. "The Most Ideal Cultural Link Between the United States and Poland," *Polish-American Studies,* Orchard Lake, vol. II (1945), pp. 67-69.

Love, N. B. C. "Me-She-Kun-Nogh-Quah, or Lttle Turtle," *Ohio Archaelogical and Historical Publications,* Columbus, vol. XVIII (1909), pp. 115-148.

McKee, Oliver, Jr. "The Father of American Artillery," *National Republic,* Boston, vol. XXII (1926), pp. 30-31.

Marraro, Howard R. "Philip Mazzei and his Polish Friends," *Bulletin of the Polish Institute of Arts and Sciences in America,* New York, vol. II (1944), pp. 757-822.

Tacitus. "Characteristic Sketch — General Kosciuszko," *The Daily Advertiser,* Philadelphia, April 12, 1797, p. 1.

W. H. "Kosciuszko," *The Magazine of American History with Notes and Queries,* New York, vol. VI (1881), p. 383.

White, Israel Losly. "The Truth About General Kosciuszko in America," *The Connecticut Magazine,* Hartford, vol. XII (1908), pp. 375-382.

ICONOGRAPHIC NOTES

The oil portrait of Kosciuszko reproduced here as frontispiece, was painted by a Polish artist, Joseph Peszka (1767-1831) circa 1817. It is considered a very good likeness of the General in his seventies (see: Gumowski, *Portrety Kościuszki*, 55). The original is in the Archives and Museum of the Polish Roman Catholic Union, Chicago.

The Italian Scenery by Kościuszko shows him at his best as an artist. It is a water color, 9 by 7 inches, painted during his sojourn in Italy. The original is also in the above institution.

Cabin Boy is one of those numerous sketches the drawing of which Kosciuszko made his pastime, usually throwing the drawings away. It was made aboard the Adriana in 1797. The original is in the New Haven Colony Historical Society, New Haven, Conn.

The watercolor sketch of Miss Lucetta Adelaide Pollock pertains to Kosciuszko's second sojourn in Philadelphia when it became a fad among the city's inhabitants to visit the sick General. Miss Lucetta, then a girl of 15 years, was a daughter of Oliver Pollock, "distinguished in the Revolution for his zeal & services in the American cause, while a resident of New Orleans." Miss Pollock died in 1804. The drawing has little value as a work of art (conf. Hayden, "Kosciuszko as an Artist," *Mag. of Am. Hist.*, IX [1883], 73); it is mentioned in Watson's *Annals of Philadelphia*, II, 279. The original is in the Historical Society of Pennsylvania.

The original of the first draft of Kosciuszko's American last will is in the Massachusetts Historical Society, Jefferson Collection.

Portrait of Captain Lee of the Adriana is a watercolor, oval, 6 by $4\frac{3}{4}$ inches. Evidently it was also made aboard that ship in 1797. The original is the property of the Henry Whitfield State Historical Museum, Guilford, Conn.

Kosciuszko's portrait of Jefferson is reproduced here from a rare colored engraving made by Gen. Michael Sokolnicki (1760-1816) of the Polish Legions at Kosciuszko's request. Most probably this is the picture of which a few copies Kosciuszko sent to Jefferson in 1802. Dr. William Thornton, a friend of Jefferson, author of the plans for the United States Capitol, was indignant when he saw the picture. "Never was such an injustice done to you except by sign-painters and General Kosciuszko . . . when I saw it I did not wonder that he lost Poland — . . . ," he wrote to Jefferson (Wilstach, *Jefferson and Monticello*, 156-157; see also Green, "Kosciuszko as an Artist," *Mag. of Am. Hist.*, IX, 73). The engraving is in the Archives and Museum of the Polish R. C. Union, Chicago.

The map of Kosciuszko's land on the Scioto River, drawn by Samuel Smith, in 1803, is reproduced here from the original in the Massachusetts Historical Society, Jefferson Collection.

INDEX

Accabie, plantation, S. C., 70.

Adams, Abigail, 58; letter to Mrs. Warren, 61.

Adams, John, 33, 43, 59, 73, 129; feted at New Brunswick, 58-59; on Partitions of Poland, 29; letters to: Jefferson, 29; Kościuszko, 49, 57; from Jefferson, 29.

Adams, John Quincy, 60; letter to King, 100.

Adams, Samuel, 20.

Adriana, ship, 36, 42-43, 80, 129, 137, 168.

Africa, 126.

African Education Society of New Jersey, 126.

Age of Enligtenment, 112.

Aland Islands, 32.

Albemarle County, Va., Circuit Court, 125.

Alien and Sedition Bills, 73 and n., 137.

Alexander I, Emperor of Russia, 104-106, 154.

America, 4-5, 7, 11, 16-18, 20, 25 and n., 29-31, 34-36, 46, 49, 60, 68, 71, 74-76, 80-84, 86-88, 96-98, 102-103, 113, 116, 118, 127—30, 138, 140-41, 144, 155; economic conditions in 1809, 145; in 1812, 150, and in 1814, 119-20; political conditions in 1790, 40; in 1797-8, 40-41, 45, 63, 68, 73-74, 137, 140, and in 1800, 89-90, 142. See: United States.

American, archives, 117; army, 1, 68, 92, 97; artillery, 92, 97, 147, 151; attitude toward France, 28, 40-42, 73, 85-87, 89, 138, 141; citizens, 127; courts, 126-28; Democratic societies, 28; education, 87, 90-92, 99, 125-26, 143, 145, 147, 149-50, 154, 156; military literature, 92; militia, 6, 17, 90, 92, 145, 147; press, 42-45, 50, 64; public opinion, 28, 44, 89, 140; seamen, 41, 86; ships,

36, 41, 43; sympathies for Poland, 28-30, 42, 44. See: United States.

American Declaration of Independence compared with Kosciuszko's Act of Insurrection, 18-22.

American Revolution, 1, 3n., 4-6, 16 and n., 17-18, 20, 40, 47, 51, 58, 63, 68, 111, 121, 129, 168; foreign officers, 71; French officers 4n., 83n., 116; influence on Kosciuszko's Insurrection, 26-27; Kosciuszko's services in, 1, 5, 7, 11 16-19, 29, 32, 34, 40, 42-43, 47, 49, 55n., 63, 68, 70, 97-98, 111-12, 121, 129. See: United States.

Americans, 2, 3, 6, 28-29, 32, 98; in Paris, 86-88, 100-102, 113, 116, 138; put as an example to Poles by Kosciuszko, 10, 17, 87, 103.

Amsterdam, Holland, 7, 70, 138-39; banks, 75 and n., 137.

Anna, ship, 39.

Argus, 62.

Aristides, 88, 98, 122, 149.

Armstrong, John, Gen., 4, 57, 67, 83, 88 and n., 125, 128, 129 n.; letters to Gates, 44-45, 57, 67; Jefferson, 88, 117 n.; from Jefferson, 117 n., 125; Kosciuszko, 117 n.

Armstrong, John, Col., 129-30, 140-41; letter from Jefferson, 130 n.

Armstrong, Kosciuszko, 88, 125, 128.

Aschenholz, Johann Wilhelm von, letter from Lafayette, 101.

Atlantic Ocean, 32-33, 39, 64.

Austria, 15, 63, 110, 141.

Austrian, agents, 101; capital, 105; government, 15; Poland, 15; prison, 26.

Avon River, 36.

Bacchus, 25 n.

Bache, Benjamin Franklin, 42-43, 80 and n.

Baillie, Matthew, 34, 136.

Church, Angelica, letter from Jefferson, 79 n.
Cincinnati, O., 117.
Cincinnatus, 101, 129 n.
Clarkson, Matthew, 47.
Clay, Matthew (presumably), 140.
Clayton, John Middleton, letter to Fendall, 127 n.
Clifton, England, 34.
Cline, Henry C., 34, 136.
Clinton, George, letters from Gates, 55 and n.; Kosciuszko, 87.
Cobbett, William, attacks Kosciuszko, 42-46, 59 n., 72, 80 n., 83-84, 101, 129 n.
Cocke, John Hartwell, Gen., 125-26, letter to Jefferson, 125.
Codman, Richard, letter to Otis, 86.
Coit, Joshua, 70.
Coles, Edward, 145 and n.
Collot, Victor, Gen., 62, 73 n.
Confederation of Targowica, 10-11.
Connecticut, 70, 72 n.
Constantine, Russian Grand Duke, 105.
Cossacks, 127, 135.
Cosway, Richard, 33.
Courland, 23, 26.
Crancé, Dubois, 101.
Cracow, Poland, 47, 117; Kosciuszko's sojourn in, 15, 18; Criminal Court, 132; Free City of, 117; Palatinate, 132; Senate, 117.
Custis, Elizabeth Parke, 80 n.
Cutting, Nathaniel, 85-86; letter to Jefferson, 85-86.
Czartoryska, Isabella, Princess, letters from Kosciuszko, 22, 24.
Czartoryski, Adam George, Prince, 104-105.

Danton, George Jacques, 16.
Dantzig, Poland, 26.
Danube Legion, the, (Polish), 101.
Davie, William R., Gen., 92.
Dawson, John L., 46, 76, 83, 89, 142; sponsors action in Congress in regard to Kosciuszko's arrears in pay, 70-71, 72 n.
Dayton, Jonathan, 83.
Delacroix, Charles, letter from Letombe, 46.

Delaware, 55.
Delaware County, Ohio, 129 n.
Delaware River, 51.
Democratic Societies in the U. S., 28.
Devonshire, Duchess of, 33.
Dickinson, John, 29, 59, 69; on Partitions of Poland, 29, 59; letters from Kosciuszko, 59-60, 69.
District of Columbia, Orphans Court, 125, 127.
Dnieper, river, 154.
Dombrowski, John Henry, Gen., 39, 64.
Dombrowski, Stanisław, 50, 79.
Dresden, Saxony, 16 n., 71.
Drouyn de Vaudeuil de Lhuys, Angelica, see: Zeltner, Angelica.
Dubienka, Poland, battle of, 10.
Dublin, O., 129 n.
Dunlap, William, 58.
Du Pont de Nemours, Pierre Samuel, 86-89; letter from Jefferson, 145 n.
Dutchess County, N. Y., 44 n.
Dvina, river, 154.

Edwards, Evan, Maj., 70; letters to Kosciuszko, 60; from Kosciuszko, 60.
Egypt, 101.
Elizabethtown, N. J., 54, 83; Kosciuszko's sojourn at, 58.
Elliott, Nancy (Mrs. Lewis Morris), 3, 70 n.; family 70 n.
Ellis, Margaret Vanderhorst, see: Mrs. Anthony Walton White.
Ellis, Mary, 51-52.
Ellis House, New Brunswick, N. J., 51, 54.
Emmet, Thomas Addis, 87.
Engestrom, Lawrence, Count, 7; letter from Kosciuszko, 16.
England, 12, 20, 32 and n., 33-34, 40, 86, 97-98, 105, 138, 148, 150-55; Kosciuszko's sojourn in, 32-36. See: Great Britain.
English, constitution, 104-105; ministers, 74; physicians, 34; romantic poets, 33, 117-18. See: British.
Englishmen, 75, 149. See: Britishers.
Erie, Canal, 98, 156.
Erie, Lake, 98.
Essex Junto, 47, 86.

Estko, Anna, 1-2, 128; and her family, 1; letters from Kosciuszko, 2, 15.

Estko, Stanislaus, 15.

Euphrates River, 45.

Europe, 2-3, 5, 8, 23, 29, 39, 54, 57, 61, 71-72, 74, 84, 90-91, 98, 100, 102, 107, 117, 121, 131, 138, 142, 145-46, 150, 153-56; indifferent toward Poland, 18, 27, 105-106; Northern, 131.

European, banks, 71; continent, 106; estate of Kosciuszko, 114; governments, 29, 47, 98; political situation, 39, 61, 63, 106, 108.

Europeans, 92, 99.

Evans, Rudolph, 79 n.

Fairfax, Sarah Cary, letter from Washington, 48.

Farquhar, William, 136.

Faustin, Kosciuszko's servant, 15.

Feast of Reason, 42.

Federal City, D. C., 80, 91. See: Washington, D. C.

Federalists, 28, 29, 40-43, 45, 59, 70, 72 and n., 73, 80 n., 83, 86, 89, 102.

Felix, Louise Francoise, 130.

Fendall, Philip R., letter from Clayton, 127 n.

Fenno, John, 43, 59 n.

Fenno, John Ward, 62 and n., 108.

Ferdinand, Prussian Prince, 60.

Finland, 32.

Fiszer (Fiszerowa), Wiridjanna z Radolińskich Kwilecka, 9-10, 32 n., 64 n., 87, 110, 112.

Florida, 96.

Fluvianna County, Va., 125.

Fontainebleau, France, 103, 149.

Foote, Henry S., 128.

Fort Mifflin, Pa., 42.

Fouché, Joseph, Duke of Otranto, 104.

Fourth of July celebrations, 28, 110.

Fox, Charles James, 33, 109 n.

France, 3 and n., 8, 15-16, 33, 40, 42, 46-47, 56, 63-64, 68-69, 74, 80-83 and n., 100, 105, 110, 152, 155; attitude toward Poland, 15-16, 23, 47, 100-102, 104, 120; and toward the U. S., 40-41, 73-74, 85-87, 89,

102, 138, 141; confers honorary citizenship on Kosciuszko, 12; Kosciuszko's sojourn in, 15-16, 83-106, 111, 113; attitude toward Kosciuszko, 100-102.

Francis II, Emperor of Austria, 63, 68 n.

Frankford, Pa., 51.

Franklin County, Ohio, 129.

Frederick William II, King of Prussia, 131; in the Second Partition of Poland, 19; defeated by Kosciuszko, 26.

French, army, 3 n.; Committee of Public Safety, 23; Consulate, 109; Convention, 15; Council of Ancients, 100; Declaration of Human Rights, 18, 20; Directory, 64 and n., 73, 85-86, 100-102; emigrants, 33 n., 130; government, 149; Legislative Assembly, 12; ministers, 74; National Assembly, 56; officers, 4 n.; police, 103-104; public opinion, 83; Revolution, 16, 22, 27, 41, 155.

Frenchmen, 64, 87, 96, 116.

Freneau, Philip, 42.

Fulton, Robert, 88-89, 144.

Gahn, Henry, letter from Kosciuszko, 57.

Gallatin, Albert, 72 n., 73 n.; letter from Jefferson, 106.

Garat, Dominique Joseph, 109.

Garden, Alexander, 69; letter from Kosciuszko, 70.

Garnett, John, 53.

Gates, Horatio, Gen., 4, 35, 42, 50, 53, 59, 129 n.; entertains Kosciuszko, 54-57; letters to Clinton, 55; from Gen. Armstrong, 44-45, 57, 67; Jefferson, 63-64, 118; Kosko, 53-54, 58-60, 67; Mrs. Montgomery, 56.

Gates, Horatio, Mrs., 50, 53-55, 60.

George III, King of England, 21.

Georgetown, D. C., 75, 119.

German, banks, 72.

Germany, 64, 74; Emperor of, letter from Washington, 68 n.

Gerry, Elbridge, 73, 85 n., 89, 138-39; his peace mission supported by

172

returns to Philadelphia, 60-62; invited to France, 64; strives to settle his financial affairs in America, 67-72; leans toward Republican point of view, 68-69; accepts peace mission to France, 73-74; prepares his will for the benefit of Negroes, 76-79; goes secretly to France, 46, 79-84, 100, 116, 137; intervenes with the Directory in behalf of America, 85-86; writes *Manoeuvres*, 92; works for the rebirth of Poland, 100-107, 154-56; deceived by the Directory, 100; renounces allegiance to Tsar Paul, 100; his arrest ordered by the Tsar, 101; watched by police, 101, 103; refuses to cooperate with Napoleon, 101, 104; again intends to return to America, 102-103; demands restoration of Poland from Napoleon, 104-105, and from Alexander I, 105, 154; disappointed by the Congress of Vienna, 105-106, 154; settles in Soleure, 106; death, 115, 120, 125, 128; eulogized in the U. S. Congress, 116; his body transferred to Cracow, 117.

Kosciuszko, Thaddeus, his character as a man, 1, 10-11, 24, 108-14; full of simplicity, 1, 52, 56, 109; modesty, 12, 15, 53, 56, 68, 89, 101, 109-10, 113-14; refuses a gift of an estate, 15; dislikes to speak of himself and the past, 111; averse to attempts to portray his features, 52-53; full of love and mildness, 25, 56, 87; natural charm, 11, 110; good humor, 10, 52, 54, 87, 109-10; compassion for the poor, 15, 76, 87, 106, 112, 114-15, and for Negroes, 76, 113, 116, 129; gratefulness, 32, 36, 52, 58, 70; kindness, 85, 87, 95; friendliness, 4, 36, 39, 50, 54, 67, 87, 96, 102, 109-10; friendly toward Washington 48-49, 67-69; attached to, Gates, 50; Greene, 4; Jefferson, 63, 75-79, 84, 88-89, and Zeltners, 108; courteous, 1, 111; to women, 108, 111; his life free from love scandals, 108; his love for children, 52, 109-10;

as teacher of Zeltner's children, 111, 114; writes advices for a boy, 113-14; stresses the need of education, 15, 76, 90-92, 99, 112-13, 143, 145, 147, 149-50, 154, 156; his philanthropy, 96, 112-13; honor, 116; honesty, 101; ready for sacrifices, 3; considers himself of no service to humanity, 113; not a man of business, 121; careless with his papers, 64 n., 112; likes music, 109; and gardening, 1, 24, 110; likes to draw pictures, 39, 52, 62, 110, 168, and to turn snuffboxes, 57, 110; likes coffee and strawberries, 111; his recreations, 111; his order of the day, 111; obstinate in prejudices, 111; taciturn, 56, 110; not eloquent, 11; of reserved nature, 79, 89, 110-11; his religious life, 112; never a Freemason, 112; orders a modest funeral, 114.

Kosciuszko, Thaddeus, his character as military leader and statesman, 11, 24, 26-27, 101; political idealism, 23, 56, 96, 113; patriotism, 2, 9, 10-12, 17, 21-22, 24, 28, 46, 56, 100-107, 113-14, 116, 126, 156; democratic leanings, 3, 5-7, 9-10, 12, 15, 17, 21, 56, 96, 111; pure republican, 58, 101, 118; averse to kings and aristocrats, 101; champion of rights for peasants, 3, 15, 17, 22-24, 103-106, 110, 113, 154; defends the sanctity of law, 22, 26; free from lust of power, 24; reluctant to renown, 64 n.; shuns politics, 1, 12, 24, 43, 68, 111; purity of his motives, 27, 56, 96, 101, 106; symbol of national virtues, 27; longing for Poland, 114; hostile to Napoleon, 101-103, 109; his devotion to duty, 9, 23-24; bravery, 11, 24, 26-28, 39, 45, 56, 97, 116, 126; valor, fidelity and skill, 97; care for the soldier, 9-11, 23, 101; advocates strict discipline in the army, 97, 151; virtuous, benevolent and devoted to the cause of liberty, 115, 121, 126; his life devoted to the freedom and happiness of man, 112, 116; his place in Poland's history, 22, 26-27, 118, and in world's history, 116, 118.

Kosciuszko, Thaddeus, his opinions on the American, army, 97, 151, 154; cities, 91, 149; defense, 92, 97, 147; education, 90-92, 99, 143, 145, 147, 149-50, 154, 156; Federalists, 72; government, 91, 99, 149, 156; improvement of social position of Negroes, 76; national character, 87, 97, 149, 151, 154, 156; political conditions, 75, 83, 91; power of Presidents, 90, 141, 145, 147; republicanism, 90-91, 142-143, 145, 149, 154; Revolution, 16-17; rural population, 91, 149; difficulties of the U. S. with Spain, 96, 144-45; war with Great Britain, 97-98, 150-51, 154; conquest of Canada, 97, 151; Erie Canal, 98, 156; Dickinson's works, 59-60, 69; Gates, 54; Greene, 4 and n.; Jefferson, 88-90, 95-96, 98, 141-43, 147, 150, 153, 155; Logan's mission, 85; Washington, 48, 67.

Kosciuszko, Thaddeus, his opinions on Poland's, education, 9, 15; emancipation of peasants, 3, 15, 17, 22, 24, 103-106, 113, 154; government, 9, 11; internal reforms, 2, 5, 17, 22, 23; justice, 26; liberty and law, 22; political situation, 2-3, 9, 64, 98, 107; Polish-Russian war of 1792, 16; principles of the Insurrection, 26; Stanislaus Augustus, 16 n., 131.

Kosciuszko, Thaddeus, his opinions on, France, 47, 64, 85, 100, 103; Treaty of Campo Formio, 63; Napoleon, 102; European powers and ministers, 98, 155; European politics, 106, 153, 156; Holy Alliance, 106, 155; Pestalozzi's system, 144; personal independence, 107, 156; strength of nations, 95, 145.

Kosciuszko, Thaddeus, opinions on, of John Quincy Adams, 60; the American press, 42-44, 80 n., 81; Gen. Armstrong, 44-45; Arnault, 116; Bache, 80 n.; Barnes, 75, 115, 122-25; Barnet, 116; British physi-

cians, 34; British Whigs, 33; citizens of Bristol, 35; Cobbett, 42-46, 59 n., 72, 80 n., 83-84, 101, 129 n.; Dawson, 70; English romantic poets, 117-18; Federalists, 45-46, 83; John W. Fenno, 108; Garden, 70; Gates, 58; Harrison, 116; Humphreys, 5; Jefferson, 63, 73, 80, 89, 96-98, 102, 104, 112, 115, 117, 121; Jones, 7; Keats, 118; King, 35; Lafayette, 61, 116; La Rouchefoucauld - Liancourt, 56; Lear, 126; Logan, 85; Monroe, 110, 117; Mrs. Montgomery, 56; Gouverneur Morris, 16; Morse, 29; John A. Morton, 120-21; Moseley, 34; Ossolinski, 24; Thos. Pinckney, 71; Polish Diet, 6; Poniatowski, 10; Stanislaus Augustus, 11; Thornton, 168; Washington, 49; Webster, 29; Mrs. White, 52; Mary Williams, 113; Francis X. Zeltner, 113, 115.

Kosciuszko, Thaddeus, attached to America, 2-4, 7, 25, 85-99, 102, 103, 113; considers the title of an American as sacred, 26; considers America as his second country, 43, and as a land of freedom, 102; strives to introduce American ideas in Poland, 6, 17-22, 27, 87, 103; affectionately remembered and respected in America, 5, 7, 12, 28-30, 42-45, 73, 98, 102, 121-22; toasted in America, 28, 42, 59, 80; his home in France a mecca for Americans, 87-88.

Kosciuszko, Thaddeus, revered in, England, 32-36; France, 12, 100, 109; Sweden, 32; Poland, 11, 12, 22, 27, 118; by the world, 116-18.

Kosciuszko, Thaddeus, his American estate, 1, 3-4, 16 and n., 46-47, 67-72, 75, 88 and n., 89, 95, 119-30, 138-42; European estate, 114; bequest for the benefit of Negroes, 76, 125-26, 128; land grant in the U. S., 129-30, 140-41, 168; in financial difficulties, 1, 4, 12, 71, 121-22, 151-53.

Kosciuszko, Thaddeus, nicknames, assumed names and agnomina: Bieda, 15; Count of Poland, 4; Father

177

Moseley, Benjamin, M., Dr., letter to Rush, 34.

Mountain, the, French party, 16.

Mount Vernon, Va., 49, 68, 69 and n., 83 and n.

Muhlenberg, Henry M., Lieut., 42.

Murdoch, William, 152.

Murray, William Vans, 141 and n.

Napoleon I, Emperor of the French, 1, 39, 63-64, 101-106, 109; tries to win Kosciuszko for his plans, 101-104.

Nassau-Siegen, Charles, Prince, 25 n.

Neef, Francis J. N., 87, 144.

Negroes, 76; Kosciuszko's bequest for the benefit of, 76-79, 113, 125-26, 128.

Nero, 41.

Newark, N. J., 54, 58.

New Brunswick, N. J., 47, 50-51, 54, 58-59.

Newburgh Addresses, 129 n.

New Castle, Pa., 83-84.

New City Assembly Room, New York City, 59.

New Hampshire, 28.

New Jersey, 126.

New Orleans, La., 168.

New York City, 50, 54 and n., 55-57, 59, 69 n., 87, 128.

New York State, 35, 89, 141.

Nicholson, —, Miss, 55.

Nicholson, James, 55.

Nicoll, Susannah, see: Mrs. Marinus Willett.

Niemcewicz, Julian Ursyn, 32, 35, 44, 46, 50-51, 53-55, 57 and n., 58-60, 62-63, 69, 73, 75-76, 79 and n., 80, 104, 137, 139; visits Washington, 83 and n.; letters to Jefferson, 25 n., 69, 79-83, 85, 104; from Jefferson, 67, 73, 85, 101, 104.

North Carolina, 129 n.

North River, 98; seen Hudson.

Ohio, 116, 129.

O'Connell, Daniel, 109 n.

Oraczewski, Felix, letters to Gouverneur Morris, 3 n., 16.

Orleanist Princes, 62-63.

Orloff Palace, St. Petersburg, 31.

Ossolinski, Joseph, letters to Thugut, 1 n., 24.

Otis, Harrison Gray, letter from Codman, 86.

Oxford, Lady, 33.

Paris, France, 4 and n., 5-6, 8, 25 n., 29-30, 64, 83, 85-86, 105, 110, 121 n., 137-138, 140, 148-51, 153-54; Americans in, 86-88, 110, 116; Kosciuszko in, 15, 84 n., 85-103.

Park Theatre, New York City, 58.

Parker, Daniel, 3 n.

Parker, Josiah, 70.

Paszkowski, Francis, Gen., 86, 110, 114.

Paterson, William, 53, 58.

Paul I, Tsar of Russia, 79, 100-102, 114; frees Kosciuszko 31-33, 42, 46; letter from Kosciuszko, 100-101.

Peak of Otter, Va., 155.

Peale, Rembrandt, 79 n.

Pennsylvania, 64, 72 n., 127, 140-41.

Perry Township, Ohio, 129.

Pestalozzi's educational system, 87, 144.

Peszka, Joseph, 168.

Petropavlovsk fortress, 31.

Pettit, Charles, 75; letters from Kosciuszko, 62, 75.

Philadelphia, Pa., 34, 39, 53-54, 57, 60, 69 n., 70, 73, 75, 76 n., 80, 87, 137, 139, 144; Kosciuszko's sojourn in, 40-50, 62-80, 95, 129; yellow fever, 42-43, 48-50, 60.

Philadelphia Society for the Information and Assistance of Persons Emigrating from Foreign Countries, 43.

Pickering, Timothy, 35, 47-48, 57; letters to Biddle, 48; Kosciuszko, 57; Washington, 48; from King, 35; Kosciuszko, 57 n.; Washington, 41. 48.

Pinckney, Charles Cotesworth, 73.

Pinckney, Thomas, 16 n., 70-72; letters to Willinks, Van Staphorsts and Hubbard, 70 n.; from Kosciuszko (probably), 64.

Pisa, Italy, 17.

Pitcairn, David, 34, 136.

Pitt, William, 32-33.
Po River, Italy, 64.
Poinsot, —, Mr., 155.
Poland, 1-3, 6, 12, 15, 17, 20, 22-23, 25 and n., 47, 60, 64, 74, 101-105, 107, 110, 113, 117-18, 127, 154; Partitions, 10, 25 n., 29, 33, 59, 131; First Partition, 15; Second Partition, 16, 18, 25 n.; after the Second Partition, 12, 21, 131; Third Partition, 25 n., 26; during the Kosciuszko Insurrection, 18-30; effects of the Insurrection, 26-27, 29; at Congress of Vienna, 105-106; Kingdom of, 105-106, 154; diplomatic efforts of Kosciuszko in behalf of, 100-106; conditions in, 2-3, 6, 9, 18-19, 88, 92, 104, 131; eastern provinces of, 9, 106; toasted in America, 42, and in France, 100.
Polaniec, Poland, Manifesto of, 22.
Poles, 17, 22, 31, 64, 102-104, 113, 116, 156; imprisoned by Austria, 110; in Paris, 87, 109, 111.
Poletica, Peter, letter from Jefferson, 125.
Polish, Commission of Education, 2; Commissions of Good Order, 20, 132-34; Constitution of the Third of May, 9, 17, 28; Great Diet, 5-6, 9-10, 12, 21; last Diet, 12, 131; proposed Diet in exile, 64; Military Commission of the Diet, 9; Palatinates, 20; Permanent Council, 2, 132; Revolution of 1830-31, 127; Supreme National Council, 19-20, 23 n., 26, 132-34; Supreme Tribunal, 20, 132-33; War of 1806-07, 103; army, 1, 5, 9-11, 18, 23; dissidents, 5; educational system, 2, 23, 104; exiles, 12, 39, 64; magnates, 10, 17, 19, 21-22; militia, 6, 17, 20; national hymn, 64, 101; peasants, 3, 5, 15, 17, 21, 22-24, 103-106, 110, 113, 154; question, 102, 105.
Polish Legions in Napoleonic wars, 1, 39, 64, 100-102, 108, 114, 142-43, 168; under Kosciuszko's leadership, 101; the Danube Legion, 101.
Pollock, Lucetta Adelaide, 168.

Pollock, Oliver, 168.
Polonne, Poland, 10.
Poniatowski, Joseph, Prince, 9, 11; letter to Stanislaus Augustus, 10.
Porcupine, Peter, see: Cobbett, William.
Porter, Jane, 33.
Portugal, 74.
Potocki, Felix, letter from Kosciuszko, 11.
Potomac, river, 57.
Pougens, Charles, letters to Kosciuszko, 87, 143.
Praga, Poland, slaughter of, 26.
Presbyterian Church, 126.
Priestley, Joseph, letter from Jefferson, 73.
Prince of Wales, 34.
Princeton, N. J., 51.
Prussia, 10, 16, 29, 105; in the Second Partition of Poland, 18; in the Kosciuszko Insurrection, 24.
Prussian, agents, 24, 26; army, 101.

Quakers, 56, 91, 149.
Queen Square, Bristol, England, 35.
Quincy, Mass., 49.

Raclawice, Poland, battle of, 24.
Radziwill, Anthony, Prince, 60.
Randolph, Martha Jefferson, letter from Jefferson, 41.
Red Hook, N. Y., 44 n.
Red Lion Inn, Elizabethtown, 58 n.
Relfe, —, Mrs., 62.
Republicans, 28, 29, 40-42, 45-46, 55, 62, 70, 72 n., 73, 80, 86, 89, 138, 140 n.
Richards, George, Rev., 28.
Richmond, Va., 155.
Rivals, —, French agent at Bále, letter to Buchot, 23.
Robespierre, Maximilien Marie Isidore, 16, 23.
Rogerson, —, physician, 33.
Roman Catholic Church, 112; clergy in Poland, 23 n.
Rome, 91, 150.
Rose Hill, N. Y., 47 n., 50, 53, 57 and n.
Ross, James, 72 n.
Rotterdam, Holland, 28.

his opinions on, the Constitution of the Third of May, 9; Partitions of Poland, 29-30; American education, 91; letters to Brooke, 91; Emperor of Germany, 68 n.; Mrs. Fairfax, 48; Hamilton, 41; Humphreys, 9; Jefferson, 41, 91; Knox, 68; Kosciuszko, 49, 67-68; Geo. W. M. Lafayette, 69; McHenry, 48-49 n, 51; Marshall, 69; Martin, 73; Niemcewicz, 29-30; Pickering, 41, 48; from Gordon, 28-29; Humphreys, 28; Kosciuszko, 48, 57, 67-68; Pickering, 48; Stanislaus Augustus, 25 n.

Washington, Martha, 80 n.

Washington, William, Col., 70.

Washington, D. C., 79 n., 125, 127, 142-43, 145-46. See: Federal City.

Washington Tavern, Frankford, Pa., 51.

Wawrzecki, Thomas, Gen., 12 n.

Wayne, James M., Chief Justice of the U. S., on Kosciuszko and his estate, 32 n., 72.

Webster, Noah, 43; on the Kosciuszko Insurrection, 29-30.

Welsh immigrants, 39.

West Point, N. Y., 79 n. See: U. S. Military Academy.

Whig Club of England, 33, 80, 137, 139; Whigs, 33, 42, 80 n.

Whisky Rebellion, 28.

White, Anthony Walton, Gen., 50, 53; entertains Kosciuszko, 51-54, 58-60, and John Adams, 59.

White, Anthony Walton, Mrs., 51-53; letters from Kosciuszko, 52.

White, Eliza, 52-53.

White House, Washington, D. C., 127.

White Plains, N. Y., 3 n.

Wilberforce, William, 33.

Willink, Wilhelm & Jan, letters from Pinckney, 16 n., 70.

Willett, Marinus, 55.

Willett, Marinus, Mrs., 55-56; letter to Kosciuszko, 56.

Williams Jonathan, Col., 92; letter from Jefferson, 92.

Williams, Mary, 113.

Williams, Otho Holland, Gen., 4, 50.

Wilmington, Del., 12 n., 69.

Wilno, Poland, 26.

Wirt, William, 125-26; letters from Jefferson, 88, 120, 125, 126 and n.

Wlodzimierz, Poland, 10.

Wolcott, John, 33.

Wolcott, Oliver, 70 n., 71, 138-40; letter from Cabot, 86.

Worthington, Thomas, Col., letters to Jefferson and from Samuel H. Smith, 130 n.

Wybicki, Joseph, 101.

XYZ affair, 73, 140.

Yates, Jasper, letter from Burd, 49.

Zaleski, Michael, letters from Kosciuszko, 3, 9, 12.

Zeltner, Angelica, Mrs., 108-109.

Zeltner, Conrad, letter from Kosciuszko, 113-14.

Zeltner, Emily, 114.

Zeltner, Francis Xavier, 111, 113-14, 125, and his family, 114-15, 128; letter to Jefferson, 115.

Zeltner, Peter Joseph, 103, 108, and his family, 108-109, 114.

Zeltner, Thaddea, 109.

Zeltner, Xavier, 111-12.

Zielence, Poland, battle of, 10.

Zolkowska, Catharine, 128.

Zuchwil, Switzerland, 117.

Zurowska, Thecla, 2; letter from Kosciuszko, 3.

ERRATA

Page 155, letter no. 39, Kosciuszko to Jefferson: Kosciuszko's spelling of Peak of Otter should be corrected to Peek of Otter (not Puk of Otter).

Post-war shortages of materials and economic difficulties made it impossible for the printer to observe some French diacritical marks.

POLISH PUBLISHING CO.
CHICAGO